Paperback ISBN: 978-1-9993632-0-8

Printed in the United Kingdom, Aldgate Press

First Edition of 500

Designed by Hugo Volrath
Art Direction by Hélène Selam Kleih and Hugo Volrath
Logo by Nina Carter

Prosperitee Press

www.himandhis.org

HIM + HIS
Hélène Selam Kleih

Contents

There is no order, there is no filter.

Our mental health is a burden to our brains; to our souls, to the souls of others. We must not speak; expression is neither for the strong, nor possessed by the weak. Expression is undesired, it is taboo, adverse to productivity. Expression stunts us, us as a functioning economically driven society - emotions are hindrances, feelings are a burden.

Feelings are reactions to events, and when stifled result in trauma.

We need to talk about men.

From a young age, men are taught to be strong - and strength is demonstrated not through words or creative expression, but through actions.

"From the moment little boys are taught they should not cry or express hurt, feelings of loneliness, or pain, that they must be tough, they are learning how to mask true feelings. In worst-case scenarios they are learning how to not feel anything ever." bell hooks, *All About Love*

So, what happens when our mind overrides our body, when the mental is stronger than the physical? Do we continue to act? Or do we stop to partake in an internal dialogue, a questioning of our mental stability and fragility? Do we progress further to spark overt conversation? Is action in fact addressing the root before the rot?

As a contributor expressed to me: 'We (men) struggle to have a voice when it comes to this subject until it's too late and we suffer in silence. In many cases, it's vital that we have the assistance and camaraderie with women in order to promote healing and growth.'

It is this same female camaraderie that instigated the creation of HIM + HIS.

After my twin brother was diagnosed with psychosis and clinical depression, myself and my family looked for comfort in the situation and found little. Working with an over-stretched NHS, as much as they have helped, has not eased the trauma of having a loved one sectioned in an institution. He has now been in a psychiatric ward for young adults since January 2017, the longest he has ever been sectioned.

During his time there, I have been able to speak to his fellow inpatients about their mental health, illness and what they felt were the issues leading to their sectioning.

The majority of the young men responded, saying that it was actually the normal everyday constraints of society that infringed on their mental health. It was the normative expectations of sexuality, of masculinity, and the inherent fear of not fulfilling the role of the 'man' that pushed their already fragile minds towards mental illness.

The problematic discourse around men and mental health reinforces the prejudice and the stereotypes in place that drag the male self and ego into the ground. Vulnerability, fragility, weakness are seen as defects, flaws, marks of instability. Mental health is often accompanied with unfavorable language: 'Problem', 'sufferer' and even 'patient', all lead to a victimization of the person, and a sense of detachment from the agency they have over themselves. This invalidation only fuels more self-loathing and denial once in the institution.

Although men's mental health is being addressed more and more by professionals and the media, many men are still reluctant to seek help, and signs of distress are often left undiagnosed until it is too late: the root is rotten. In the UK, only 15-19% of men would seek help from their GP for anxiety or depressive tendencies.

My cousin passed away last July, after committing suicide. He was in his 40s, a charismatic, loving father, friend and brother, yet could not find support and comfort even in his own family. He now makes up a statistic: 76% of suicides in the UK are by men.

He was my backbone; he gave my brother hope. He had a circle around him, he had space and time to speak, and yet the shame still consumed him.

Shame breeds silence, and silence breeds nothing. A relentless attack on identity, shame knows no boundaries of race, sexuality or class. It is the most oppressive threat to the mind, to life.

Can we stand by and let shame consume another?

-

HIM + HIS is an exploration of what identity means to the male: Him, signifying the physical being, and His, symbolising the mind and the journey to acquiring agency over one's mental state.

HIM + HIS holds many versions of voice and all contributions have been welcome; whether you are a man yourself, and have experienced mental health issues and mental illness, or whether you are a family or friend, like myself, who has watched their loved ones eaten alive by their minds.

The brief was intentionally loose - express what you can, in whatever way you can. The performative act of speaking, and of crying, are only two forms of expression, of sharing, and not a universal indication of healing.

Whilst I have edited contributions and gone back and forth with drafts, HIM + HIS remains unfiltered. It is not about taste, but expression. The focus is not on the product of creation, but the act of creating. Of language and expression: verbal, physical and spiritual. If there is no existing language to describe your trauma, why not make your own.

Each contribution varies completely in style, in perspective, in experience - yet they are all the same in truth: silence is the killer, prevention is key. Mental health, like this anthology, ebbs and flows, it is not a straight road. There are no chapters, no boundaries, no identifiers or separators of each contributor and contribution, but there is a working towards hope. A hope that in the darkness there is light, and a hope that mental health is not a loaded term.

This is their story, and my transferred pain. For all of us: our mental states are forever changing and it is this very uncertainty that is sometimes the most overwhelming - the extremity of never being certain of the next high or low.

HIM + HIS is more than paper - it is a community, a network, that I hope can provide some sort of relief for men and their families. A platform to speak honestly, however dark; HIM + HIS is a reminder that whilst things may not get better, they are manageable and don't have to be tackled alone.

'Unfortunately I've been going through a bit of a relapse over the last 2 weeks. My depression has gone back to unmanageable levels and I've been really struggling to function. But I am still really interested in being involved in your project. Actually my most recent setback has made me realise just how important a project like yours is. I find that writing about my experience is really therapeutic. Fortunately for me I now have an amazing support structure in place. But so many people are suffering in silence and on their own for no good reason.'

As this contributor highlighted: community is crucial and acceptance is basic. We must not avoid the uncomfortable, the terrifying, the uncontrolled and uncontrollable, instead we must face mental health head on, discuss it honestly and openly and unflinchingly. We must applaud growth and healing; we must applaud the men around us for the strength in their vulnerabilities.

There is no absolute solution, yet creating and creation can be a prevention.

There is clarity in the confusion.

How was your day Helene?

Good, so we were just talking about mental health. Why, do you think men have more difficulty expressing themselves?

Because we think... men are the type of person... they think that they are the tougher person than to women... and that's the difficulty that men have with mental health, to talk about it with other guys, or their family members or friends. Or to strangers even, just to get some advice. That's why there are mental health clinics and support groups in the community, anywhere you go.

Do you think there is enough, for men?

There should be more for men.

What would you like to see... for yourself, for example?

To feel a lot better, to do my own hobbies that I used to like in the past, because I don't feel it inside, I feel like a different person. I don't feel like the Yohannes I used to be. And it confuses me sometimes, and sometimes I cry a lot at night and I try to remember the good memories I had in childhood. But now I am in adulthood. And I ask myself sometimes, how did my mental health happen? I didn't take a drug or anything. It just happened in the middle of the night, and I was terrified. And... I'm trying to say to myself, I'm a strong person, I survived when I was born. It was more serious when I was born. And, I want to make an effort.

Still from 'Network' , a video by Josiane MH Pozi and Hélène Selam Kleih

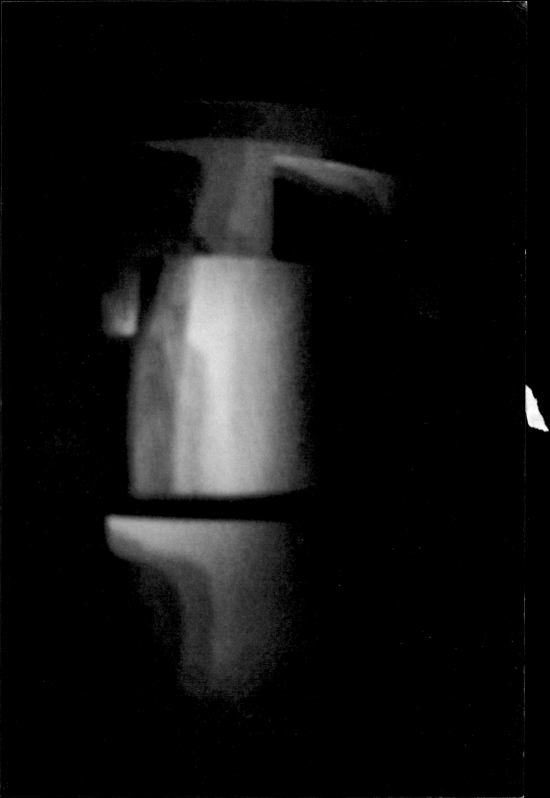

'I wrote a letter to Benga a couple of years ago, trying to get him on my radio show...he didn't ever respond but I remember weeping when I read the words back to myself.

This was after I heard he left music due to anxiety and mental health issues.

from 21/09/2015', AKINOLA DAVIES

-

Hi Benga

my name is Akinola, I tweeted you the other day to briefly mention about my bout with depression and mental health.

Since the age of about 12/13 I started smoking weed (skunk), at the time it was what my mates did and as the only Nigerian kind in an all white school in Kent, I also wanted to fit in. My first experience was great as I'd never had that feeling before but over the next decade or so it became all encapsulating.

Don't get me wrong I was still very social and active but more reserved in my communication. At about 20 or 21 I had my first panic attack, it was triggered by something so mundane. I was in a club in Lagos, as I often would go visit for christmas and was talking to a beautiful girl at the bar. Insanely high at the time, we must have spoken for about 30-40 minutes. Everything was fine, but then I asked her age and she was about 15/16. For some reason I panicked and paranoia kicked it.

Was everyone staring at me? did they think I was hitting on a kid? did she think I was a creep? was I being a creep? - literally 0-100 I was gripped and freaked the fuck out, I basically asked my homie to leave straight away. That night round his place, I locked myself in the bathroom and called my brother and told him I felt like i was going crazy, that I'd never felt like this before, that I might actually be mental.

He laughed and shrugged it off, telling me to calm down, sleep and come home.

The second time was with friends, as I went to school in Kent all my mates DJ'd drum and bass (personally I hated it but was around it all the time) so when we'd be at anyone's house there would be a cypher. You know kids grabbing the mic, it was like country grime almost. Fancy equipment, kids in reebok track suits all clamouring for the mic.

Again insanely high, we were in this back room and all the guys were having a go on the mic, and for some reason I thought they were all mocking me when they took turns to emcee. There was a lot of giggles and sillyness and I held it together but inside I was screaming and crying without showing it. Why would my friends do this to me, why were they doing this? should I react? how do I leave? I can't leave, we're in the fucking middle of no where? Am I making this up? Are they really talking about me? Fuck, what is going on? How did this happen? Am I crazy?

I'm not sure how that situation ended, all I know is I lost 2/3 really good friends that evening, one was my bestfriend who I confronted about it a few days later and he swore that they were not talking about me. Till this day I don't know but I know I stayed clear of all those individuals mentally and physically since then. Which saddens me but I guess I was too mentally fragile to address it and maybe see it as solely just being my mind playing tricks on me.

At 21/22 I was in my second year of uni in brighton, lived in a huge house with 8 others. All i remember was going to Uni and wanting to come home, get into bed, smoke weed and watch movies. I did that on repeat for about 4 months and then realised I didn't want to get out of bed. I would drag myself to uni each day for the one lecture but go straight home. I became sad, very good at not showing it, always high on skunk. I would feel bad for feeling sad because I knew my life was fine, much better than many others, after all I'd lived in Nigeria. I mean I was in uni in Brighton for fuck sake, doesn't get more middle class than that.

But the sadness consumed me, it gripped me. It felt like the sadness was my best friend and was the only thing that could understand me. But it was also like an abusive relationship, if the sadness cared for me so much why was I sad. I mean, there was no reason at all, I was fairly good at school, I was still very much part of my social group. I went out, got drunk, spoke to people. But would always run back to be alone and sad even in a house filled with 8 people. I never interacted with them.

The Irony, I lived in a house with 8 people but felt extremely Isolated, My friends and family love me but yet I felt unloved. It got to a fever pitch around 6 months in, I remember it being an extra dark winter. I started thinking of how to kill myself. Being the coward I thought I was I didn't want any drama. There were 3 options I thought. It would be to hang myself, I'd heard of a kid doing that in halls. Although I didn't have anything to hang from. My light fixture would definitely not take my weight and my roommates would probably not get their deposit back.

Number 2 was to slit my wrists in the bath tub, I mean I didn't know much about this other than it would hurt and probably be a lot of blood. I also thought that I live with 8 people, someone would definitely need to use the bathroom, so I'd get knocks on the door and it would totally fuck my shit up, then I'd just be bleeding everywhere (too messy basically).

Number 3 was marylyn monroe, I heard she took a whole bottle of paracetamol and went to sleep and never woke up. Yes, this seemed like the one for me. Simple, I could do it in bed, no interruptions. I was already good at swallowing pills simple I can do this.

Then I thought about my mother and my sister and my brother and said would they miss me, I mean I know they would but at what cost? Me being unhappy forever? Maybe I should talk to a psychiatrist, how the fuck would I find one? Maybe they'll just section me? I don't want to be sectioned? People talk about that shit, I'll be labelled crazy forever? Nah I have to talk to someone.

I went round my best friends place (RIP), the whole gang were there and we were smoking skunk all cracking joke, which mainly involved bullying this mate of ours. Which i found a bit uneasy but I went along with it because I knew we all genuinely liked him. When me and him had a moment alone, I told him I feel weird that I don't feel my self and I'm unhappy. In hindsight we were 2 guys in Brighton, so I might excuse him for thinking I was coming out. I wasn't, I was just desperate for help, desperate for someone to tell me it was fine, I'd be fine, it'll pass.

It pains me to ever write this as It's bringing tears to my eyes. 21 year old me just needed help. I remember his saying you're just being silly Ak, you're fine mate, don't be stupid. So i thought I was being stupid, sadness put its arm around me again. I thought that I'm gonna have to do it, I'm going to have to kill myself. Right there and then that was the only option. If my best friend can't understand then no one will.

I went home and wept in the arms of sadness, in the arms of my shame, my embarrassment. I had accepted my mortality and was ready to call its bluff. I cried a lot and thought who? who can I talk to? Who will listen? I have to make one more attempt before I commit to this pack of paracetamol, I just have to.

I picked up my phone and called my brother, who lived in Brighton. I mean I basically went to uni there to be closer to him and somehow forgot that he was actually around physically even if just living on the other side of town. I was terrified, what if he didn't understand too? I almost wished he wouldn't answer. Funny I'm in the same position I was in then, replace the phone for a laptop and age me younger with tears coming out of my face. (obviously I'm over the whole ordeal for the better) but I was there, and he answered "hello"....

I told him I was sad, so sad, I had no reason to be and felt stupid for being sad, but I can't control it. I cried and cried, and he listened. I remember it feeling like I'd just dropped this fucking commercial plane off my back fuck a monkey. It was sooo heavy. But after that convo, I felt better, my brother said. Whenever u feel like this call me. Please don't hesitate, call me or come over either or just reach out.

He doesn't know about the suicide strategies I was making up or that I was at the bottom of this pit, covered in vaseline so I couldn't even crawl out. The phone call was like someone shining a torch in this darkness. It was like a shimmer of light and changed my life forever. I'm crying as I write this because this is the most I've gone through, all that.

I wouldn't wish that level of sadness on another human being, no matter their circumstance. No matter if they were a bad person. Depression and mental Illness is so consuming.

What I realise is that being alone with your thoughts however natural can imprison you. If you have no outlet to release you become even more isolated in your mind. The pretence in public isolates you even more. Your thought becomes a shell in a shell in a shell, buried in the ground inside a bigger shell. Where sad & dark ideas can begin to manifest. We all have these thoughts but if we share them then we won't be alone with them.

I'm not sure why I've written all this to you. But You shared so much the other day online and I thought to share back. I try and help people now. In my own little way. through personifying being however strange or weird I can be.

I realise there are so many like me, especially people of colour who don't have an outlet. I've lost a friend last year and my uncle early this year to suicide, they both hung themselves.

I feel their pain, as they were both so loved and surrounded by love and even their closest must have realised how isolated they were that they couldn't share.

so now I share, I share everything, every thought.

Thank you for using your platform to help, I hope & I'm sure it will make a difference to many.

I hurt for anyone going through depression or mental health.

Everything is temporary

We are not alone, love is the power

Best

Akin

p.s. I don't solely hold the weed accountable but I know it played a part. alongside a truck load of insecurities, in regards to myself and my environment and constantly trying to compare myself to others. I kept on smoking for a few more years less and less, not skunk tho. Hash and thai Now I don't smoke anymore - the odd puff here but very very rarely.

There are people who function on weed my bestmate (RIP) did.

But it didn't work for me or at least because it was traumatic rather than enjoyable.

I'm over a lot of things now and thankful for the whole experience - literally what doesn't kill you only makes you stronger.

'it's a letter to yourself almost...'

I was about 29/30 when I wrote to that letter to Benga. I wasn't ever really expecting a response to be honest. I just wanted to share. I've always cultivated a habit of reaching out to people and letting them know how their work or words have impacted me. It actually is a process I've adopted to help aid my on-going recovery. As a means of showing gratitude to myself and whoever I write to. In a sense I would have loved a response but that is never what motivated me in the first place. I thought I was writing him a letter but really I was writing to myself and letting go of a lot of what I felt about myself and that period of my life. I cried when I wrote it and initially read it back. It still leaves a lump in my throat when I read it back but I have since realised I'm not the only one who has experienced these overwhelming feelings of not being good enough or worthy of life. I arrived where I did through an accumulation of my nurture and what I was battling with innately. Which is the person I am versus the person I'm supposed to be. I'd like to think the person I am won, or is winning. I don't think it's that cut and dry with those feelings. They never really go away, they just become less pertinent and smaller in size. Should i ever shut down again fully it might regain its strength and become bigger again but I decide every day to challenge myself and be open.

Since then I've seen a spiritual enhancer/ or therapist to others. I've also lent my story to a few people who I felt needed some form of support as a bridge to empathy. I'm a little cautious of who I tell it to. I mean I've not really ever had any of these conversations with my family. It's not that I hide them but it's more like I worry that they might internalise some of what i felt or feel responsible. That's not to say they didn't play a part but the situation was low self-esteem coupled with needing to always project a certain type of confidence. A macho or whatever it means to be a man type of confidence. I never really identified with that and still don't.

I wrote because he shared something personal, and in some sense my understanding of psychosis induced through what wasn't actually weed but skunk, has grown. I wrote because I was making a radio show about people being sectioned and trying to understand an extremity of mental health. Those who are sectioned aren't these sensationalised types. They just have an episode which people are not capable of understanding - therefore they are sectioned. Also we have a mental health system that is already being squeezed to its death.

I'm not sure what advice I'd give to myself because this largely shaped the person I am today. Had I not experienced any of this then I would potentially be totally different. Although, I would have been a little less harsh on myself, and probably should have maybe been exposed to more art. As for the conversation with musicians and celebs coming forward. Yes, I guess so, I'd hate to trivialise anyone's story and I guess if you have a platform then it's important to let people know there is help available. My concern is when it becomes a trend or buzzword. It can have a capacity to leave people who really need help behind. I would like to see more social enterprises who help people recovering from mental health issues get back into work and find structure and routine. Like the Centre for Better Health - http://www.centreforbetterhealth.org.uk/

Also maybe for mental health to be taught more in schools and normalised. Whilst it's great to get the word out, it's more important to back that up with those who are on the ground doing really important work and taking practical steps; teaching people skills and introducing them to structured social settings.

'Above', HÉLÈNE SELAM KLEIH

In Tigrinya your name means gift from above.
Your selfless love and joy were these gifts.
You infected the world with your grin, your laugh, your shining smile.
Your smile gave us strength throughout all of the struggles.
Your smile brought only light when darkness threatened to defeat.
You were a wonderful man, father, brother, cousin, nephew, friend
and role-model.
You are a man who cared more for his neighbour's heart than his own.
May our, our gift from above, continue to guide our lives towards joy.

When I talk to our father about it, I don't really talk to him in depth because like... I don't think he wants to talk. He wants to be with younger people and not like...be patronised.

It's better talking to him than anyone else but I also feel like he doesn't want to talk about it in sadness?

I didn't really have a chance to talk about it with anyone other than our father. He has his picture on the wall in his flat and he talks to it in the morning. He says "oh good morning" to him. And whatever he has to say, he actually speaks to him. I was struggling at one point and I did kind of half break down... sort of teary eyed more than actually crying and he was telling me how he was coping with it and I was telling him how I was coping with it... but I can't explain the conversation properly because there's so many different feelings... it's like a never ending amount of feelings, you feel sadness, you feel pride... so it's like only tears can describe how you feel. You can't say it.

I had no clue of how it would feel to lose someone close and I hope people hear me.

There have been times where he kind of tried to kill himself whilst I was in his flat - whilst I was there. A couple of times he told me he tried to and again like I said about seeing things differently... things started to come together and I started seeing the bigger picture... what he felt, when it happened, who he had around him, how he felt... and so it's taken me a long time to piece together... to come to terms with it. I'm still nowhere near. I have to kind of pretend that he's still alive in order to cope. And by cope I mean... breathing... you know?

So, that's what I do. I have to play mind games with myself to avoid it and to not think about it. Everything reminds me of him.

The thing is we weren't talking much. We had a bit of a falling out. He said this, I said that, he felt a bit bad about it, I felt bad about it and we kind of had this up and down, stressful friendship.

It was like that for a few years. We had a big falling out and our father was there as well and he was trying to cope with this and that and so on... we were trying to help each other but we'd butt heads a lot...

He wants all this... I'm trying to do something else... we were kind of here and there. When we clashed, we clashed. I thought he was still away, I didn't know he was in London. It's frustrating. For a while I felt guilty.

-

Addressing mental health is not only challenging, but courageous. There are many sub-genres and facets to mental health which are yet to be covered, and we must help bridge the gap from the taboo, to the normalised.

Within the spectrum of mental health, depression and suicide have hit home the hardest. Within the UK, the suicide rate is 3 times higher in men than women. In addition, global statistics prove that those in the lowest social class are 10 times more likely to die from suicide than middle-aged males in the highest socio-economic backgrounds. This being the reason why we must provide support for those without.

We must not only lend a hand to those in need, but to those who wish to develop their knowledge on mental health and its correlation with masculinity.

The more that we address the stigma surrounding mental health in males, the higher the result will be of boys and men accommodating themselves or others to receive the correct support.

Safety

As a teenager, the subject of mental health was unspoken, yet somehow I found myself completely engulfed in a world surrounded by it. Growing up, I was dealing with my own mental health struggles, family and friends mental health, including friends who had attempted suicide. Shortly after turning 18, I then lost my step-brother to suicide. Subsequently, his death did not trigger an uproar of discussion, neither did I feel that our education system was taking responsibility for their present and future students regarding mental health and its extremities. It was then, that I took upon myself the task of contacting local charities; calling in requests for posters, leaflets, and cards for advice on where to seek help. Once received, my study breaks were spent pasting the new information up in the corridors of our school. These events

became the catalyst to trying to generate a change.

Over the past 8 years I have worked alongside various mental health charities to raise awareness, each year holding the intent to build a larger audience. This year, I decided to use social media and my online platform to promote a conversation catered towards men.

Societal expectations of masculinity are warped, it is not a weakness for a man to cry, nor a young boy to feel pain. Abuse, depression, and eating disorders are some of the topics society states men do not understand, let alone accept that they personally experience such issues. It is up to us to change that, and start this conversation.

My aim was to curate a visual series with the purpose of creating an impact specifically to draw the viewer in. So, I cast an all-male beauty series, an unconventional choice, to raise awareness for mental health in men. Paired alongside each post are statistics and advice from Samaritans for those in need. The comment section then allowed a safe space for males to further discuss this topic, and ultimately find that they are not alone.

The decision behind choosing Samaritans to collaborate with on this project was an obvious choice. They currently stand as the only mental health charity in the UK where you can access help 24/7 free of charge. Samaritans vision statement reads that fewer people die by suicide, and that it can be prevented by reducing distress and crisis that can lead to this result by increasing support for those in need.

Contacting Samaritans is anonymous, leaving you with complete control over what you discuss and the details you wish to tell. It's an environment that is full of care, whether it's over the telephone, online, or in their walk-in branches.

Photography - Piczo (represented by We Folk)
Make Up - Athena Pagington (represented by Bryant Artists)

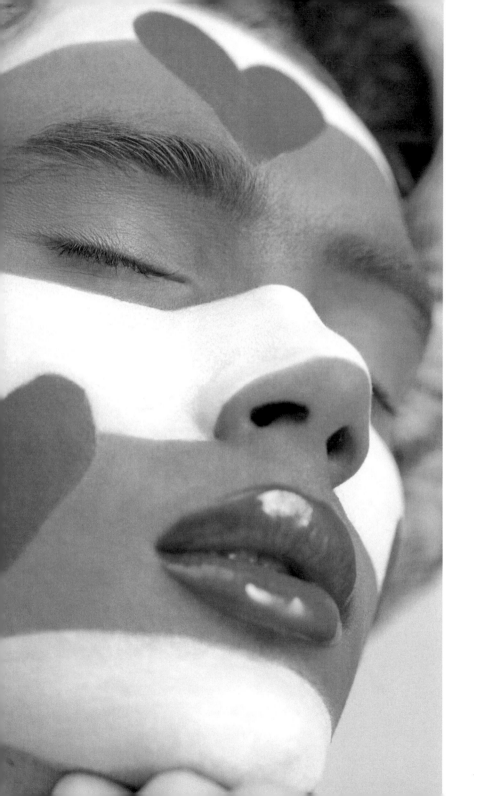

'Telephone Lines' — '91

-

The topic of mental health is typically more difficult for men to discuss, but speaking about the issue is often the thing that could help the most. In many cases, speaking about feelings isn't considered "manly," causing a lot of men to keep their feelings to themselves. This is why mental illness within men goes undetected more often than within women. During my research I saw a lot of videos that addressed the issue of mental health but did it in a way that didn't make me want to engage with the topic. The videos were factual and hard hitting, but did not encourage or make the issue understandable at all. They lacked empathy and I struggled to find anything relatable - that's what led me to create this animation.

I want to normalise the topic of mental health through the use of personal storytelling. The narration conveys the feeling of what it is like to suffer with mental illness and the pressures of being a man, contrasted with everyday imagery that we can all connect with. Through the narrator confidently and openly speaking about his experience, my aim is to encourage my audience to do the same, making mental health a common conversation topic.

It is set as a car journey because quite often the best conversations happen during car journeys, it's a moment of privacy between two people, and there's not much else to do but talk. However, it can also be quite a solitary thing to drive alone at night.

By ending on the hashtag "talking helps", the animation encourages men to share their experiences online and hopefully build a community on social media where they can connect with other men that may be experiencing the same feelings.

"It's A Long Road Home" won Creative Conscience Award 2018.

Just because you can't see it doesn't mean it's not there, it doesn't mean it shouldn't be taken seriously. It's easy to feel as if you're alone and that nobody would understand what you're going through. The thing with mental health is, it is important to identify that you've got a problem and openly talk about it.

Not everybody's journey in life is the same, but this is my journey.

You hide things away; you don't let people know anything's wrong. I always felt I had to provide for my family, I was the main bread winner, the man of the family, the one that's meant to be strong, the one that's meant to be able to support their family and provide for them and that just pushes you on. It's not so easy to just suddenly stick your hand up and say, I want to get off this treadmill, I can't cope with it anymore.
I suppose it is difficult to ask for help, because you don't think you should feel like this and you can't see the way forward. I don't look ill so I must be OK. But I feel as though talking to someone was the most important first step, it made me realise that I wasn't alone,

and there's always someone you can talk to.

I don't feel mental health is something to be ashamed of.

Audio of "It's a Long Road Home",
Conversation between Amy
and her father

31

-

> "One of the greatest barriers to empathy is the fear of saying the wrong
> thing or the need to make everything better... What we all need when we're
> in struggle is the ability for other people to look us in the eye, to be with us,
> to embrace us, and to be willing to be with us."
> Brené Brown, *Men, Women, & Worthiness*

Just yesterday, I was thinking about the mental health of men as I've not been around many men who outwardly express how their mental health affects them. I have a lot of male friends and I'm always in spaces that are very male dominated and yet only two men I know express how they feel, one more than the other.

I do think men are put under immense pressure to uphold the unrealistic standards of what a man should be, which is ruining a lot of lives.

I worked in a step down unit for a few years and with my time there I spoke to all different types of men who had done some terrible things, but had some of the best, loving personalities when they were treated well and didn't feel the pressures of the outside world.

Working at that step down unit taught me a lot about my own mental health as well as other people's. Being in an environment where you're constantly helping people control and understand their thoughts and behaviours you see that communication and understanding goes a long way.

I don't think 'working' society realises how much in common they have with people who they consider 'crazy', it only takes one mishap, one misunderstanding or even slight miscommunication for a person to go into a downward spiral of negative emotions, causing them to act out in many ways. Being a person who has and still does at times struggle with my own mental health, falling into a lot of dark places and most of the time finding a way out on my own, has always made me want to raise awareness about how to keep a healthy mind.

I've recently started a hashtag #CourageousMindz. My aim is to encourage people who suffer with their mental health to cope in healthy ways, and educate people who don't suffer so they're able to understand more about people who do. The many stigmas attached to mental health, especially concerning men and masculinity, is something that still lingers within 'so-called' discussions. I want to reach out to people to change this, so I plan to make a relatable platform with information about mental health for anyone and everyone, as we all suffer at times but largely in silence. Most of all I want society to have a better understanding about the things they can't see. We can all help each other with the right information, communication and patience.

"One of the greatest barriers to connection is the cultural importance we place on "going it alone." Somehow we've come to equate success with not needing anyone. Many of us are willing to extend a helping hand, but we're very reluctant to reach out for help when we need it ourselves. It's as if we've divided the world into "those who offer help" and "those who need help." The truth is that we are both."
Brené Brown, *The Gifts of Imperfection: Let Go of Who You Think You're Supposed to Be and Embrace Who You Are*

Brainstorm is a project set up by Sophia Compton, Max Hayter and Dulcie Menzie, after Dulcie's dad committed suicide: "His family had no idea of what had been going on inside his head. He hadn't felt able to talk about it, even with them. The gender role assigned to men actively encourages this." The collection of responses explored the "failures of communication around male mental illness and try to envisage a masculinity that isn't toxic." In support of CALM: Campaign Against Living Miserably, the *I'm Fine* exhibition "set out to investigate and challenge this brittle gender role... no man will ever live up to masculine stereotypes."
I'm Fine ran from the 15-17th December 2017 at the Copeland Gallery, London.

50 artists have come up with personal / irreverent / angry / witty / contemplative responses to questions about masculinity and mental health - using embroidery, sculpture, performance, knitwear, illustration and beyond...

1: INSIDE MY BRAIN

These sensitive, evocative works illustrate a crucial part of the problem; they convey the isolating experience of having thoughts trapped inside your head. Many of these works present men alone, in silence. With a close family experience of suicide -men are shown sedentary, slumped, heads in hands.
They seem miles away emotionally. Cold, solid and fragile. Silence, in these works, can be harsh and cutting - being surrounded by it can make you feel small. But being in silence can also create space for the subject to discover things about themselves.
Sometimes we feel most acutely alone when surrounded by other people - uncomfortably tactile works are intimate and isolated in the same moment, the artist/ storyteller is plagued by melancholia. 'Extrovert positions within a group' demonstrate the repeated failings of protagonists to draw on the people around them offering to help, fortifying isolation.
But these works don't just hint at the problem. Their honesty and emotive power itself moves towards the solution: they are doing just what the subjects

are finding difficult, communicating this claustrophobic aloneness. Works lay him bare: destigmatizing depression, 'he demonstrates great bravery by being so vulnerable here'. It is vital for us to probe the emotional depths that these works hit upon.

2A: MASKING

This section looks at the barriers men put up: the masks they hide behind.

In investigating the performativity of the pro-wrestling subculture and the 'dual exhibitionism and concealment of such a disguise', the knotted layers of this paradox resonate through a blow up sex doll, and the repeated imagery of isolated male heads.

Contact with the world of wrestling is formative. 'I grew up watching WWE': hero-worshipping the son of a pro-wrestler or locked into physical combat with a 70's arm-wrestling champion. Looking back, these incarnations of masculinity are clearly extreme, but this way of being a man was persuasive when these men were consciously registering their own masculinity for the first time, as teenagers. It is important that these artists acknowledge how these ultra-hyper-masculine worlds influenced their own growth into manhood.

Donning a mask is a type of self-policing: the constricting pressure to fit into what Grayson Perry calls 'default man'. People of all genders feel this in patriarchal society; and female, trans* people and those of non-binary gender perhaps feel this most forcibly. What men seem to lack, comparatively speaking, are forums and spaces dedicated to discussing this impetus. With nowhere else to go, these thoughts are violently internalised.

Words seem to build as many barriers as they break down: they strengthen this internalisation. Sardonically despondent or part-concealing words with visceral intensity feels like a brutal suppression. Abstracted gaming symbols suggest how male communication can work sideways rather than front on: communication, via a screen, does not always amount to direct contact that delves beneath layers.

In almost all these works, feelings seem to be bubbling under the surface, dangerously liable to spill the bounds of their self-imposed containers.

So how can we move forward? Where are the sites from which we might be able to peer over a ridge to make out routes into a masculinity of the future? Poised on moments of change: these works point to openings that are just in reach. A poem unfurls from a solid frozen place to one of breadth and possibility, and the shift seems to coincide with the use of direct address - 'you'. In an installation we see photos of men touching themselves: 'Sounds more scandalous than it is. There's a sort of self-comforting touch I've seen a lot. Something lonely and lovely and seeking of the mother'. In presenting this he makes visible the closely-protected vulnerability that so desperately needs an outlet.

We cannot try to describe or label a work: you have to go and read it for yourself. Its unflinching honesty, and its generosity, are very powerful. What is displayed does not just move beyond past stereotypes of male strength or solidity, it renders them completely irrelevant.

Also highly personal, certain works look 'into my past', at the tensions and dynamics of father, son, brother, sister. They are self-critical, observing moments when he wishes he'd spoken but didn't. Looking into one's own family or mind to observe the workings of masculine stereotypes is a powerful tool; it forces you to confront how you too are implicated in creating these mechanisms.

A poet has created a work that moves beyond discussing how words can forge points of contact two between people, in forcing them to enact in cooperation in order to read his poem. A would be reader needs a helper to hold a light behind pieces of paper marked with vegetable oil, 'promoting and literally making space for communication. So that the writing emerges out of the contrast between the opaque and translucent in the paper.' As the poet says, 'the problem of communication, then, sits at the heart of this whole thing'.

3: WHAT MAKETH MAN

Things. Pint glasses and football shirts are the stage upon which gender is played out on: what you give a baby boy vs a baby girl, who does the dishes, which car you drive... These instantly familiar gender tropes are clear targets for deadpan irony, but also deserve our attention. These are the building blocks of our gender, and determine how we live within it – as his layered and endearing journey into his boyhood fascination with traffic jams reminds us, these symbols and ideas are knitted into our identity from the earliest moments.

What ashes before your eyes at 'exhausting' pace is like a masculinity starter-kit: bulldogs, boxing, sunbeds, snooker. Tools are similarly crucial pieces with the items' materiality continuously manipulated. Works subvert expectations by mashing up objects from different gender camps. Found objects – made into headdresses – androgynously blend male and female stereotypes; casting old-school manly tools in soap, the realm of the metrosexual male, smashes to fragments the notion of masculinity.

Certain artists hone in on certain words, placing them in unexpected environments. Illustrations re-examine male-dominated spaces, using perfectly chosen phrases. The image of male bodies leaping and tumbling riff on what one artist aptly terms 'the most idiotic, malignant phrase', Man Up; with another artist reclaiming words – 'poof', 'mummy's boy' – 'that used to make me feel de-masculinised' by putting them in the context of the 'ultra-hyper-masculine world that I don't fit into'.

He is not the only one. This is a resounding message across all the works: that no man will ever live up to masculine stereotypes. Each will be differently alienated and marginalised from this so-called 'ideal'. It is this ideal that we need to dismantle.

4: NAKED

We want to lay things bare. The works are naked in every sense: they are electrically aware of the vulnerability of our bodies.

The body is the site of many of masculinities' anxieties – and must not be falsely severed from discussions of mental health. His works – based on microbiology scans of malignant pathogens, and inspired by his own difficulties with physical health – call into question 'the senseless paradigm of strength and resilience championed in western culture'. They show that nobody will live up to these brittle notions of intactness and solidity.

With medical precision, some of these works deconstruct the dualisms of interior / exterior, physical / emotional. A PET scan of the literal workings of an artist's own brain; and another's placement of a cut out of the brain has been informed by what happens in the brain neuroscientifically. The skin is highlighted, the boundary between inside and out. How we orient ourselves in the world is determined by how we feel within our skin - our sense of having an inner life, and whether we want to retreat or escape.

Bodies have a sensuous, erotic feel, seemingly inspired by Classical Greek statues. Naked men in the positions of female nudes - arms draped across shoulders, faces looking demurely down. These works pose questions about what gaze we use to look at naked male bodies, trained as we are in viewing the female form. In a copper advertising structure, the solid frame is left empty: while gendered advertising (the realm of inhumanly proportioned biceps) is certainly vacuous, it has real, felt, physical effects.

What we need are masculine bodies that can flex, bend, cry; that are porous - even leaky, the ultimate patriarchal insult. Forensic probing of physical/emotional fragility must play a central role if this is ever to become possible.

Edited catalogue of works, written by Sophia Compton.

"There's a time and a place to be supportive and create safe spaces for women etc. but there's also a time and a place where you have to think about how feminism might have ways to interact with men and masculinity and bring that in. They don't need to happen at the same time or in the same place. That's not right and relevant. That's why I was so happy to do Brainstorm. That's also, like I'm sure your finding, what made it so difficult. It's a minefield. On one hand I don't want to alienate anyone, on the other hand I don't want to impose my vision on this topic that I do not intimately know. On another hand I also don't want to compound platforms for men who already have most of the platforms in the world... I don't want to just make another show which gives another load of male artists space to discuss what they feel about stuff when (men and women) are not on level playing fields.

... there was no method. Things kind of snowballed in a really nice way. What I found really surprising about Brainstorm was... ok, I hoped that it would have a positive impact and I hoped that it would have done well. My worry with the exhibition wasn't that people were not going to come but that they were not going to truly engage... that it might be a thing that people just attend and don't kind of really investigate. I hoped that it would have an emotional impact, but I was completely unprepared for the level of emotions that it…

But yeah… the number of people that said… especially the number of men who had not had the time or the space to think those issues through… they've always been pressing but… they've never really been able to join the dots. The amount of men that suffer in silence.

Because of the lack of communication, they're not connecting what they're individually feeling with a widespread issue. That can be subtle relief when you start to think that there are reasons for why you feel so isolated - the society you're living in is expecting and demanding that you deal with these things on your own because of outdated ideas about strength and vulnerability. Learning about that can help encourage people to not feel so isolated in that situation.

The element of Brainstorm that didn't come out as strongly as I expected was the thing about communication. There was a lot about isolation and expressing but there wasn't so much about the… policing of language in an all-male world?

…I think it might be interesting to go slightly hypermasculine and stereotypical just 'cos that's where you'd see patterns more clearly. Then to observe these worlds and see if you can draw a pattern of the interlinked language that it being used? Either positive or detrimental. I bet if you did that you'd find - within some worlds, words and phrases that pop up all the time, like "man up" or whatever."

‘*Wilson*’, JOHN OGUNMUYIWA

-

“*I'm good thanks, fine.*”

“*Works fine.*”
“*I'm fine.*”

“*You'll be fine.*”
“*Great, so you're all good.*”

If no one says what they really think, what does real really mean? There's a fundamental difference between what we say and what we feel. If a person is sobbing on the inside and smiling on the out, what's weirder, holding it in or expressing it in full to the world? This is a film about being trapped behind fake words and the disconnect between our feelings and our surroundings. Our perception of reality will always be a little out of touch if we're not honest with ourselves right? Whereas some people can't speak freely due to circumstance such as disabilities and oppression, many of us can and are free to express ourselves but in fact choose not to.

My father suffers from aphasia, which is an impairment of language, affecting the production or comprehension of speech. And my experience of this condition with how it affects speech has informed my perception of language and emotion. It always made me think how frustrating it must be to be trapped in your mind. All the things you could say but can't. And that led to the thought that although we may be close to people physically, the reality is that our inability to speak freely or feel freely keeps us so very far at the same time. And this isn't a case only unique to my dad, but it's something unique to how I see the world. For my dad, not being able to speak freely is an unfortunate circumstance, so I now find it odd that there's a similar social problem that we act out intentionally. The masks we wear, the facades in which the feelings we present do not match the feelings in our heads. It's wonderfully strange, a proper dichotomy. Our society encourages emotional openness yet it's actually out of the norm for someone, particularly men, to say how they really feel. This is the story of

Wilson, a seemingly composed man, whose battle with his inner thoughts leads to a dark and truthful outburst when talking to an old friend.

'Wilson' screened at ICA Playback Festival 2018 and aired on Channel 4 Random Acts.

'*Reassurance*', JAMES MASSIAH

Nothing wrong
With anything
Especially me
My body is just
The way it's meant to be
So is my mind
At any time
Drugs I take
To change it: fine
Always fine
And always me
Never not
That's right indeed
Thoughts I think
Are always mine
Even those that I don't like
Things I do to
Switch it up
Wind me down
Back to ground
Orange, blue
Green and brown
Wow! What the
Why? How?
High as heaven
Low as hell
As my heart swells
And my heart swells
And my heart swells
And my heart swells

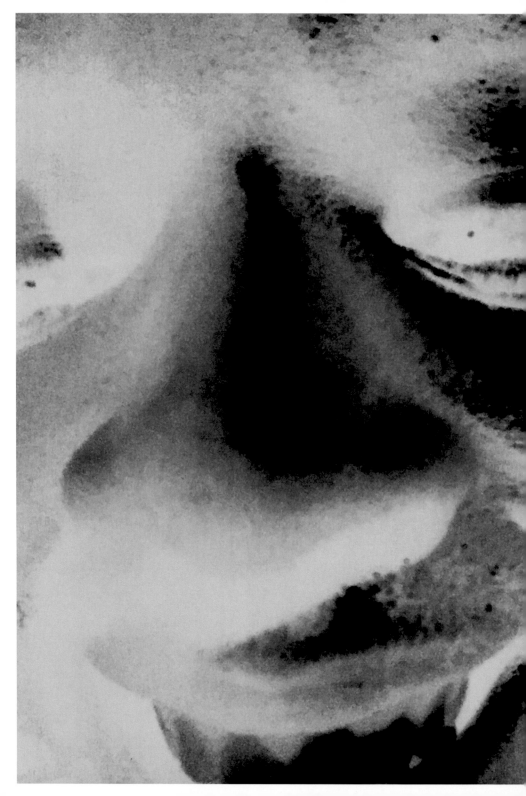

'There's a lot more to say, but this should suffice for now',
WILSON ORYEMA

-

Stuck between
A hard place
And a harder place
With nowhere soft to lay my head,
I bathed in the violence,
And with the vulgar,
We made a bed.
One of thorns.
As such,
I rarely stayed over,
Instead,
I ran home,
To the cold, wet embrace of fear.
But the latter rendezvous was never shared...

I mean

I came out the womb with a full head of hair and a straight face.
The 3-4 times i shed a tear,
It was like there were feathers near.
Uncontrollable laughter,
Or what happens,
When the lone zebra meets the hyenas...

The moral of the story,
Be careful what you trade for your freedom.

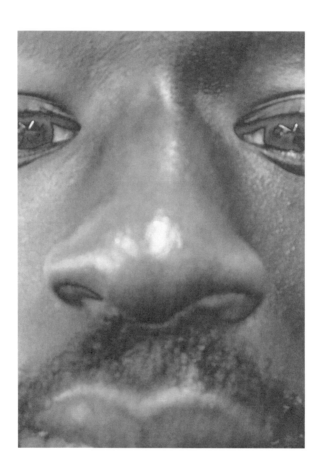

'People always ask me how I destress and let out my emotions and honestly, poetry is the only way I know how. It's the only way I can make sense of my emotions and where my heads at because I actually have to think about it and think about the words that could/can describe how I'm feeling. I don't go therapy or do like a sports where I can physically/emotionally get all my feelings out so this is the closest I get and honestly... it works for me.
I don't title my work tbh.' , CALEB KUMIKO

-

Been fighting with myself so long my mirror don't look at me the same
And my black eye looks at the world with disdain and a pain that could only derive from my broken relationship with...
I haven't been the same since New Year,
I changed my name,
And my age mates and old friends ain't treating me same.

I can see it in your eyes you don't like me,
You despise me
And I feel it.

I really do.

It's really not fun to hang out with me no more,
I couldn't fake a smile,
Even if you put me on trial and said do this or it'll cost you your life

I've tried twice to be the man I used to be
But the new me ain't having it
Ain't letting me go back to that depressive ass tragic shit

But as luck would have it,
Like an addict,
I've circled back to old habits
Quite tragic how I fiend for the heartbreak

The ups ain't felt high enough
And your advice can't save me
Been feeling lost around my friends
I know their drugs won't aid me

I know your God won't save me

My prayers keep going to voicemail
And I know me and God have a connection but my signals been lost for a while now

47

Say a happy poem Caleb
Look you're doing so well now
You're on a show
You're getting money
See you're even getting girls now

You don't know what I've been through
You don't care where my mind's at
You've just peeped game and seen clout
And jumped over my back

Treating me like a joke
But I ain't wearing no high hat
So get off your high horse
Say you're sorry like you mean it

And the funny thing is you probably all think I'm depressed,
But recently I'm feeling like my very best.

This was just yesterday.

*

I would cry if I knew what I was upset over.
I would scream if I had a clue what I was feeling.
But with all these cards my minds been dealing it makes sense why I'm always left the joker.

You have it all you should be happy now
Well happy how?
I've worn sadness all my life
Happiness don't fit me well

It's uncomfortable
To always see you looking up at me looking down
I wouldn't of aimed so far if I knew I was this scared of heights

But now I'm here I'm wondering if I'll ever accept it
Because my body naturally rejects it
And my mind always deflects it
And the people that always doubted me never did suspect it

The flower that grows from the concrete doesn't have the luxury of feeling camera shy

But it's that flashback that makes me run back to my roots,
The roots that run deep filled with turmoil from the soil and deceit from mothers teat.

Can I speak?
No because we demand your silence.
Just smile and wave and please leave all emotions on autopilot

*

I feel like I'm falling into routine,
Life nowadays feels like I'm stuck in
a scene
And in the seams of the fabric of
my mind I find myself to have fallen
outta favour with the lord
(send help)

I'm a stranger in my home now,
Searching for attention whilst
screaming leave me alone now

On the phone but never pick up
All alone
    - I rarely am
But when I'm home I'm finding ways
to escape far from this land

I'm a stranger in my mind now,
Can't put two words together

Am I really living fine when my mood
sways with the weather?

I'm still not eating
U can see my body changing
People say I'm looking skinny
But they can't see the stress I'm
gaining

My mum don't look at me the same
Stranger in my own home
She looks at me with fear
Cause the boy she knew was
homegrown

And that breaks me to the point
where I can't even form a sentence,
Can't put two words together

Still I'm happier than ever.

How does that work?

*

Do you know how painful it is that
your face now only reminds me of
how undeserving I am.

And the fact that you have to deal
with that

One day talking to a brick wall and
the next day I'm breaking it down
for you.

I could love you more than anyone
else.

I could hurt you more than anyone
else.

No one man should have all that
power.

Clocks ticking, I'm too scared to
count these hours

U deserve more than cold showers
and epiphanies,

I should be your wake up call.

You're stronger than I am.

I should be stronger than you.

And no, not because I'm a man but because you need me to be.

But I am undeserving.

I could surprise you but I always hide away

And no one likes a jack in the box;

Only able to stretch out of it for the joke just to reel back in until the next.

I can't/won't finish this poem.

I'm still living it

And it's not due to lack of I
But lack of U

Fake love and the multiple times U
left me thinking I needed U

Young Valentine
Thinks a rose might save the day
But the thorns down her stem
Will sting when the salt of the tears
hit the sores in your heart

*

My tears aren't really used to falling
on a smile,
And it's not that I haven't seen them
in a while,
It's that they're usually paired with
a trembling lip
And a tip telling them that men
don't do that shit.

I am Mr. Lonely

PETALS FELL OFF THE TREES
AND TRICKED ME INTO AN AUTUMN
I MEAN GREEN SHOT THROUGH TO BE
SEEN AND MY FACE WAS CLEARED OF ITS
EXASPERATION. YOU SUFFOCATED MY
SUMMER THOUGHT I TO ME BEFORE I'D
TIME TO BE, AND BE SOLD AND BOUGHT BE
FLAUNTED + TOLD
YOU'RE ONLY YOUNG ONCE SO
NEVER GET OLD
PRUNE YOUR BUSHES AND PERK UP YOUR
BLOSSOM - I'LL REMEMBER YOU BEFORE YOU'RE
FORGOTTEN. BEFORE YOU FALL TO THE
DAMPENING GROUND LIKE A USED OLD
TISSUE BUT WITH LESS SOUND. YOU'LL
DISAPPEAR INTO A SMUTTY HAZE, BUT AT
LEAST ONCE YOU WERE PAID AND AT LEAST
BEFORE YOU HIT THE SKY YOU HAD A REALLY
REALLY GOOD OLD TRY.
WELL DONE OLD PAL AND SMACK ON BACK
YOU'VE MADE IT FROM WHERE
I AM SAT
YOU'VE MADE IT FROM WHERE
I AM SAT
YOU'VE MADE FROM
WHERE I AM SAT

'Love #5 ', LILY ASHLEY

-

Love #5 was written in response to the pressure imposed on men
(and now women) to be successful, as "time = money", when in fact both of
the latter are made up. It's a brief study on the disconnect from nature and
how it has created a strengthening anxiety - the poem acts as a resolve to
these worries.

I like using watercolour as you can wash it away with more water, nothing in
permanence, it encourages absolute uncertainty.

-

'*Grey Man* is a publication exploring the social and psychological effects of the world of work on men. Each issue tackles a stereotypical attribute from the working world and explores its impact on males;
issue one interrogates the concept of uniform.

I - Barney Fagan, Emma Teasdale and Evie Godwin decided to create Grey Man in response to reading the rates of male depression and suicide which are employment related. We began to question which central elements of the world of labour and our wider society lead to this mentality. With no obvious answer, we decided to launch *Grey Man* in search of an answer. To tackle the working world at its core, we decided to take the format of one of its primary elements, the broadsheet, and tried to subvert it in the same way we were trying to subvert the way we think about work. Through a flipped landscape format, expressive and emotive articles, non-traditional typesetting, tailored illustrations and a custom typeface we created a language that contrasts the traditional newspaper and attempts to question work and what it means to men.'

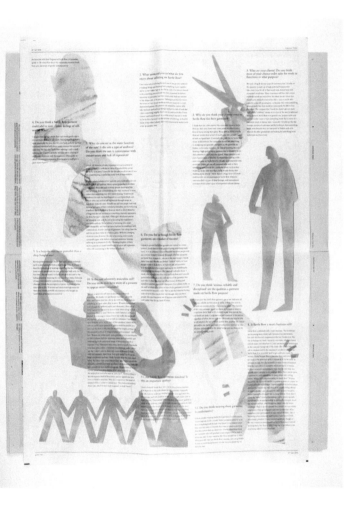

-

The shirt, we're here for the shirt. My father got me my first shirt when I was a kid, and now my little one has one too. He barely knows what a ball is as yet, let alone what the shirt means - its myth and its history - but everything we do, we do for the shirt. And he and I will sit here, when he's old enough for a season ticket (I've already put his name down), and over our packed lunches I'll tell him about the first time we did the double, about all those European nights, and about how the shirt is more than just a shirt: it's a tradition and it's a community.

I don't have every shirt, no. I mean, some of the new seasons' shirts are barely any different to the previous seasons', and it's not like I'm flush enough to drop fifty quid on something that I've essentially already got. But I'd think about it every time that there's a change - you know, like when there's a new shape or new sponsor. I'd definitely get one every time there's a new manufacturer.

The new Nike ones, for example, are pretty much completely different to the old Umbro ones. I have picked up a few of the old collector's ones - you know, the vintage style ones, the ones that you see in the old pictures, where you've got a whole team of these shirts, a line of soldiers marching up Wembley's steps to collect the FA Cup from the Royal Box. I love these shirts. But it's really infuriating because my partner doesn't like them. I think they're proper retro but she won't let me wear them out when when I'm with her. And then you have those pubs that say 'No Team Colours', and they're not the kind of shirt that you can wear when you're having a kickabout with your mates, and they're kind of itchy if you're just going to sit about in them at home. They're too synthetic, too plasticky for that. So they end up just sitting in the cupboard. Even if I could wear them, I wouldn't know where.

'No Team Colours'. They have it lettered on the doors of their pubs. Our pubs - or they should be, at least. They're the pubs that line the way from the station to the ground - the pubs that you want to drink in. The pubs with the real fans: the hardcore, the dyed-in-the-wool. They're the guys that stand behind the goal in the home end. They're always on their feet, always singing, and you can always see their hands - up in the air, pointing to the sky; masked across their face, biting their nails in frustration; or despondently holding their heads when things aren't going quite right. And they're the pubs that won't have us, and the people that won't even talk to us. They just have the sign: 'No Team Colours'.

These are the pubs - the ones for the locals - that always end up having the most trouble outside of them. I remember reading in The Guardian last year one report that was particularly bad. Four guys (older than me, you'd know) all ended up hospitalised, three of them with stab wounds. And you never see none of these guys in 'team colours'. These are the old fellas in their short-sleeve Fred Perrys or the young lads in Topman. These are the kinds of guys that drink in the pubs that say 'No Team Colours'. You know you'd find me in one of these pubs on any game day - but, come on, you have to wear the shirt to matches.

The pubs on the corner don't have any real atmosphere in them. They're pubs but they're not real pubs. They're full of tourists on their one day out at the football for the year. And you know literally everybody in there is gonna be in the shirt. Everyone's gonna be tanked up and chanting. And it's these pubs that'll have the bouncer at the door, even though the guys inside are nothing more than your travelling prawn sandwich brigade. But to everyone walking past, all the people doing their Saturday shopping, we look like an enclosure at the zoo, full of sound and fury - but actually signifying nothing.

We take the shirt seriously. I remember at the start of the season, on opening day, our big number nine banged in the winner and he ran straight to the home end and kissed the badge. The passion in his eyes! It was palpable. You could feel it. But he ended up getting a lot of stick for that from the fans in the online forums. Apparently, they didn't like the fact that he flirted with one of the European clubs in the summer. We offered him a massive new contract - almost double what he was on before - and he stayed, he's committed to the shirt for the next five years. And in today's market, that's as good as a lifetime.

grey man

-

How do you change when wearing your uniform? Do you act and react in a certain way depending on your clothing?

Yes, I think the phrase that best describes it, you've heard of suited and booted? It literally feels like I've put my suit on and it's not just my suit, it's all of my business attire. It's my shirt, tie, pocket square, suit, formal shoes and then it's literally me then switching on, ready to do business. There's something about bringing your true self to work and it's something that my firm really labour on. I'm not going to work relaxed, I'm going to work switched on, so I am into that sort of work mode, ready to face the day. I have prepped, I know which meetings are coming up, I know for the most part, which people I am going to be dealing with and the challenges that I am going to be facing throughout the day.

How would you change when you put on your RAF uniform?

It's much the same, the RAF uniform came first, so I joined the Air Force at 18, so literally a month after my 18th birthday. If you think about how the forces work and how fire training works, effectively it's to break you down and then build you back up again. It did teach me independence, resilience, but you also get treated a bit like cac, because that's part of the breaking down part and that's very formalised by the uniform in the armed forces. Alongside that, it's a very hierarchical organisation and necessarily so.

The forces are effectively preparing for times of crisis, to defend the UK and it's in the national interest. You can't defend by committee, if you're given an order, particularly at the lower ranks, yes you are taught to question it, in terms of is it the right thing to do, but generally it is. The ranks above you are demonstrated by the uniform they wear and the badges of rank on that uniform. They have earned that through demonstration of their own capability, both in terms of leadership and their ability to engage with their troops and their subordinates. So the original question of how did that differ in the RAF, well for me the RAF came first, it was what I knew as an 18-year-old. I joined at 18 and I was very immature, I grew up in the Royal Air Force and spent 20 years there. Particularly for the last 8 years of being in the services, it prepared me for going out into business and equally taught me the relevance of what I was doing in the forces to business. Just changing my RAF uniform was symbolic, so I left the Air Force and set up my own company and bought 5 business suits as my new uniform for my new company.

Why do you wear your pocket squares?

So going back to the previous questions we've just been going through about comparisons of uniform and rank, it is funny how similar business is to the military. In the military it's obvious where you sit in the hierarchy dependent on your rank, what badge you are wearing and literally how many stripes, how many crowns and pips you have on your uniform.

Within business it depends on the context of where you're working, so I have worked with the creative industry, it's almost like their uniform is casual dress. I can remember turning up to do a piece of work with Boden clothing, I turned up wearing my normal attire, as in what I believe was expected of me as a senior executive within management consultancy firms. So I had on, a pinstriped suit, shirt, tie, pocket square, my normal rig, turned up and all their executives are wearing, jeans, shirt open, converse trainers, kind of thing. I was standing out like a sore thumb and I was very conscious of what the uniform was in that situation.

In my normal business, I work with very high level defence and with the cabinet office, there is an expectation, an organisational culture, so the uniform is suits, shirt, tie. I walk into a room and nobody has met me before, but what I am wearing conveys to the people in that room, or so I perceive it, that I am of a certain level of seniority and I am to be taken seriously.

They associate what I've got to say with what I am wearing, they shouldn't do, but unfortunately that's the prejudice that exists within that organisational culture. Why I wear my pocket squares, is almost my little bit of individuality, if you're wearing a pocket square, you've got to have some nuts to do that.

'No Team Colours'. They have it lettered on the doors of their pubs. Our pubs - or they should be, at least. They're the pubs that line the way from the station to the ground - the pubs that you want to drink in. The pubs with the real fans: the hard-core, the dyed-in-the-wool. They're the guys that stand behind the goal in the home end. They're always on their feet, always singing, and you can always see their hands - up in the air, pointing to the sky; masked across their face, biting their nails in frustration; or despondently holding their heads when things aren't going quite right. And they're the pubs that won't have us, and the people that won't even talk to us. They just have the sign: 'No Team Colours'.

I love my pocket squares, they're pretty, they say something about me beyond a blue shirt, a standard tie and black leather shoes. My pocket square is my little bit of individuality, it's my little, just have a look at me. I used to be self-conscious about who I was and my personality, but I have now realised that I'm now comfortable. My god it's taken me bloody thirty odd years to do it, in fact thirty years in business this year. It's taken me thirty years to be comfortable with who I am and effectively people can draw their own conclusions, but I'm content with who I am and that pocket square is part of who I am.

How much do you feel your job constructs and represents your identity, or your past job in the RAF?

Let's talk about restricting personality. I mentioned it before in a previous question, bringing your true self to work - I think is really really important, to us as people and being happy, content and satisfied with our careers and what it is we do and how we make a difference in life. When I first joined the air force at 18, I did basic training and then went off and did a three-year technical apprenticeship, three years is a long time. I found it quite difficult, but I enjoyed the technical aspects of it. Bearing in mind there were about seventy-odd of us, we had a full uniform in terms of our RAF ranks and we had uniforms as apprentices, so we all looked the same. I used to get quite frustrated and never felt like I fitted in, because out of work, the vast majority of my colleagues, my fellow apprentices, their uniform out of work would be a football shirt, jeans and trainers. I really never subscribed to that, I will be honest, I can remember about 6 months after joining in an attempt to fit in and be part of the crowd, I actually bought a football shirt and jeans, I probably wore them twice, out with that lot, but then sort of had a look at myself in the mirror and realised I wasn't being true to myself. That made for a tough time kind of thing, so I used to get mocked in terms of wanting to wear nice things, about having my hair, not just a skin head or flat top kind of thing. I did stand out slightly.

There was this culture of unless you were wearing a football shirt, jeans and trainers, you were somebody to attract suspicion, it was that thing of "you think your better than us because you're not wearing a football shirt" and that's something that has always rankled with me.

In that regard, it wasn't until my second job that I actually fell in with a bunch of five guys, who did like similar things. We sort of dressed similarly, we liked the same sort of music and we just clicked literally, we were thick a thieves and had the piss taken out of us because we were known as the clique. Here we are bloody 25 years later, we all got together in London a couple of months back and it still sticks, it's the clique reunion, but that was great, really got on with them. I felt like I was starting to bring my true self to work in that regard.

I then went off and got commissioned and went off to university. Studying Aero-Mechanical Systems Engineering, I felt I had gone back to the apprentice type crowd. Funnily enough all of those guys that were studying the degree with me, (nineteen officers in total), but away from university, the guys would be wearing, football shirts, jeans, trainers, talking about bloody football all the time. They would be playing golf, smoking, playing darts and I just wasn't into that and I felt I was driven to behave in ways that weren't me.

It wasn't until I left university and did my officer training that I was with people that literally had just qualified from university. There are no preconceptions with the royal air force, I was just thrown in with a load of graduates, no preconceptions and suddenly it felt like I could breath. I am an extroverted person, I know I'm quite loud and brash and sometimes my extroverted nature can be misconstrued for arrogance. I'm very self-aware of that, but there I was on my officer training and found that I felt like for the first time I was really able to be myself in my job and I was actually getting lorded as part that. However, in my RAF career, there were periods when I didn't feel I could be myself, there were times when I felt like I had to behave a certain way. It's not until I joined my current company, in January last year, it's quite hard for me to talk about because joining this company, it now feels like I have come home. I am bringing my true self to work, I'm happy in my skin and actually people want me to bring my true self to work and I'm adding a lot of value to the organisation and my clients by doing that.

Growing up, my father is what I would call a conservative conservative, I know he had a very tough upbringing from his mum and dad and not a lot of love in that family. Luckily enough my father met my mother who's Italian and is very emotional and she would always be an ameliorating influence on dad and his man's idea of being a man. I'm the oldest of three boys, so my younger brother is 19 months younger than me and I have got a youngest brother who is 10 years younger than me, but my younger brother and I are very close and have sort of shared experiences of growing up. As teenagers we used to go out and we were good lads, you know we weren't tearaways. We would push the boundaries, any teenage boys would, but actually dad's mantra to us as we were going out independently was, go out and have a good time but don't bring shame on the Checkley family name. It was all linked to that sort of values that dad believed that he had you know indoctrinated us into. Throughout my career I've been lucky enough to do a lot of stuff on self-awareness, on reflection of self and reflection on the behaviours of others. I have a lot of work around the Johari Window about my hidden blind spots. As I've gone through my career I am certainly very very aware of just how important diversity and parking things like biases and prejudice is. We are the product of our parents' biases and prejudices and the culture in which we are surrounded by.

I count myself very lucky and the education that I have had and the experiences I have had both in the services and after leaving the Air Force. My masters in particular introduced a criticality of thinking, so I feel now that I do step beyond any of those sort of patriarchal bounds and the degree of influence I have at work. I am able to call into question some of those patriarchal poor behaviours. I think the best example I can give was when I had my own company I was working on the improvement of the nuclear submarines maintenances and it's at a navel dock yard which is a fairly robust place.

It's pretty much like stepping back into bloody 1940s Britain kind of thing, so much patriarchal hierarchical leadership, it's all about shouting.

I can remember seeing a young graduate who was in charge of a team of guys and just basically was shouting his head off at them. I took him to one side and I asked him what he was doing and he said I'm their manager and leader and that what is expected of me. I said well why do you think that is, and he said because my leader and manager shouts at me and therefore that's what we do.

It was really sad to see that sought out perpetuation of leadership, whereas being in the forces, I had been lucky enough to study leadership. For me leadership is very much about getting people to want to do what you want them to do and actually them understanding the benefit of them doing that. They may not always agree with it, of what you have asked them to do, but you've managed to convince them and they've got enough respect and trust in you as a leader to do it without you balling and shouting and being directive and autocratic. There are times when you do have to be directive, particularly when the chips are down in situations, I'm a firm believer in a dare's model of testing an individual.

You change your leadership style based on the needs and the context of a certain situation, but in terms of a patriarchal rigid idea of a man and I think it's something that I've been lucky enough to step well beyond. I work in an environment where, particularly in management consultancy, there is diversity of what we do and who we work with across all sectors. We are very diverse, in diversity and all of its forms of age, background, ethnicity, sexuality, religion, all of those kind of things, we understand how important it is because it's part of engineering of creativity.

Men's and women's uniform

Thinking about my current role in management consultancy, we particularly look into defence and we do work across government. I actually get quite jealous of ladies, because there is a far greater degree of latitude with lady's business dress then there seems to be with men. That said, I imagine if I had a conversation with a female colleague she would probably say, "well all you men have to worry about is just wearing a suit" and you know what that's fine. With women it's a bit of a mine field because there is a greater degree of latitude. It can range from trousers and a blouse through to formal dresses such as belted dresses, I've even seen people wear what I construe as evening wear but they can carry it off because they're ladies. Equally I've turned up and if I was to wear a kind of open necked shirt without a tie, chinos and a blazer I will get looks, particularly in my office. They will go: are you not seeing any clients today?

I can remember talking to female colleagues in the forces and what was quite interesting in the air force is that men and women's day to day uniform was actually very similar. You'd wear a shirt and you don't necessarily need to wear a tie, but you can wear tie and a jumper which is the same for men and women. Guys had to wear uniform trousers but the women could choose to wear uniform skirts or uniform trousers, which was pretty much the same as guys but cut for women. When it came to the mess dress, which is the very formal, posh attire, I can remember female colleagues absolutely moaning and do you know what they are absolutely bloody right.

The guys mess dress was actually pretty spot on, you'd have high-waisted trousers, a formal waist coat and a sort of short fitted jacket. We used to call the women's mess dress circus tents, they were very wide and then they moved to having a similar jacket to the guys, but massive floor length skirt just looked bloody awful. It was almost that the forces used to struggle with what to put women in but that has changed a lot, I know it has changed a lot. I left the forces ten years ago and I know it's a lot better now, it used to be a floor length skirt made of suit material.

I have reflected on this, how would a woman be interpreted if she turned up in a full business suit with a shirt and tie and effectively wearing what man was wearing? I think it's quite interesting that the general impression would be, "well that looks quite odd", but why should it look odd?

Do you think the suit is synonymous with conservatism and lack of expression?

No I don't, whilst I said a pocket square is sort of my symbol of outward individuality associated with the suit, actually the suits I buy themselves, I'm very conscious of. I want to look good in a suit, so I have previously bought suits that I know didn't fit me very well.

I've got quite broad shoulders for my frame, unfortunately the only suits I could buy that would fit me then were suits for much larger gentlemen, that would hang off me like a sack of potatoes.

I could pull the suit jacket right out which was quite comic. I'm now in a position where I can buy suits that are fitted for me and I think actually in the last sort of three to five years, I think the market has really woken up to that. Not one size and shape fits all, especially guys of business. I'm proud of the way I look, I want to look nice, I want to go out and look good, not least of which I spend a lot of my time in my suits.

I don't just go and work in my suits, my job involves that I'm quite often at evening functions straight after work. I want to be comfortable in something that I know if I'm sitting in a bar or a restaurant or actually at a formal dinner - I still look good. I'm sorry if that's vain, but I have got pride in my appearance and I think it's important that I do look good, both for me as a person and having my self-esteem because my self-esteem supports my confidence and my ability to actually represent my company and do good work.

Do you feel the suit is a status symbol and do you feel they are a marker of success?

They can be, I think it is more important how the suit is worn. I've seen guys that I know use an inordinate amount of money on bespoke suits looking like an absolute bag of turd. In that instance I would say definitely not, probably in their heads they are thinking, right I've got a bespoke suit from Savile Row or wherever, therefore what a great status symbol. They would say it goes with my watch, my trophy wife and my Lamborghini, but actually that's all going on in their heads. Unless you know that you are looking at a bespoke suit that cost x thousand then it's, well you wouldn't know, it's only a status symbol for those who have status. I think it's far more important about how you look in the suit and how you carry the suit. I'm not a great believer in spending an inordinate amount of money on clothes and for me the suit is something I need to wear for my work, but it's a functional piece of attire. It goes back to that argument with women, saying, well all you have to do is put a suit on but they are right in that regard that I know if I'm going to a meeting with a cabinet officer, I've just got to put a suit on, a good shirt, a good tie, make sure the combo looks good, polish my shoes and I'm ready to go.

-

I'm hardworking, I'm determined, I'm inspired, this is clear when I say I'm the man, this means I'm big and strong and will carry on. I can't let you down, it's not in my nature, my biology, my gender.

I do it for you, for me, the kids, as well as for my mental stability. I need to keep working, stay stable, make money, even if I have to sacrifice my own joy, this is the responsibility of a boy.

Wait...
not a boy, a man, I'm masculine, which means I'm the breadwinner, it's up to me, why don't you see. My darlings, I'm working away so that you get to play.

The arguments are a strain, but I'm to blame. They're right, as the man of the house it's up to me, it's my responsibility. The bills are flooding in, the money is rushing out, and behind it all I'm losing it all... in my mind.

There is another voice in my brain saying "why not give in". Not again I say to the many thoughts that are rushing around causing more strain.

It's everyday life, so why is this so hard? On the outside I'm the man you have always known and loved, but tragically inside I'm lost.

I want help but it's all wrong to ask, it's a burden on all who I love, I'll keep things to myself, it's my responsibility... I'm the man.

But, why don't they notice... no this is progress, if they don't see, then I've got stability.

I'm not struggling, leave me alone, I can deal, you reap what you sow.

No... no leave me alone, I can manage on my own.

Leave then I don't need you, the kids I'll see once in a blue moon?

It's all wrong, there's no way out, and there's no doubt. My next move needs to be swift and short, end this suffering inside and out.

They speak so loud inside my mind, with no ability to rewind. Do I do an act so permanent, it will scar the lives of those so close, but end mine? Do I take the rough path and seek a guide to help me through the troubles that come in and outside of my mind?

I'm at a crossroads with no ability to think, can I make this 50/50 bet to get out of debt?

I can't be this lost surely, I'm the man, but perhaps I will, I won't, I can't, I can... because after all my dear ones... I'm the man.

One succumbed to the darkness of his brain, one took the path less travelled and struggled and strived to break out and survive.

It's not obvious to see how toxic the term masculinity. Men are men when they beg, scream and cry, who are we to deny.

When are men not boys? Whose to say when and if they put away their toys. It's tragic when they grow up so fast, all to be later burdened with so many a task.

More and more the years are shorter, especially when it's because their lives have faltered. No sympathy, except when statistics are as high as we now see.

What happened to the man that died, that remains with the ones he left behind.

From what I have seen it's left those so close broken and fragile, in a constant state of turmoil. The others lesser known, are the mates and dates of the man who would always come home.

Keeping it all in, that's how they win. Remember the day, all we now all think is "wish he had stayed".

Stories are told through the memories that shine bright like gold. As of course he was bold and brave, but we still can't help wondering why he let his positive mind-set fade.

Mentally and physically a man should be strong, therefore it's essential they know it's not wrong to seek guidance and sympathy in order for that stability.

Friends, family or professional care, why is the attitude that they're not there?

The man that survived has thrived, it's day by day, but even he still says "I'm doing fine". He knows how to admit when he's down and when the bad thoughts are there, but he is still a man. Through crying, through fighting, through the support of loved ones and care, he is still there.

Tragically, what's physical of the man who was, is and now, like him will always be gone.

'*The Male Gaze*', **SAM COLDY**

Rome, 2017

-

Cyanide and Happiness

Broken wings
with the ruffled feathers,
freedom seems so far away.
But don't you cry,
don't you cry,
eternity is
but a second away.
Your wings will soon spread,
and flap in the wind
when life is nothing more.
So wait my child,
Please be patient,
eternity is
but a long way away.

Faceless Woulds

A shell of my former self.
Empty beer cans and
cigarette snubs,
series of unfortunate events,
bad news never wonders alone.
I am haunted by the shadow of
death,
Frightened by the looks I will get.
From ashes to ashes
Dust to dust
As I shoulder my cross
My burdens
My loss,

I pitifully concede.
My heart bleeds,
in my darkest moments
yet I do not speak up
I do not speak up
For reasons I cannot admit.
I am already weak.
It's been a week
And you haven't heard me speak.
Still one day I hope,
One day I pray,
You can take this pain away.

The Final Stand

Living in an abyss,
free-falling into darkness...
My thoughts are suffocating my soul;
strangling my heart;
destroying my mind...
Tired of looking for peace in a world
that thrives on our pain.
Death isn't a choice.
It's merely a formality to the other
world.
A better world.
Where the grass is green,
and peace is not just a word,
and pieces of our hearts aren't just
toys
for the world to play with.

No longer seeking clarity from
others,
only the reaper has the answers.
Call my words grim,
call my actions sins.
Still, our final breath
is like the sigh of an angel...
A sigh of relief.

Existing is Lonely, Depression is Warm

Existing is pretty scary. I mean, to exist is to accept an emptiness I can't quite yet explain... but to live, well that's the tricky part. Living requires a certain je ne sais quoi. It requires purpose, drive, ambition. It requires everything absent in this life of mine.

It has been a while since I have written anything like this, so forgive my incoherent stream of thoughts. Often it helps to just put pen to paper, or, in this instance, press a few keys on my laptop and hope the sentences formed make sense.

Plastered over a book of mine 3 years ago was a quote by Nietzsche. "Man's misfortune is that he was once a child", it said. I didn't understand what it meant then. I still don't understand what it means now. I thought I did. I thought I knew everything. Bold and brazen, I spoke of things I half knew. Like Dr. Jekyll and Mr. Hyde, half-truths and half-lies were two sides of the same coin to me. A coin I would frequently toss. My faith, fate and future was left twirling in the air, a telltale of a man no longer in control of his life. Or maybe I never had control.

It's frightening. Frightening realising you know nothing. Frightening realising you are lost. Frightening realising you spent most of your childhood chasing wind, only to constantly gasp for air as an adult because you have nothing keeping you afloat. So what do you do next?

You run. You hide. You isolate yourself. That's what I did. I ran away from my emotions. I hide myself away from my family, my friends, the world. You don't even realise what you have done. It just happens. The replies get slower. You become less bothered. Disinterested in anything and everything. The numbness takes over. It becomes a part of you. And you become comfortable in your isolation... warm, almost.

Numb to my achievements, my emotions, everything, I accepted I would never find the joy and happiness I once had when I was younger. Attempts at finding what made me happy became torturous. Tormenting myself over the thought of what makes me happy prevented me from accepting I could find happiness in new things.

The truth may set me free, but sometimes I need the comfort of lies surrounding these four walls, within which lies my deepest fears. I spent the best years of my life chasing memories of a time when I was happier. Little did I know, my happier moments existed before my depression; and me chasing after those moments only made me fall deeper into the pit I was trying to climb out of.

I love having my space. I love being alone. Or so I thought.

Being under the impression that I loved independence, I seeked all the components of Independence to be more in her likeness. I did everything alone. I avoided anyone who would take my Independence away from me. I became reclusive. Little did I know; I was cheating on Independence with Loneliness. My time alone was a cover. It was a way for me to hide my failings. Hide my lack of growth. Hide my lack of achievements.

If you know me, you'd know I say "i'm tired" a lot. Funnily enough, no one has ever really asked me why I say I'm tired. And i've never bothered explaining. I say that because I genuinely am. Mentally I am exhausted. Physically I am exhausted. I mean, i'm not exhausted to the point where my muscles are aching; but if it's between going for a walk or staying in bed, my warm and comfortable duvet will be right beside me as I finish a whole netflix series in 2 days. Often I wish I could explain why I'm tired. Often I wish people cared.

To be black, to be a man, and to suffer from a mental illness is lonely. Taking turns to talk about mental health amongst ourselves is like seeing a unicorn in the middle of Brixton market. We are stuck with Loneliness, a mistress we did not ask to sleep with. Yet we return to her bed time and time again. We keep this secret to ourselves, confiding only in those who won't judge us for cheating.

Often we use our depression as a blanket to insulate ourselves from further pain. Accepting the darkness we have become accustomed to, we comfort ourselves with the knowledge that things can't get worse. Because, truth be told, what could be worse than black? The world doesn't care about black. The world doesn't care about anything.

Scary are the days the voices in your head go silent. When the deafening silence screams, and you can no longer run away to another world with music from Spotify or Apple Music, you turn inwards. You see what you have become. You feel both free and frightened to know the world doesn't care about you, and you haven't cared about yourself.

Do you decide to change? Or do you continue along this path. A path many struggling with a mental illness have walked but have never had the strength to move away from.

I have been struggling to piece together my thoughts. I say this, but, in all honesty, I have avoided even listening to my thoughts. Whether it's feeling numb, incompetent, defeated, confused or feeling like I will never reach the level of happiness I once had before, I have allowed myself to remain this way. I am not living. I am existing. And that's what frightens me.

Hell Isn't So Bad When You Have Music

The sweet symphony of uncontrollable sobs can be so soothing when all you've known is the sound of silent suffering. When the effort of existing becomes unbearable, and the white noise surrounds you (and no, i'm not talking about Disclosure), you come to realise hell isn't so bad when you have music.

It's dark down here. "My mind is dark. Or maybe blank? I don't know." Silence. It's excruciating.

"Now everybody tellin' me a lie. Lordy give me something for my soul. See I don't wanna think of suicide. So please don't take the lock key off my door."

It begins. The lyrics living in my head have awoken. They bounce across my skull, jumping from ear to ear as though my mind is a playground. The devil's playground. And it was theirs. Theirs to control. Theirs to destroy. They had become so comfortable here. They knew things about me I didn't.

They knew my deepest thoughts, my deepest fears, my insecurities.

"See you can't handle pressure on your own, so why you carry boulders by your-self?" Who told you I shouldered all my burdens? How did you know I was crumbling under the pressure? Like crabs in a barrel, my own thoughts pull me down - deeper into hell I go.

The lyrics speak to me. They tell me things I would never tell myself. I know *"I just need some guidance in my steps"*. I know *"i'm not the only one alone"*. I know *"i'm not the only one who felt"*. But can I heal? Black boys aren't supposed to cry...or so I was told. Black boys weren't taught to cry...a myth I was sold.

Is it wrong *"I'm praying that I make it to twenty-five?"* I've lost friends. Friends who didn't see another year, another week. Friends who should have seen tomorrow, but tomorrow never came.

Call the doctors. Call whoever you want.

I know I've been having problems with myself. I know love doesn't live here anymore. Before you take me away, just tell me this: where does this "love" everyone talks about reside?

You claim to love me but you don't know my issues as a child. So what if I've been losing more than just my mind? So what if I don't want to be like any of you no more? I am coping my own way. And if I'm doomed to die young, my only wish is to receive an answer from our Heavenly Father. I want to ask Him, why are you so far away?

I am grateful Isaiah Rashad spoke to me in my moments of darkness. Days when I chose not to listen to myself, you were there. Music was there. There to support me when I let myself down.

It's true, I guess. Hell isn't so bad when you have music.

– To better understand this, listen to Isaiah Rashad - *Heavenly Father* –

Mental Health Week

In February 2016, a small group of friends and I, disappointed by our University's lack of focus on mental health, created our own Mental Health Week. Centred around the black community, we held five events. From workshops to safe spaces for people to talk openly, we tried to create a comfortable environment for people to speak and learn about mental health.

After seeing so many men close to me at university suffer from depression or bipolar disorder, holding the 'Men and Mental Health Session' was imperative. Men don't speak. Often we blame patriarchy, we blame upbringing, we blame our environment. Yet, though we may know the source, men still don't speak. That's what the event aimed to change. We wanted men to talk about their experience in a safe space. We wanted them to create their own support group. We wanted them to feel liberated. Free. Unfortunately, the disconnect between men and mental health still exists. Many felt no need to attend. Turnout was low. The cycle continues.

I wish more men became comfortable speaking about mental health. I wish things could change. The pressures men face are often made worse by university. Many men feel they are alone in their journey. But that is the myth I know HIM + HIS will dispel. Filled with personal stories and more, HIM + HIS is a reminder that we are not alone. There are people dealing with the same mental health struggles, and it's so important we come together to support each other. We don't always have to be strong. It's okay to cry. It's okay to pause. It's okay to breathe. Don't let it be too late. Please.

'Skull and Phones', JAMES MASSIAH

\-

you should have been 10 years ago
should've been dead 20 years ago
but you're here today and it is what it is

death will come for you like it came for the 26!
die now or in a few ticks, either way, it is what it is
death will come for you like it did for di'
and the thought of it might change the colour
of your bed sheets in the night!

you are the royal fresh heir to the throne
not quite ready to be pale white skull and bones

so tell me, kid -
tell me why you never take your eyes off that telephone?
"well, to be or not to be that is the question my g
and it fucks with me eternally - but this here
is another world man - i can suspend the pain
for a few scrolls and at least wait the length of
a story before i hear mine read out
plus i'm waiting for my life man to holla back
so i can put that white powder on my face
and forget it all again" -

yo clown what's up? you look down
i've seen you around - with that fake smile
your make up's been coming off for a while
you're thinking about that kid's birthday
where you entertain the little version of yourself
and they stare back into your eyes and say

"nigger you're gonna die!
what you gonna do with the rest of your life?"
i can't say i know kid - whether i die poor or rich
it is what it is - well or sick - free or stiff
what's differential? we're all just collateral
and then we die alone

it's that mortgage, baby!
but at least you like house music! so dance your fears away
take two of these and call me when the clocks go back
a billion days to when everything was black
and white was just the life you hadn't yet known
a light at the tunnel at the end of your nose

'In a world ruled by the dead, we decided to start living',
EMEKA COLLINS

-

Growing up as a Millennial, although very positive
and filled with opportunities, life can also be a burden.
We share pieces of ourselves religiously on social media
like bread at a holy communion, we're exposed to so much
reality online that we become numb to the reality in the world.
In all of this commotion, we tend to get lost in the "sauce"
 and most people have no real outlet to express real emotion.
This collection is inspired by friends that give me support, laughter,
annoyance and happiness in times of need.

January - September 2018

'Better Out Than In', ELOISE KNIGHTS

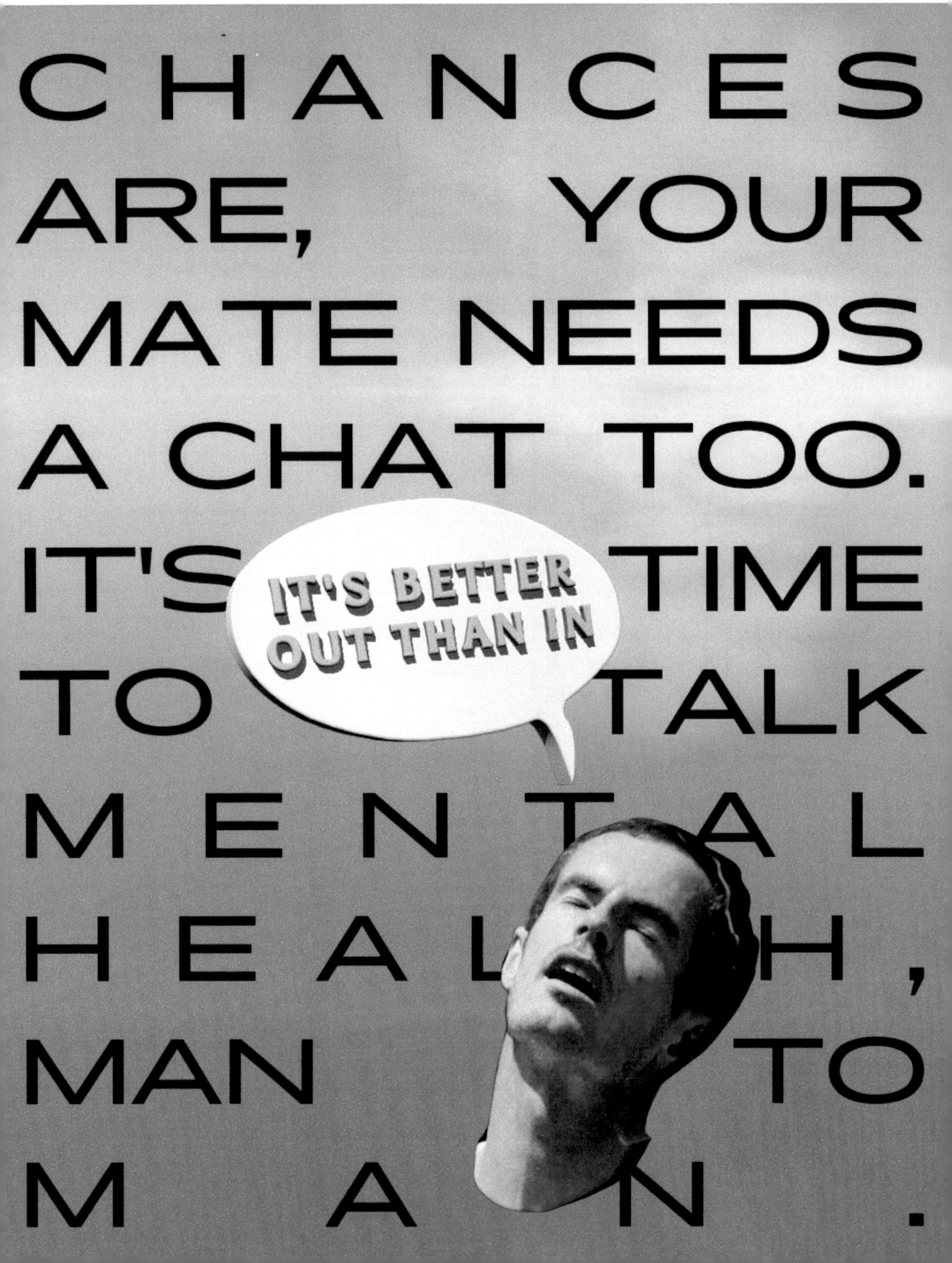

'*What I think of Men*' , DALJINDER JOHAL

-

What I think of men.

When I think of Sikh Panjabi men, I think of a bottle.

At our weddings, the dhol would beat and the clink of the glassi. I'd hear the cry of "one more" for the songs and the sips.

Growing up with my sister in the South Asian community taught me a lot about how harmful gender roles can be.

Most obviously was the fact that I quickly realised that I should stand in the kitchen with my mum at big family events. From under her chunni, I'd practise how to listen without seeming to listen.

Behind painted smiles, I'd look up and see the women of my community lie that they'd made the sabzi, that their husbands weren't hitting them, that each sneaked swig of vodka meant nothing even when vermillion red petals would smear on the lip of the bottle.

In fact, this was the closest I'd see to a lover's kiss. Instead, wives would be in one room, men in the other. True to their namesakes, the Singhs would sit around while women did the feeding.

Only my sister, ever the tomboy, the carnivore, would perch as usual, like a little ladybird in the crook of my dad's arm.

Here, the chatter of men would buzz like a swarm around her. But when the bottles would begin to sprout up to stand proudly on the table, she'd be shooed away.

Then the men would guzzle the precious nectar until they'd sway like drunken honeybees. They'd frighten me as they'd be sweet and fuzzy one moment, clumsily patting my curly head.

Yet then I'd watch as one misstep from a wife or sister would send them into a frenzy, their words stinging now, if not their fists later.

There was always a particular smell that still sets me on edge today.

———

It wasn't that I didn't enjoy teenage and university life. I loved heady late nights out, lazing at festivals, to dance until my feet ached or to stay up until 5am talking about our childhoods, our feelings, our futures.

But there was still a haunting undercurrent. A tiny female housemate stumbling towards me, eyes unfocused, arm swung lazily around my neck and an open-mouthed slur rambling in my ear.

Even then I'd smell it again.

———

Under my mum's wing, I practised how to watch and listen. I learned to understand the hardships of the women who fed me, hugged me and came before me.

My rite of passage into womanhood means that I'm now allowed to show that I'm listening and reach a hand out to dry tears or pull my fellow sisters into a comforting embrace.

But my mum also gave me the chance to fly above these so-called natural roles.

And by doing so, I learned to appreciate not only did I not have to be the prey, the princess, but men weren't necessarily the predator.

I grew up quickly to realise the reality of Sikh Panjabi women in our close-knit community. However, I have only now absorbed the lesson of what happens to our men.

Many Panjabi men are so bound up in their role as so-called lions that they so often struggle in silence.

Our community teaches them to be strong and be the pride of their family and community by working hard and uncomplainingly.

Yet whether it's in this country or "back home", they're not allowed to be human and just talk.

Instead, our inheritance is addiction, our bloodlines run sluggish and corrupt with rum rather than red health. Instead, that same poisoned liquid helps spill the blood of women in a vicious cycle of hurt and violence.

So many have drowned in the bottom of a glass and I should know, I've seen it.

This doesn't have to be our inheritance. These aren't natural instincts but taught behaviours from a culture that makes a man bottle up a feeling while unscrewing another.

My own family had a personal bereavement recently, sadness and alcohol was at the root of it.

My quiet dad thought it was his responsibility to stay strong, to keep us as one like the steel bangle on his arm.

He'd sit in his usual spot in the living room. The weekend beer hissing open in front of him, whilst he'd be there closed off.

My sister is in America and my mum was hit hard with the shock of our loss, usually a cocoon of blankets, tissues and tears.

I walked over to him from under my mum's blanket and so did she.

For a few moments, we all stood there, all pulled into one embrace. One ring, not of steel but love and words.

"It's okay to let it out".

And while only a few tears escaped, it's a start.

Dhol - Type of Drum
Glassi - A shot of alcohol
Chunni - A veil worn to cover the head
Singh - Lion
Kaur - Lioness/Princess
Sabji - Vegetarian dish
Steel bangle or Kara - A symbol of faith typically worn by Sikhs

*

-

It feels like a very long time ago I suffered from chronic depression, and yet, when life gets rocky, it can all come back in an instant as if it never left. In fact, it is because of this that I have been able to discover the power in vulnerability. Knowing that, no matter how "sorted" I may think I have life, at any point it could come crashing down. But that's not to say one should live in fear of what is to come, rather, live each moment with whole hearted fucking gusto as if it's our last - no fear. Instead, being driven by an authentic desire to discover life.

The depression - what did it look like? Like faux smiles, repeated over analysis of every aspect of life, toying with repeated suicidal thoughts, comparisons in my head to what "a real man" looks and acts like... just beating myself up for being me. A constant feeling of not being enough. Forever acting how I thought people wanted me to be - so much so that I completely exhausted myself and lost any sense of identity.

One of the biggest things was that amidst all this negativity, I felt completely normal so would then beat myself up for having these down moments. There was just no acceptance of myself. It's tiring even reading all this, isn't it? Imagine it being the narrative of your life - I truly was a victim to unconscious traumas.

"You're being stupid, there's nothing even wrong".

"Your life is great. What have you got to moan about? You have great supportive friends and family, a sweet set up, there are people with real issues in the world, stop feeling sorry for yourself".

Little did I know that it was these thoughts, this lack of acceptance of my own being, that was depression in action. All these "normal" things we think everyone has handled, and so that internal dialogue tells us we are stupid for thinking them - they're the killer: (and if at any point you're wondering what I mean by that "internal dialogue" - I mean the voice reading this back to you in your head. The thing that doesn't stop chattering all day and you must befriend lest it become your enemy).

This negativity would then manifest itself into self-sabotage too and before I knew it, I had formed a new identity WITHIN this depression that would feed the depression further! Thoughts of inadequacy, leading to acts of inadequacy, leading to beating myself up for the inadequacy... annnnd repeat... herein a new negative cycle was born. A cycle within which I could strangely seek comfort. All of a sudden people were feeling sorry for me. I remember my girlfriend at the time started being super kind and loving towards me when I was down - but more so than usual. Looking back, I can now see my mind/ego was just thinking, "yes! I've found a way of being that will make people care about me and feel sorry for me". Very fucking slippery slope to be on. All these things just brewing away in the background and I was none the fucking wiser.

It is only upon reflection that I can see just how negative ALL my thoughts were. How trapped I felt and defeated I was. In my mind I regularly had the thought, "no matter how bad it gets, I can just kill myself and that'll teach everyone!". Lol. My own life was a mere bartering tool to teach people a lesson, and I was totally fine with it. I was convinced it was an absolutely ok thought to harbour, as if somehow I could benefit from it. Man, that's what I used to think?! Madness. Big madness and yet all too common.

It took acceptance of all of this, and a true rock bottom feeling to then begin to see the true beauty in life and be thankful for my own existence. Once you hit the bottom and experience that feeling of - "I can feel no more", "I am untouchable, nothing can be worse than this" - it seems like there's no point in living - however, context twist - when you are that low, the only way is up. When you realise nothing can touch you, holy shit that's so powerful! NOTHING CAN TOUCH YOU! There is serious power in the vulnerability of it. Total surrender to life's will almost.

Getting that everyone is on their own journey and seeing the world through their own perceptions and interpretations. All we can do is train our empathy muscles and let go of opinions, and just be how we want to be. Accept others however the fuck they want to be too.

Oh, re the suicide... just to quickly share, I could never bring myself to do it, because I couldn't do it to my family. I couldn't put them through it, and though that made me feel like I was just existing, not living and too scared to die - it kind of highlights that innate loving aspect of our souls. That each and every human has in them so we know we can relate. We are so connected.

These thoughts we think no one else thinks, but we all do... if you share something that no one has yet experienced, it's real for you so it's as real as anything else in this universe. Who knows, you may have answered a question that someone else didn't even know existed in their space until they heard your share.

In a bid to share some raw vulnerability myself, I personally was enslaved by the "is my dick big enough", "how do I look?", "am I funny enough?" concerns. Thoughts I hear all too often from other young males, instilling a desire in me to globalise an open dialogue around the matter. In sharing this shit and not holding it in one's mind, it frees up so much space and creates this empty canvas that you can then just go forward and fill with beauty. Share love, share beauty, share joy and smiles. Celebrate one another's existence and emanate light as one.

The truth is that anxiety, depression, disconnection; all these things are massively common because WE. ARE. HUMAN. BEINGS. There is nothing to hide or ever be ashamed of. There is power in sharing, in vulnerability, in allowing ourselves to align with the truths our intuition and soul guide us to.

-

I was lucky enough to find patience and compassion when going through my mental health struggles at University. My housemates provided an essential foundation from which I was able to discuss my difficulties in an open and honest way. However, I know many are not afforded the luxury of being so open in such situations. I looked back home, to the Punjabi community in which I grew up, and I saw that mental health was often pushed aside, silenced, and used as a point of derision.

Taraki wants the Punjabi community to understand mental health in a different way. By being more open and honest about our experiences, I hope that we can all begin to understand the mental health struggles of others, and be in a position to offer support when needed. At this moment, I am particularly looking to the Punjabi male community, who have a distinctive relationship with mental health tied up to notions of self-understanding, involving gendered, racialized, and sexualised forms of expression. A Punjabi man is confined by the notions of masculinity, what it means to be a brown man in a white world, and the fallacious link between expressing 'feminine' traits and a non-heterosexual identity.

By platforming the experiences of Punjabi men and mental health, we look to break down these preconceived notions which increase suffering within the individual, families, and wider community. Before developing formal, structures of support, we need to understand mental health in a different way, debased from notions which look to oppress those suffering.

Taraki means being 'forward-facing', or 'progressive', but I prefer it to be a continual movement, a non-stop phase of learning about ourselves and the world around us. Working towards something better, we look to the community to provide the systems of support the government have failed to construct. This is a model I hope to consolidate and share, working with non-Punjabi communities to tackle mental health within their lived experiences as minority communities in Britain.

"It was difficult to talk to anyone at the time; a cloak of silence seemed to have masked all attempts to understand why my father's death occurred. Religion mixed with custom, soaked in culture. Suicide was taboo,
a stigma to be avoided at all cost.
Eventually I began to seek some professional help. Thankfully, I was referred to a Mental Health therapist who helped me set foot onto the road to happiness. A person who listened without prejudice,
unblemished by society's taboo."

Kalwinder Singh Dhindsa, 38, Writer and Activist

"I've had depression on and off for years due to a number of reasons. But recently, it's the worst it's ever been. I would overthink everything to the point that sleeping for 14 hours straight was my only escape from my obsessions. I suffered big breakdowns every other day. I lost dozens of 'friends' in my life. I would lash out at people including my family to the point that it was affecting their health. I would only eat one meal in a day. I showered every 3 days.
I planned my suicide on multiple occasions.
Eventually, I decided to cry out for help as a last resort. Literally hundreds of people showed their love and support for me which gave me one last hope. I've been to many other therapists before but then I was directed to Sikh Coaching - they're a life saver. I am currently in the process of reinventing myself and taking slow steps upwards. I still have many bad days, but I have been to hell itself, and I realise that there is light amongst my darkness."

Gindy, 21, Student

Submissions to Taraki, featured on the Instagram page
*@taraki_*

'28 / Duty Manager / Wolverhampton / Freelance TV Artist / British Indian', **Arun Kapur**

-

I am a strong firm believer in supporting mental health. I myself have spent many years dealing with my own experiences, and coming to terms with each one. I believe that we can all support each other on an everyday basis, and encourage each other to be more vocal about what we are going through. I have learnt that I should not be ashamed of what I am feeling, and it is perfectly normal to feel vulnerable and ask for help. Let life inspire you, and tell yourself it is okay, to be okay. I have seen myself rise from the lowest of lows, to finally seeing daylight again. I have been in the position of taking my own life, sometimes you feel there is no way back up. Never give up the fight, if you need a shoulder, we are here for you. The World is ours. Keep smiling.

Blindside

People like to think they can play God. They like to think they are puppet-masters. We are strung under every whimsical yet unimaginable command by these so called 'Gods'. Feeding their greedy - addiction, power. Power is a fragile tool to contain regardless of the possessor. I am left blind-sided by thought and yet again I am lost. No one is the almighty no matter how high; we are created as one so why would you command from your own flesh and blood? Crimes against humanity, you are just a hypocrite. You pounce upon your blood-lust for every sin which is tattooed on your skin, whilst you shower your filthy gold and possessions. Offer no cost of you to any of the puppet masters, there is a reason to still hold on and see the light again.

Alive

Don't cry for me, for before you I was dead anyway. You brought me meaning to why I exist, you gave me something which I been craving, when I was broken, you glued me together, holding me long as you could. Life gives us lessons and blessings, you will always be a blessing, one I take soon to the grave with me. You made me feel alive, gave me the reason to rise once again and believe in myself. You stopped me from drowning, you stopped me from slipping off the edge. My heart does, and will always ever belong to you. You will be with me for not in this life, but into the next. I just want your star to always shine bright, even if it is not in my sky. I am alive once more, tears will stream of sadness forever, but you freed me and gave me my wings to help fly again.

Warrior's tears

Even in the face of battle, the warrior may still shed a tear. Through the suffering, the pride, we are finally here. Broken, shattered, we urge amongst even the strongest of people, never run away from your fears. The path becomes blind, allowing darkness the ascend. The warrior will never back down, for they are so near. No one will understand the path of another warrior, for they are being submerged submerged inside. Fallen so far deep, they become unable to at times prevent their own peril. A warrior's spirit will never die, even once when they awake from hell. A Warrior will live again, to us all. Be true, live through the pain and it will become never more.

'Untitled', ZEBIB K. ABRAHAM
PGY-3 PSYCHIATRY RESIDENT
MOUNT SINAI PSYCHIATRY, NEW YORK

-

We sat around a table under fluorescent lights, in between lectures, waiting for a meeting with one of the psychiatric attendings to begin. We were psychiatrists in training, out of medical school, learning psychiatry in inpatient psychiatric wards, outpatient offices, emergency rooms. We saw behind the veil, and we worked with the most ill patients. Our attending soon walked into our lecture room, appearing tired and somewhat resigned, his hands clasped before him as he sat down to address the room of trainees. He had an issue to discuss with us, one he did not know how to address exactly, an ethical, cerebral sort of problem he thought we might be able to help address.

Medical students were beginning their rotations on the psychiatry floors and in the emergency room, and they too were entering the world behind the veil for the first time. They began to see how we handled patients who were mentally ill. And these students, these naïve students, thought that there the doctors were biased. Things were not sitting right with them. How white doctors seemed to treat some of the mentally ill, often black patients, disparage them, make jokes about them. The way they saw it, black patients were seemingly treated with more disdain and judgement, were medicated more aggressively. Things did not seem fair. Overall, they felt that us doctors might be, well, racist.

To my surprise, my fellow psychiatrists in training did not think these medical students knew what they were talking about. The students were young, naïve, "too idealistic". We had to be responsible for the safety of ourselves and our patients. Sure, we made jokes, got jaded, but we cared a lot and worked really damn hard to ensure the best care. To an extent, the students didn't really understand all the facts. It is a hard job that required tough decisions. Seeing the periodic patient held down and medicated is never nice, but it is sometimes necessary when a patient is acting dangerously. But how come we couldn't address it, the *race* of it all?

Psychiatrists don't talk enough about race. We give superficial credit to the racial biases that have been researched and proven. We claim we know how race affects risk for certain disorders, the different cultural understandings of mental illness. We acknowledge that, the facts of it, in passing, in resigned sighs and nods. Yeah, we know about "implicit bias", about "systemic dis-enfranchisement", "access to resources", "stigma". We were well-educated, liberal, full of social justice, medical knowledge, and higher callings. But in my experience, doctors and psychiatrists are just like the rest of us, and just as uncomfortable as anyone talking about race in depth. We get defensive and scared when asked to acknowledge the possibility that our collective and individual biases affects our work - psychiatry.

It's hard enough for us to understand and empathize with the experience of being depressed, being anxious, having a psychotic spectrum disorder. To take on the burden of people's pain, to turn it over in our minds. To know what to say, what approach in treatment to take, what medications to give, and to navigate the intimate yet vast territory between you and this other person in the room, this "patient". We train for a decade to begin to under-stand the field of psychiatry. How do I help this person, reduce their suffer-ing? We believe we are compassionate, objective, intelligent, perceptive, and yes, powerful. How can we reconcile this idea of ourselves and our field, with our own racial, gendered prejudices? How does race fit in? (and it does, de-spite what we think we know, despite what insight we think we have).

As a psychiatrist in training, I have grappled with trying to understand how blackness, masculinity, and mental health are interwoven for black men with mental illness. It's a question I cannot and do not want to avoid, as a black psychiatrist, as a provider for many black male patients (cisgender males, transgender males), and as a human being trying to more comprehensively understand the experience of other human beings.

We help people, how could we be racist? Do we see black male patients dif-ferently? Can we ask ourselves this question, and answer it? The world may not be post-racial but psychiatrists have to be, right? Maybe there are whole swaths of our patients lives we are not attuned to, not even curious about. Beyond our biases, how does being a black male change your risk factors for mental illness, your cultural context for mental illness, how you pursue care?

Many studies have documented the differences in access to care, diagnosis, and treatment in black men. Black men are shown to receive more diagnoses of schizophrenia versus mood disorder, and to end up presenting to emergency rooms more often, getting hospitalized more often, being admitted involuntarily more frequently, and disproportionately receiving higher doses of medications. More mentally ill black men are imprisoned versus receiving mental health care in alternative settings, which illustrates the huge issue of how mental health intersects with the prison system and institutionalized racism. Racism in America has cultivated long standing prejudices that associate blackness with madness, and black men with danger, violence, and anger.

A study by the CDC showed that people of color are less likely to access or receive mental health services in the US, as are men. Specifically, black and Hispanic men aged 18-44 years old who reported daily mood and anxiety issues are less likely to use mental health care, as opposed to their white counterparts who reported the same symptoms. Amongst the uninsured, black men with mood/anxiety issues are less likely to use mental health care, and across incomes the same differences were observed. Black men have less access to mental health care and utilize care less.

Regarding racism in mental health care, black men have a history of prejudiced treatment and actual harm inflicted on them by the medical system, from the Tuskegee study and to individuals amongst such as Henrietta Lacks (not a male I know can fix). Psychiatry exists within a medical system with a history of racism towards those in need of care, and a society built on racism: unequal access to resources and institutionalized racism.

Black men view mental health through a different lens, through their own biases. This is crucial for us to understand. Not only beginning to examine our own biases and our system's biases, but beginning to think how it feels to be a black man navigating this world. This does not imply all black men view mental health the same way, that all black men have the same barriers and biases that can be conveniently understood and utilized in blanket terms. Overall, there are racial, gender, and cultural expectations that tend to be placed on black men, including stigma against mental health and toxic aspects of black masculinity.

A quantitative study involving interviews with black men showed they viewed psychotherapy as associated with weakness, not demonstrative of the strength they were expected to show. Despite the biases that exist with black women in mental health as well, black women were shown to have more favorable views towards mental health care.

How about the world a black man has to navigate, outside the care we give them? The mental health of black men is influenced by the expectations of black masculinity, perpetuated in varying degrees by black communities and cultures, and by the larger world. Black men are expected to contain emotional angst, to bravely and stoically hold themselves together. From a young age, black men are encouraged to limit expression of emotion, verbally and nonverbally, and taught about the pride and dignity of the roles they are expected to fill.

Yet, as we hope for more room for intimacy and vulnerability in young black men, how do we reconcile this with the real dangers and prejudices black men are arming themselves against? We ask black men to relate openly in a world hostile and dangerous to them, and to a medical system that has prejudices against them.

The problem we can address is reflected in that awkward discussion around that table, the unwillingness to acknowledge racism or perceptions of race, the knee-jerk defensiveness. The well-meaning but presumptive statements of young, liberal (often white) doctors.

How do therapists and psychiatrists and psychologists engage in an open dialogue about race, on a larger scale, more in depth, and consistently? We need to confront our own racism. When we are talking to a black man, we need to at once allow race and masculinity and gender into our minds (because it is there anyway, prejudicing and influencing us), and simultaneously not allow identities to fully define the wholeness and humanity of the person before us. We are not objective or above reproach. Black male identity affects how you experience your symptoms, how you hide them, how and if you ask for help, and how you receive help.

I want to know what an intersectional discussion of mental health looks like, particularly amongst young black men who struggle with mental health problems, who struggle with the expectations and perceptions of a racist world, and struggle within and against a mental health system that has so much learning to do.

We care about the mental health of black men, and as providers we are full of knowledge, empathy, ready to work diligently, and devote our lives to others. We are capable of greater, more complex thinking. We should have a more sophisticated conceptualization of mental health in men, and specifically young black men.

We must use our privilege as providers on a larger scale too, to raise awareness and conversations about mental health in disenfranchised and marginalized communities, the conversation residing amongst all men.

https://www.ncbi.nlm.nih.gov/pmc/articles/PMC4215700/
https://www.cdc.gov/nchs/data/databriefs/db206.htm
https://psychnews.psychiatryonline.org/doi/10.1176/appi.pn.2013.11b16
https://ajp.psychiatryonline.org/doi/full/10.1176/appi.ajp.2009.09101398
https://psychnews.psychiatryonline.org/doi/full/10.1176/appi.pn.2013.10b22
https://www.huffingtonpost.com/ernest-owens/what-we-ignore-when-talki_b_7580034.html

-

"*Blue/Orange* is seemingly a simple plot about Christopher's diagnosis of either Border Personality Disorder or Schizophrenia within a NHS psychiatric department. This is a play that literally lends itself to the metaphor of an orange. The layers to all three characters have multiple dimensions, leaving an often sour or sweet taste in the audience's mouths. From mental health, profiling and hyper masculinity, there are a range of issues that are addressed. The play remains comedic and yet raw. And after watching, you'll often question your own sanity because there is a Christopher in us all.

I was Christopher, the main character."

Blue/Orange is a play written by English dramatist, Joe Penhall. It went to London's West End in 2001. It was performed at the University of Warwick in Week 10 of Term 2, 2016.

Act 1 Page 39 - "They're blue oranges...bright blue."

"An obviously poignant part of the play - the reason for the name. Yet, we found no solid meaning to it. Chris seeing the oranges as blue was significant because it showed how what you see is like a mirror image of how you've been treated. Chris makes multiple references to him being treated differently; and that no-one is truly colour blind - something audiences should meditate over. Even oranges aren't seen as orange to everybody. Are black men seen as just humans in a society that ranks them last? Even in the same environment, do people see each other in the same light. Do other black people see each other as the same when one is faced with internal mental issues? People are the oranges and unfortunately, we are not all seen the same. For what you could see in the fruit basket as orange, another could see as blue. Joe Penhall is a truly talented playwright in being able to use an orange as the connotation of the black mental health experience."

"Here, ties into the whole idea of black men and fatherhood. Christopher avoids the question, on the surface, because it makes it out like his father is this "powerful man" (Idi Amin) and no one would believe him. But it reminds me of how there is a stereotype and statistic for black men being without fathers. Christopher is the product of a fatherless black man in the United Kingdom. Many do end up with a false sense of identity and while others don't tend to have the luxury of imagining their Dad as a celebrated man, they do try to fill the void in other ways. Playing Christopher allowed me to step into the shoes of what it was like to be a black man with the weight of the world on his shoulders, already destined for failure, and then facing the consequence of that through mental health."

Act 2 Page 59 - "People stare at me. Like they know...like they know about me. Like they know something about me that I don't know."

"We are exposed to Christopher's sensitive side and the reason why he has made an image of his dad up in his head. There is a real sense of longing for a home, somewhere he can feel safe. When he says people are staring at him, at first you see paranoia (which is probably not inaccurate as Christopher has shown signs of schizophrenic tendencies) but it reminds of the stereotypical image of old white women clutching their bags and the judgement that Christopher/ black men must face. He walks around on the streets and he doesn't feel like anyone can ever truly understand him. Firstly, because the police racially-profile him and secondly because he sees the world differently."

Act 2 Page 67 - "Do you know the average life expectancy of the modern black male? Sixty-four. What age do we get the pension? Sixty-five. It's a fucking rip-off man! D'you know what I mean?"

"I chose this because it represents the reason why Christopher is black for the play. The black man being one of the most vulnerable people in society and not many people realising it. Even Christopher who isn't supposed to be as self-aware, according to doctors, understands that he doesn't really stand a chance in the real world. It's a very saddening thought, a sad realisation."

Illustrations by Neila Czermak

-

I launched *(In)Space* on 1 March 2018 as a place for young, black men to express themselves creatively as individuals.

(In)Space came from a very personal frustration.

At the end of 2016, I was watching a Belgian film called *Noir*, which contains a graphic gang rape scene perpetrated by a group of black men. It was the final straw for me, in that I was no longer prepared to accept seeing black males being portrayed so untruthfully. I became determined to challenge the prevailing narratives.

We are often negatively stereotyped, and it has a real impact on mental health, with black men being the demographic most likely to experience depression, schizophrenia and bipolar disorders, and to be hospitalised for those conditions in the UK.

Through the medium of art, I want to shatter the illusion that there is one kind of black male in the UK and to highlight how diverse our backgrounds and experiences are. *(In)space* promotes collaboration on the understanding that we can achieve more together than alone - especially with such an array of voices.

This is why I collaborated with HIM + HIS to create this body of work. I truly hope these poems, all from different *(In)Space* artists, provoke people to challenge any conscious or unconscious stigmas they may have about black men, especially younger black men in the UK.

While looking to allow young black men to speak authentically for themselves, I am also motivated by making a broader spectrum of art more accessible to people from all backgrounds. In turn, I hope this will encourage people to come together and discuss sometimes difficult topics, from a place of understanding.

'Right of Passage' , **IGGY LDN**

-

We built this man
We built this man on white vest tops
We built this man in the image of Fela himself.
We built this man on spices and herbs firmly pressed by mothers and
fathers scattered on the poverty line
We made this off parked cars and park benches
On hope, tightly squeezed between success and failure.
We built this man so far removed from the norm that he is too close to
freedom.
Born in the underbelly of the rhythm of the central line
Just so he could learn that fear is wisdom in the face of danger
We built. We fought. We buried
Built no man more deserving than the infant man.
Too broken to fix but too functional to be in pieces
The infant man
Born by unhappy trigger happy made men that left suicide notes in the form
of love letters to the dead.
We built. We raised. We buried.
We built this man on those hands who remain accountable.
We built this man

-

I often wonder if I'll be enough,
A king raised strong to live long,
Forever walking without a destination.

This is not a path chosen, but a forced detour,
From the righteousness that I was taught to be true,
To a reality I want to inhabit as my own,
To the desires yearned for in the depths of my heart.

See, there are two of us in this life,
I am his and he is mine, one shoulder left and one shoulder right
Betwixt heaven and hell by order of the Divine.

Aged 6 moving forward, I felt a judder and then a depression.
My limp-wristedness gave birth to pressure,
A stage to perform on but no script to speak,
The audience waits expectantly for the commencement of their
entertainment.

10 years old and crushed by bereavement.
The Matriarch left on a plane never to return
Resting forever in the Nature Isle, a fact he vehemently spurns
The Act continues but still he has no words to speak; only a solitary tear
rolls down his cheek.

Aged 15 a fruity nature causes tribulation.
Out of trepidation, my mother brings ignorant confrontation,
My mind keeps pleading defence; her words sharpen with piercing offence,
My humanity exposed for all to see, left defenceless I mentally flee.

19 and free he finds himself imprisoned again.
Mind over matter they say, but it's his mind he cannot sway

Embracing his demons and their proclivities, they danse macabre,
But at 3am lights go off on the dancefloor and a house is not a home.

21 never felt better, but the nagging begins again, I see.
Police brutality, anti-Black reality, pluri-cultural fallacy,
All because of this melanin, their eyes watch distrustfully,
Moving like plantation overseers, every detail scrutinised and
contextualised.

23 and me and 23 and he.
He begins to rise, their grip tightens,
Here comes the uncontrollable mental gyration,
And neither pill, nor prayer, nor potion can save him.

2017 and corporate bullies trapped me with nowhere to hide.
Tension headaches and anxiety rule my body and soul,
Stifling tears, the damage is done - so big in mind, yet made to feel so small,
"It's just a 9-5" yet they're tearing me apart and eating me alive.

I often wonder if I'll be enough,
A king raised strong to live long,
Forever walking without a destination.

-

Daze, a heavy feeling sinks your pits
Open windows look like exit doors
Peoples' eyes' portals all leading to nowhere:
A sweet memory, completely naked in utero
Searching for hope in the present
Through boundless shades of grey
And the comforting sound of maternity
But no gifts to be born
From the depths of my soul
Oh! Melancholy and sorrow
From the highs for the low.

'On good and evil.
(My God does not look like Zach Galifianakis)',
KOJO APEAGYEI / KOJOSTEIN

-

Define: Black

I'm worried that nothing has changed.
And the next generation are growing up just as toxic as we did.

The other day my little brother was arguing with our cousin.
He snapped at her and said she was "such a *blick* girl"
with so much venom on his young tongue.
Despite being 5 years older than him,
she immediately stopped her sentence and fell silent.
I wanted to snap his neck.

Who taught him that this was an acceptable insult?
Who taught him that "dark skin" was a punchline to end an argument?
How did he know this was a button to push?
But then I thought, how did I?

Define: Growth

As a child, I remember asking my mum why she kept referring to us as
"Black people" when our skin was clearly brown. Big woman of her age
not knowing simple colours seemed ridiculous.

She looked at me with horror and said, "we're not brown, we're Black"
I recoiled my neck in confusion, twisted my head slightly and said "no..."
pointed to the oven and added, "see that's black, we're brown".
She repeated her original statement with more vigour,
and this time with a full stop.
Burnt and black became synonymous in the mind of that child.
And I was a Black boy from that day onwards.

Define: Absolution

Day number 519, Twitter just exposed another 'celebrity' who built up an identity around anti dark-skin tweets. I'm waiting for the iPhone notes apology and obligatory:

"I have unlearnt.
I sorry.
Much growing to do."

Vindication.

As a culture, we have to ask... why are dark skin Black women always our stepping stone for growth? We stand on their heads lauding the lightest versions of ourselves.

Sons praising false suns. It has grown painful to see their pain. And to know, there will never be absolution for it.

We will all return to the Earth in time. But today it's...

 "Caramel complexion - who's that lighty!?"
"Sunshine expression - who's that lighty!?"
"Redbone selection - who's that light-yyyy!?"

Was a common sentiment.

When I was growing up, girls were only interested
in guys that looked like Chris Brown and Usher.
Chadwick and Elba weren't on TV
 so Piccolo raised me. Green, with envy the closest
I could get to a representation of a coal skin kid.

At school, "blick" bumbled off the tongue like sick,
whilst Cooli actually had the word cool in it.
"Oi, init he's as dark as shoe bottoms" wasn't an uncommon line.

"Tarmac looking brudda", followed it half the time.

"OOOOH." They would cry out icily in in rhyme.

And I'd cry too, in that bathroom stall hunched up foetal,
peeling back this skin like petals.
Trying to show all these bees something beautiful.
All these sunken boats a lighthouse home.

Playing a symphony on this broken instrument of an arm.
A red requiem for the dream of a dead darkie, diseased and doomed.
The 5'Ds of Dark skin diagnosed by the dammed inhabitants of this building.

Condemned.

I remember staring at mirrors and feeling so dirty.
I remember scrubbing this home I was built-in and praying that these mud
stained bricks would clean.
But instead they just got ashier and ashier,
and those bees stung more and more until my Blood
        and my Black were the same colour of anguish.
And then they turned off the lights so they could not see me cry.
But stole guidance from the light of my teeth and eyes.
I began thinking this lighthouse was a mistake. This skin was a mistake.

It has brought me nothing but pain, and tears and blood and tears
 and pain and tears
 and pain and tears
 and ash and tears
 and pain and tears
 and ash and tears
 and pain and tears
 and pain and tears
 and pain and tears
 and pain and tears
 and pain and tears

and prayers!

Prayers for a new home.
Prayers to a God who looks NOTHING like I do.
Whose skin looks so fresh, and so clean
that I was certain this God did not make me in their image.
But then this coal skin kid grew into a coal skin man.
And learnt to stop setting himself on fire.

I learned that my God does not look like Zach Galifianakis,
no my God looks like Viola Davis. With powerfully warming eyes
which sit you down and employ you to love yourself. My God looks
like Whoopi Goldberg, locs weighted and flowing like a solar crown.
My God looks like Lupita Nyong'o, skin as soft, and dazzling
and yes as angelic, as it is dark.
My God looks like Doreen Lawrence,
and Yaa Asantewaa,
and Maya Angelou,
and Michelle Obama,
and Idris Elba,
and Trevor McDonald,
and Thurgood Marshall,
and Kwame Nkrumah,
and Betty Shabazz,
and Malcom X,
and Fred Hampton,
and Mary Seacole,
and Kathleen Cleaver,
and Frank Ocean,
and Amy Garvey,
and Coretta Scott King,
and Marsha P Johnson,
and Kendrick Lamar,
and Piccolo,
and Lebron James,
and Michael Jordan,

and Serena Williams,
and Samuel L. Jackson,
and my grandma,
and my mother,
and my brother,
and you,
and you,
and you,
and you,
and you...

No, my God does *not* look like Santa Claus.

My God looks like *Us*.

And *She*, does not care about how dark,
or how red,
or how yellow,
or how light,
or how white you look.
Because she looks like the universe.
And within her, you will always find yourself, beautiful.

'Help or Asleep', *2016,*
CHRISTIAN QUINN
NEWELL VIOTTO

'*Jidozie*', **ARNOLD CHUKWU**

-

My brother is a black man,
In a world that is unforgiving to the outline.
I'm able to manoeuvre...
Reference french new wave cinema, and force smiles that momentarily
disarm white lady discomforts and white male dispositions - Don't bother,
moments are fleeting... white devil omnipresence is not.

[*Onye Ocha ad gh egwu*].

Smile at their musings, smile too much, smile, I have dimples for stretch
marks over-stretching my own happiness - placing it in the hands of others;
"He must be happy, look he's smiling."
"What a lovely smile."
"He must be one of the good ones..."

My little brother is a black man,
I am a black man too.
Born eldest of four in a country that didn't bare our roots-
In a country that stole our fruits, resealed to;
stay back, sell back, go back,
 "You best get on your merry way."

My little brother is now a black man,
born a boy, held, praised "bundle of joy"- laughs of pure joy -
laughs he still partakes in when the clutch of life's toll decides
that it'll ease off for an hour or so.
Splashing, gasping, born drowning,
Never learnt fully to swim. It always took longer
for him to reach the surface.
Sometimes I meet him there when he arrives, I always try to.
On occasions I'm sinking myself.
I can not afford to anymore, he may have to rely on me,

He's seen you kick away, he knows you can swim.
I need to be there if I need to hold him.

My little brother is an autistic man,
I am a man too,
Manically crippled,
on body; trauma's talons tearing away throat tissue,
I am shaking -
My brother. My baby brother - bigger, bolder than I - on my back.
"Mummy, I just want him to go with me"
"I'll need him to hold me up."

'*He Whispered Softly*' , JAMES JOHNSON

-

He whispered softly

When I Stood there
With my finger nails
Seeped in the soil of the earth
Watching him gasping for air

He was jaded when I first embrace him
Cupping
My hands around his hollow heart

And slowly...

He smiled as if I was his saving grace
Like
Christening water
Anointing his body and soul

I told him endlessly that I loved him
Before the world would
And
Before the womb that birthed him
And his seed
That my love reigned supreme
Before any

I told him love is in the reach
Of his arms
That he need not stretch a little
Or to walk his body to perpetual exhaustion
To find tenderness in the crux of a distant cave

Or
To tip toe on a stall to find love
Like attempting to grasp cereal boxes on the fridge
But, instead
Grasping my hands in comfort and assurance
Where love could be his

He knew that all I ask
Is his palms to be perched around his torso and back
That we could both look into the mirror
And watch the outlines of our black skin
Naked in each others presence

Allowing me to freely lay my hands and skin
Ever so gently on the deepness of his wounds situated on his back

I, whispering softly
"You do not need to cover them in shame"
Him finding home
With his head on my chest like a baby in the hands of their father

Rubbing his back
Only to find scars that once were leaking
Blood
Similar to abandoned industrial pipes
And scars
Like
Disjointed rocks on battle grounds

Whispering softly

I found him
By the grace of God
Scooping him and his dwindling breath
From under rocks and soil
I dug for him to be found and saved

My hands around his hollow heart
Telling him that
Deep cadences of the voice
And numbness
Breed lifelessness in beautiful bodies
But
I was here
To install newness...
In him

'Statitiscs', **JEREMIAH BROWN**

-

"I saw flowers outside the park,
a memorial.
Is that to do with the tram crash
too?"

He whispered his answer like it were a dirty word
wrapped in shame, something that shouldn't be
said out loud on a bus.

I couldn't hear, none of us did.
He repeated himself   louder,
but parts of his sentence dropped
out when the bus revved.

"A young man, [killed] himself. Hanged.
[He] was only [young], thirty."

There's a hush that follows,
the one only ever broken by
"so sad."

*

I'm the only man that turned up for the talk on self-care.
I only got my ticket that morning, meaning the only man
just about turned up.

We spoke about pressures and coping and not just in theory
but really, like when it's really real.
Like *"when someone kills one of the children in my communities"*
real, after that *"I don't want to go home and meditate"* real.

Here I am the voice of men and it feels strange,
I have someone to talk to. I have my poems
unlike most men.

*

"I'm assuming you've been through depression?"

He asks me having heard my poem,
I've just performed it.

I tell him that I don't know.
I never spoke to anyone.
I never checked or got help.

I just wrote the poem.
I just wrote where I was.
I just wrote what I felt.

*

we're talking
                    "and it's mad"
we're talking
                    "to know"
we're talking
                    "to look in the mirror"
we're talking
                    "and to know"
we're talking
                    "if I'm dead in 5 years"
we're talking
                    "it was probably me."
statistics.

'Clogged Up', **PETER deGRAFT-JOHNSON /**
THE REPEAT BEAT POET

-

How do you write about something you're ashamed of?
How do you reconcile fingers with each other when they know how dirty
your palms are?
And how they've caused scars?
How can the legs march proudly forward, still feeling bruises underneath
them from stomping people down?

The chest doesn't know best, and the stomach is grumbling,
and the thumbs can't feel why the neck is crumbling.

Honest words aren't permitted when the writing hand can't be predicted.
If the soul isn't open to what the writing hand will bring,
the eyes close up and the mouth won't sing.
Will the ears turn to stone if they're shut to new tones?
And will the nose just close if it's not allowed to be exposed?

If the skin is hardened and used as a barricade, what can the sun do?
How can a clogged body connect with something that requires space to take
place?

I cannot write, I am ashamed.

This soul locked in to a body's frame.

-

I know who I am,
Once I stopped running away from that is when I found peace.

MANDEM is an online media platform that encourages young people to engage in topical discussions centred around politics, identity, race and masculinity, while also offering a space for young men of colour to express themselves creatively through writing, filmmaking and music.

I set up *MANDEM* because I became tired of the mainstream media's popular representations of men of colour. I felt that is was important to create a new space where people could witness and relate to the identities and personalities of men of colour beyond the common narrative. It's no myth that people of colour are underrepresented in the media industries, thus *MANDEM* is there to offer a helping hand to those deprived of opportunities to break into them. It's crucial that marginalised groups in society create their own alternative platforms, (like *gal-dem.com* who initially inspired me) to express their views instead of solely relying on larger, outdated platforms.

With the current media discourse on men's mental health, there was no better time to set up *MANDEM* than now. The high suicide rates among young men have captured the nation's attention, and now more than ever, it is important for us to dissect the complexities of this issue, which inevitably includes accounting for nuances such as race and class. My response to this situation has been to use *MANDEM* as a vehicle to host public events that explore this sensitive subject matter in more depth. While we have discussed several interesting topics at these events, the ones that have garnered the most attention are those based on masculinity. To tackle the dilemma of men's mental health, the darker side of masculinity must be discussed.

In March, I hosted the second part of a panel discussion series titled 'Mandem Don't Cry'. The aim of the event was to shine the spotlight on how masculinity manifests in men of colour. The event sold out the 200-seater auditorium at Bristol's Arnolfini in three days - just proving how relevant the conversation is for so many of us today. Much of the mainstream discourse around masculinity has been narrated by white men, with little reflection on the experiences of men of colour, hence the 'Mandem Don't Cry' panel offered a space to discuss what is often considered a 'fringe' conversation.

Joining me on the panel were four friends of mine, Vince Baidoo, Vicaas Hussein, Olamiposi Ayorinde and Daniel Edmund. Vince and Olamiposi have worked with me on previous *MANDEM* projects, while Vicaas and Daniel were the new comers. Daniel's perspective was particularly insightful due to his experience in deconstructing harmful notions of masculinity for his *Milk For Tea* organisation, (an initiative that through workshops, one-to-one coaching and community work, supports and encourages men to 'find their truest identity, recognise their value and live out their purpose'), and his experience in delivering TEDx Talks on the subject matter. Daniel eloquently affirmed that everyone who identifies as a man must come up with a definition of masculinity for themselves. He believes masculinity to be a notion that is at once elastic and fluid, not only differing from man to man but also along the trajectory of one life. How expectations or expressions of masculinity manifest themselves throughout a man's life will differ at different stages. Daniel defined his masculinity as the ability to be responsible, loving, kind, caring, sensitive, and possessing the power to allow himself to be vulnerable and open to those close to him.

Furthermore, Vicaas highlighted the misconstruction, that when high profile black men are outwardly open and speak about their feelings it is often confused with arrogance. He mentions that the media's representation, or lack thereof, heavily influences the crisis of masculinity that men of colour face. The limited representation of black men in the media - and much of that representation being athletes and musicians - extends a reductive expectation of black manhood. This avenue is perhaps narrow for all men, but certainly narrower for men of colour. Who a man actually is has to be mediated with who they are expected to be.

A lot of my reflections on black masculinity were inspired by American author bell hooks. She often argues that the only avenue of validity offered to black men (particularly working-class black men) is a hyper form of masculinity. Black men are inclined to accept this avenue if they are denied other routes to validate their manhood, such as access to capital, wealth, creation or prosperous employment opportunities. In contrast to this, 'progressive masculinity' is a term now used to describe a new group of men: sensitive and emotionally available - he practices yoga and can cry at the movies. This trope, however, is not as equally available for a lot of men of colour. Men of colour - especially black men, who have for hundreds of years had fantasies of hyper-male virility, strength and sexual prowess projected onto them - are not always granted the same access to this 'progressive masculinity'. As I understand it, this demonstrates how standards of masculinity can differ between white men and men of colour, yet I am increasingly interested in the similarities in notions of masculinity between men of all colours and creeds. These ideas were further discussed at a following event *MANDEM* held at the Arnolfini titled 'Do Mandem Need Feminism?'.

I recently spoke with the feminist platform, *That's What She Said* on 'Mandem Don't Cry 2.0'. During our second panel discussion, it was raised that homophobic slurs are employed to ridicule both straight and gay men with 'feminine' attributes, and questioned whether this is in fact an attack on femininity. Maria Paradinas from 'TWSS' said, 'Speaking about masculinity is fundamental as part of a feminist discourse: women often bear the brunt of toxic masculinity in platonic and romantic relationships in the form of sexism.' I agree, and as I quoted in my dissertation, Grayson Perry argues that, "men who feel isolated and alone can do harmful things to themselves and others. The appalling ubiquity of online sexist and racist abuse speaks of lonely, angry men. If we don't teach them emotional literacy they might well end up living lonely, unhealthy and shorter lives."

Masculinity is too broad a term. Men don't have the tools to talk about or understand it, as nobody has taught men how to do it.

Using the term 'masculinity' simply isn't clear enough - masculinity is something that society defines, characterises and imposes.

So far, I could not have asked for a better reception to these panel discussions on such a delicate subject matter. The people who have attended the events have been warm and patient with us, while also confident enough to challenge us where necessary. I have intentionally tried to make the events as light-hearted and accessible as possible and this has been proven by the brilliantly diverse turn outs. Women, students and people of colour from the local community have not shied away from attending these discussions and asking insightful questions in the Q&A period. This has greatly boosted the confidence of the movement as a whole and continues to encourage me to host similar events in the future. For me, it's particularly important that young people are keen to attend at a time when the media perpetuates a myth of disillusionment, un-interest and indifference within the youth when addressing politics of society and identity. The interest is there, we just haven't been presented the right avenues to express ourselves and this is the drive that pushes *MANDEM* to continue and thrive.

-

Black Boys Don't Cry (BBDC) is a project designed to deconstruct the ideals of black masculinity and manhood in the 21st century. BBDC is led by three creative mediums (spoken word, videography and photography) in order to bring to light the challenges that young black men face in today's society.

In "Black Boys Don't Cry," the colour blue was really important to me. Because I didn't want to change the dynamic of manhood so that aesthetically, other people wouldn't be able to see and relate to it. I could have had the blue background be pink, to try to subvert the ideas of masculinity, but I owed it to my audience for it to be a much more thought-out process. Using this colour, but subverting the content was really important to me.

A lot of my themes relate to manhood, and often my work is a response to social media at the given time. You know, people say "Iggy London is making black men look vulnerable," or "He is telling black men to be vulnerable."
I'm not telling anyone they need to be vulnerable, I'm saying that in your vulnerability you can showcase the different sides of yourself, and that vulnerability is a key component in representing yourself. In expressing these emotions, you can be fulfilled, you can facilitate the feminist movement, teach your children about who they are as people, as men, about what it means to feel, and unload and unpack your insecurities.

Videgraphy: Exekiel   Models:
Creatively Directed: IGGYLDN-   Tunde
Make-up: Jomelyn Ferras   Rob
Mixing and Mastering: Jake
Joe Meehan   Abolade
                    Jordan
                    Melvin
                    Alexander
                    Kailum

They said I'd inherit the earth one day, so no-one could know I was weak.

The wailing is much left to the woman to endure.

If it is not our job to be breadwinners, then we have to be feared.

We must be feared. Feared by many, feared by all. Our friends, our family.

Because to be feared, is to have the upper hand.

Society tells us to be

Heavy, never swaying,

Steady, never wailing,

Ready, never breaking.

Did you know, I choke on words like strong and power?

I trip on phrases like 'Man Up' and 'Big Man Tings'.

So I guess that I'm made of straw and hay.

I'll tell you the story of the *black boy who never cried*.

He like I, enslaved, but no slave master in sight.

Yet, I am whipped until they see red meat, stripped from my head to my feet.

No light, no saviour, no sleep.

Enslaved because we are too weak.

We are yet to overcome any emotion but that of anger, until we are behind bars or six feet under.

But why aren't we taught to drop down our barriers and pick up our pens?

We have been conditioned to think that our emotions are not permitted, but maybe it's okay for a man to feel helpless sometimes?

Instead of holding a torch for the rest to see, maybe it's okay for a guy... to roll out of bed, sleep until midday, watch day-time TV.

To be the voice of the meek.

But they said I'd inherit the earth one day, so no-one could know I was weak.

Edited transcript of BBDC spoken word

It's mad. I've never really been the greatest at articulating my feelings, and I feel like it's magnified tenfold during my darkest moments. However, when I introduce a medium, I'm great at expressing how I feel. That sums up my relationship with mental health as a man. Throughout my whole life I've always been told to put on a brave face and hide my tears, and as I've gotten older I've realised I have to unlearn these things because hiding behind a smile doesn't make you strong. It's mad. I never knew my tears could set me free.

I made this to remind myself to breathe when I feel like I'm drowning.

I am not a puppet. I am not here to entertain. I am just here. Ouchea.

-

Creativity is freedom. It gives confidence to those who deserve it and provides endless opportunities to construct and form an individual style. Time doesn't matter because creativity is patience. It builds faith within your mentality to get stronger every day. Given with a chance to shape our own imagination, creativity is a gift from God, a beauty of life. I create to show the world what I'm capable of and the reason for my existence.

Direction: Caleb Kelly
Photography: Erica Blue Kim, US, 2018

I pray for those who don't understand me, I pray for those who don't understand themselves , I pray for the suffering , nobody wants to suffer alone , at least not I - Pray For Silver

*

Early Mornings They cry For Me

*

so much pain & tears that ive gone through, then i met you . you changed me into somebody who didnt believe , now im free . im not the only one who goes through this , theres many more who deserve to feel HOPE . - ImAboutToChangeTheWorld

*

Only The Blind Can Really See What We See Today Isn't Real , There Is No Race , There Is No Icons . I Hear You Judging Them But You're No different, I Hear Their Cries But Ik We Was Promised Something Bigger , I Can Feel The Pain but Everything Heals Eventually, I Can Taste The Fruit But Don't Wanna Fall Into Temptation . Only The Blind Can Really See - trust him

*

Tough Niggas Stay With The Piece , But Don't Wanna Create Peace - Khaos

JUST LET ME BREATHE WHILE I CAN , - lack of oxygen

*

Conscious Speaks: " You Kant Hide Who You Really Are Even When The World Wants 2 Swallow You Whole ! You're tired of fighting , but you know the results are worth fighting for . There's a Light In All Of Us . " - Khaos

-

i could sit, pondering the countless thoughts racing back and forth like basketball suicides, contemplating my choice of analogies alongside the thoughts preceding it, or i can document at least one of them.
im grateful.

what these things mean to you, i am unsure, i don't even know who you are, i know as kendall/zenduh, im moving closer to myself, who that self is and what i allow myself to be capable of. im culpable of a lot as well and i think thats what keeps me from presenting my blessings and 'high' points. this was for sure one of them to me. i want others to have them as well. i want perspectives to change, i wanna grow alongside the world and I'll do what it takes for it to.

-

• Soundtracking another mental health spiral to Angels With Dirty Faces by Sugababes (2003) tracks 1 through 11.
• Reading The Sun's horoscope section and taking Mystic Meg's findings as a direct prompt to blow the bank and book a 2-week holiday self-discovery trip to LA.
• Sitting on your own writing about your feelings drinking a bottle of Barefoot Pinot Grigio (Villa Maria if on offer).
• Sitting on your own writing about your feelings drinking Aperol Spritzes (very radical self care).
• Unleashing a 4-day long internal dialogue onto loved ones in a fit of blind rage and irrationality (better out than in I always say).
• Reaching a state of numb absolution from 8 hours of back-to-back films starring Meryl Streep.
• Spending no less than 75% of your waking day on Instagram.
• Overthinking your productivity to a point of paralysis and indifference.
• Early nights.
• Late nights.
• Freezing chocolate mousse for approximately 1 hour until it has reached a consistency between mousse and ice cream (I recommend Sainsbury's own brand). Consume 1-3 pots in a single sitting.
• Redefining 'carefree' to mean a 5-minute window in your entire day when you're distracted enough not to remember that you are anxious.
• Documenting said moment on chosen social media platforms.
• Rationalising 'wants' as 'needs' (this applies, but is not limited to: food, clothes, home decor and holidays).
• Lists.
• Eating copious amounts of lactose-heavy foods (despite intolerance).
• Ignoring all the lists and articles like these and actively finding out what methods work best for you.

Fazed100

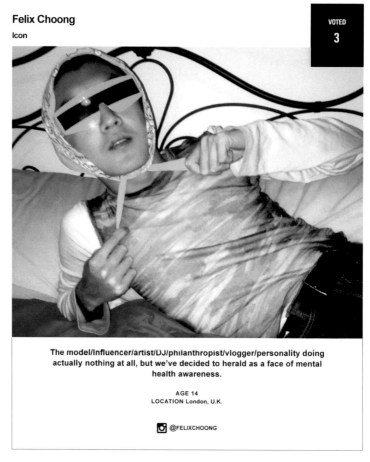

Felix Choong

Icon

VOTED

3

The model/Influencer/artist/DJ/philanthropist/vlogger/personality doing actually nothing at all, but we've decided to herald as a face of mental health awareness.

AGE 14
LOCATION London, U.K.

@FELIXCHOONG

This race fluid, age fluid, body fluid FAZED100-er is taking the world by storm through his radical acts of self care. With two eyes, a mouth, nose and one crooked tooth to boot, he's challenging mental health stigmas, beauty standards, global warming and the UK banking deficit through simply existing. Groundbreaking.

Felix's existence in itself is awe-inspiring, transgressive and authentic. He navigates the real world and the e-world through his lens of self care. You name it, he's done it on his unique, radical journey of self care. Something that we all can get inspired by. A selfie. Exciting! New! A tattoo. Inspired! Gasp! Respiring. Incredible! Gag!

He may seem like a normal millennial, but in fact Felix is quietly redefining what it means to be anxious and depressed and how to tackle it - a laissez-faire attitude where anything and everything is self care if you frame it right.

What will he do next? You heard it here first in a Fazed exclusive, rumours have been circulating that he is working on a new Instagram series of selfies collaged with pictures of trash. It's sure to be lit and definitely an exciting progression for this FAZED100 nominee that we can't wait to write far too many articles about.

Moving to London two years ago, has forever changed my life. It has become a place where I have been able to build a support system of like-minded individuals, I've felt free and I have never in my life been in a position where I have been around queer men, where we could openly discuss the battles we suffer within our own lives with Mental health. However, this was not something that happened overnight.

I'm from an African American Baptist family and I went to a prep school in New England - if I wanted to be in Stand Up comedy there I would have just got onstage, said "mental health", and sat down to a standing ovation. In high school, I had always found it interesting listening to the straight, unaccepting boys bash on mental health, then the day there would be a "Mental Health Advocacy Day" or Hashtags on Twitter, like #Bellletstalk, there would be some weird change in the simulation and everyone who would previously throw up the terms "Pyscho", and all the other derogatory terms surrounding mental health, would suddenly become the same types of people who would write op-eds about the harm in stigma regarding "Fatal Attraction".

What's interesting is that I grew up with an older sister who was able to be so open about her anxiety - and she was severely bullied for a long period of time. I would never devalue her struggle as I know how hard it was for her. She wrote about it in papers, and college essays, but the day I told my mother I was anorexic when I was 16, and was body dysmorphic before my voice dropped, it was like I had joined the Black Ops. "Operation get Trey to and from the Therapist", "Find a code word for the Nutritionist", and "Think of creative ways to get him to and from the hospital". I imagine this level of secrecy is only rivaled by Beyoncé's team. While I found this annoying and obviously it was awful, I just thought that was how it always was and would be.

During this period of my life I was like the Karen from Mean Girls, but Black: sweet, nice, not the brightest and with enough vodka I could indeed fit my whole fist in my mouth. I hung out with very pretty white girls so people would invite me out, leave me alone, and help me to a bed if I got a bit wild on a Saturday night. During this time my mental health plagued my school work, was wrecking relationships and my social life. I remember one day, one of the suddenly popular 'mental health advocate football players' referred to me as: "The nicest mean person" he'd ever met. I remember saying to myself: "No shit Sherlock, I am doing the best that I can in dealing with all of this alone".

Like many closeted queer men, especially one of color, I had what I would call a 'one' complex. Survival of the fittest. When you are in a situation, where you only see one of yourself, you feel as though every action and step you can take has to be about coming out on top. I was strategic in making sure my social status, and secrecy of my mental illness and sexuality were hidden. Before diversity became a hot topic in the entertainment industry, I weirdly related to the one token gay character. And if a show was really trying to put all of their eggs in one basket they would make them: gay, a person of color, adopted, and give them a religious background. My depression, anxiety, and eating disorder were not things that were up for dialogue because in my closeted Black Christian household those were things that were not discussed and made one look inferior. I've always found this fascinating because as the son of a minister I have never seen more adultery, fraud, men on the down low, and unplanned pregnancy than I had in God's own house. Yet, with all of that being addressed in a secret code: mental health is something that is looked to as something that can be prayed away. You mean to tell me there were Twelve Disciples and not one had body dysmorphia, or PTSD[1], or dealt with Seasonal Affectionate Disorder?[2] Really? Nothing was behind Judas' betrayal?

That year of out-patient treatment was a lovely joke. Twice a week I saw the kindest Little Nutrition fairy, a sweet little woman with raven black hair who

1   PTSD - Post-Traumatic Stress Disorder is an anxiety disorder caused by stressful or distressing events

2   SAD - Seasonal affective disorder is a type of depression that comes and goes in a seasonal pattern

would beg me to eat a carb - get down on her knees to get me to eat a sweet potato. The therapist I was linked with was a former 80s film star who just gave me T Magazines and we talked about her Birkins. Until I was "all better" and went off to college.

I spent my entire youth playing down my mental illness, to a point where I trained myself to internalize my panic attacks after my friends once told me they were "weird" and couldn't tolerate them. Again, my panic attacks were weird but when, for example, a college basketball player who was a recovering Heroin addict came to the school, they all became the spokespeople for mental illness. Even Marissa Cooper from The O.C wasn't that annoying. So like any son of a minister I moved across an Ocean to study fashion. But here is the kick!

By the time I had come to London from America, I was ready for an Upgrade to be the Black Regina George. Fearless, Unafraid to survive and conquer. Now imagine this formula. Take a boy from a small town, where he was once ridiculed for liking a said pop star - mine was Britney but you can fill in the blank. A boy who ran to the nurse's office when gym was split into boys' and girls' teams. A boy trying to suppress their sexuality along with their mental health. And then put all that boy in one place: Fashion College! The dysfunction. The distrust, of other queer men. If you have spent your entire life suppressing who you are and your struggles like depression, when you see someone who you can tell has had a similar life trajectory, you may not be willing to be an open book. I was not. Though I knew we were stronger united than apart, I did keep my distance because subconsciously I had this feeling as though there was only room for one: the 'one' complex. And when I was getting push back from other men I was meeting, I could tell they probably experienced the same situations, same stigmas, same suppression of their emotions.

A two years before my move to London, a boy two years older than me, who was obviously in the closet, created a rumor that I, a boy who could barely read a poem out loud in class had tried to date him, as an attempt to dissuade people from talking about his own sexuality and instead have people question my own. It made me so irate, but now being around men who were so secretive, I began to empathize with the fact that he probably didn't know how to react in a healthy way and his feelings of isolation probably played into his fears and anxiety.

But where this changed for me and my peers, was when we began to talk about it. We often forget how common our experiences are, and when that feeling of being the only one who is dealing with a pain that is not visible to the eye is unlearned, we can begin to support one another. So many men deal with this darkness in silence, but because of this complex that I've witnessed, I've seen how people can be timid to speak up and reach out to their community of peers. *What is vital is that we stop acting like lone wolves and act like a pack.* As human beings we are more alike than we are not, so when we begin to embrace our support systems the better off we will be.

-

Am I Depressed, Yes?
Is it true I want to die? That's a Yes,
Yes!
This is not a test. Stop trying to fact-check!

My exterior is like a porcelain doll
But my inside feels like it's been- re-called! Shut down- Like Toys-R-Us
My names not Barbie but I can skip
a meal.

I'm a Vegan but You can't buy coke
at whole foods!
But it comes from a plant, so please
let me lament!
They comment "skinny legend" but
they don't know the rest!
Skinny holds me back; it doesn't
keep me with the back!

Making mountains out of mole hills,
That's the real real!
The black church thinks depression
is voodoo, that's some real real!
Like I'm Azealia Banks slaying
chickens for my meal deal!

But C'mon Pastor, I know your own
real deal!

They check my mental illness for
inauthenticity!
Like I'm a fake Gucci Blouse, but the
flowers are real, real!
And the tears that are flowing are
near and dear!

CUT THE BEAT

BUT AM I THE BADDEST? Yes!
Will my illness bring me down?!
Bitch-u-guessed it!

I'm a Survivor- shout-out to
Michelle!
My Bag will stay secure like a
Hermes Kelly!
My spirit is like Beyoncé- It's Crazy
With Love!
I'm No Lauryn Hill so my Mental
Illness isn't an Ex Factor, c'mon
trust!

So don't factor someone out cuz
they ain't "Feeling That Well"!
We are more than our illness, and
that much I will tell!
Never count us out, fam we always
down for the count!
Mental Illness is my son and I'm
sending it away!
My depression is going to Hogwarts-
Go on & Slyther AWAY!

'*Autoportrait*' , HARLAN HUE

-

I undertook the project for a few reasons...

I originally just wanted to paint someone every day but I realized my own self was the only person consistently around enough to do that, so I chose to paint myself out of a sort of necessity/easiness.

I also just wanted to see if I could be "disciplined" and committed enough to take on a project like that.

Lastly, I was going through some really bad skin issues at the time and I began to find that painting the self-portraits allowed me to

... Lighten up about those issues and direct the stress or sadness from that, and funnel it into a joyous and therapeutic activity like painting.

In regards to my style, the only thing I noticed changing was that as my skin issues improved, I began painting portraits that felt a little happier, they were more vibrant in color and less distorted.

I think the last one was painted 9.9.16.

Also I should probably say, another intention with it was that I would eventually do this again towards the end of my life and be able to compare the two.

My dad is a photographer and when I was a kid he showed me this photo project by Nicholas Nixon. He has photographed 4 sisters once a year since 1975.

It's still going.

I guess I'm emulating him idk. I just was always fascinated by that concept.

I've always enjoyed time-lapse, and the before and after.

It's definitely not just about what I looked like in that year compared to later in life because I could just use a photograph for that. The project is more comparable to a daily diary I suppose...what I felt like that year, how I painted, how I depicted feeling, being able to see what I felt on a particular day.

This is funny though cuz these questions are making me realize new things about it.

Don't want to be too invasive / intrusive.

No, it's good - Those are the questions I enjoy answering.

'NUMBER 1 - 9.20.15', 'NUMBER 14 - 10.3.15', 'NUMBER 17 - 10.6.15', 'NUMBER 2 - 9.21.15', 'NUMBER 36 - 10.25.15', 'NUMBER 39 - 10.28.15', 'NUMBER 47 - 11.5.15', 'NUMBER 107 - 1.4.16', 'NUMBER 74 - 12.1.15', 'NUMBER 124 - 1.22.16', 'NUMBER 126 - 1.25.16', 'NUMBER 292 - 7.10.16', 'NUMBER 279 - 6.27.16'

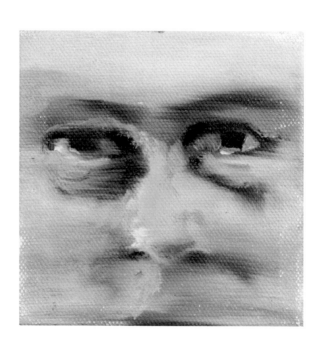

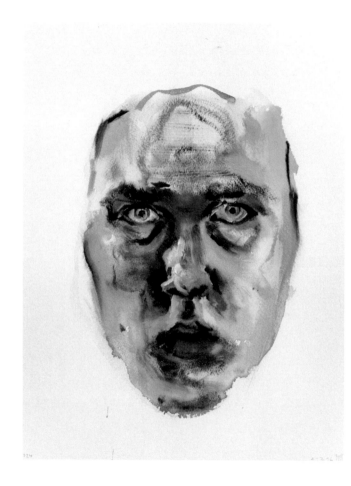

'I worked across male and female wards and the difference was very striking. Men were far less willing to talk overtly about what was bothering or distressing them. And yet, they expressed distress more covertly, and after a time would begin to talk. This was uniformly when they are aware they are in control of the conversation so the topics, pace and timing is chosen by them.

The approach I use is called the 'Method of Levels'. It is a-diagnostic and the background principle is that distress occurs when people lose control of what's important to them - similar to HIM + HIS' notion of power and possession. The key to regaining control is having an opportunity to talk freely, without fearing the consequences, and having someone there to help us pay attention to what is in our minds as we talk.

HIM + HIS comes at a time when I've been reflecting on my own willingness to talk about my mental health publicly. I feel reluctant ... I just wrote a few lines and then thought again and deleted them. Perhaps I can write about my experience of offering help and receiving it.'

-

'Surviving Hour by Hour in Here', **VYV HUDDY**

-

Brixton prison was built by the Victorian's and is still in use today. It houses around 800 men in conditions typical of prisons around the turn of the Millennium: cramped, noisy, alive but with a predominant sense of futility, boredom, angst and barely hidden rage.

I was there in 2012 and worked in the mental health team. For many men remanded it was their first experience of prison, and consequently a period of adjustment and stress. Mental health difficulties are common in prisoners, with the majority of men meeting the criteria for at least one mental health problem.

My job was to help support these men, they were distressed by a variety of things: thoughts of suicide, hearing voices or seeing visions, suspicious preoccupations, and feelings of emptiness or meaningless.

Before too long, I was struggling to find a way to be useful. It didn't start this way. I was initially fairly confident I could do something to help, by listening to their difficulties, helping them come to a different understanding of their problems by using some of what I had learnt whilst training as a clinical psychologist. Surely I could offer something of value.

I quickly found out that this was a completely naive assumption. One meeting brought this home to me. I had been sent to meet one of the men but couldn't find him in his cell. His name was Jake. An officer told me that he'd gone to the chapel for a theatre production. I thought to myself that this indicated that he had at least some motivation to engage in some activities, that perhaps this was a positive sign.

When I arrived, the theatre session was in a break and Jake accepted the invitation to meet with me. This meeting has stayed with me over the years and I think this is because it reveals something about what really matters when we try to help others, the central importance of the patient's or helpee's perspective.

We'd been talking for a while - I was finding it hard to get what I felt I needed: some idea of what the problem was and where I could intervene. I switched tack and I began to ask Jake about his goals. "Sometimes it can be helpful to define some goals", I said weakly. He replied, "Ok, sure", but looked uncertain. I asked what came into his mind when he thought about what I just asked him and he replied, "blank, I guess". I felt stuck, floundering, whilst thinking to myself, "how do I get him to talk about goals? That's what we need to talk about". I tried another approach, "when you look to the future what do you see", he replied, "I'm surviving hour by hour in here".
It was a number of years ago and I don't recollect much more on what we talked about. Looking back, I wonder if Jake took anything meaningful from it. But it highlights my lesson. Never again would I assume what the other person wanted from the meeting with me.

Around that time, I met another clinical psychologist and researcher, Warren Mansell. We were at a conference in Liverpool that was focused on an obscure sub field of psychosis research. In one of the coffee breaks we began chatting about my work in the prison. I was bemoaning the tendency for psychologists to use technical language in therapy. I was arguing, passionately probably, that the main job of the helper is to help people define their problems from their own perspective and in their own words. He said, "You might be interested in Method of Levels".

I followed his advice and bought the first book on the approach that I could find. It seemed esoteric and abstract. But there was no description of the client's problems or how they were caused from an outsider's point of view. No chance for the therapist to take an expert stance because the main thing that is expected of the therapist is for them to leave their expertise at the door. The focus is instead on a stance of continuous curiosity, questions that open up new perspectives for the person answering them.

I returned to the prison the next week and began to try to apply this new attitude. I was excited by the ease that the men took to the approach. They seemed to value the openness of questioning, the control they were offered on the session content, duration and intensity; most of all it was the chance to find their voice.

This new and open way of offering a thinking space to the men of the prison had helped me to see their perspective on mental health in a new light. Many of them had never had an opportunity to express their own perspective on their hardships, what was wrong and what they wanted to be right. The goals they were told to pursue by health practitioners, probation officers and courts didn't allow them to express their own dilemmas and fears. Indeed, throughout much of the therapy they'd previously viewed their problems from an external perspective - anger, drug abuse, and violence - things that someone else sees: which necessarily neglects their inner perspective. From the inside there was futility, boredom, frustration, ridicule, loss and a myriad of other personal struggles. Voicing these latter experiences seemed to be helpful to them.

I may not have found the solution to how to be more useful. But I knew where to start.

Vyv Huddy is a Lecturer in Clinical Psychology
at University College London.

I CAN'T ~~REMBER~~ REMEMBER YOU.

YOU'VE CHANGED

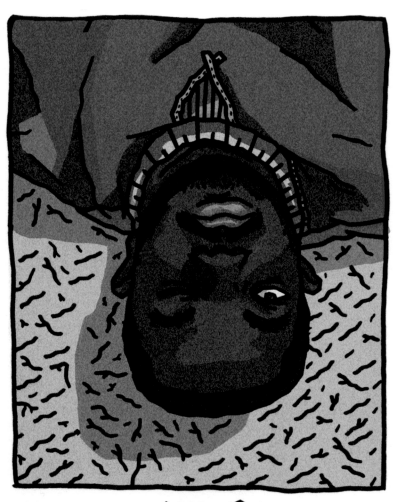

WHO?

'Diversifying methods of treatment: using philosophy to practice self-care', HARRY KALFYAN

-

'Men are disturbed not by things, but the views they take of things.' - Epictetus.

CBT (Cognitive Behavioural Therapy) is the standard NHS prescription to tackle illnesses such as anxiety and depression. One of the founders of CBT, Albert Ellis, credits the programme to the practice of Stoicism, believing it to be the most powerful tool for understanding the human mind. The average waiting list for treatments such as CBT on the NHS is six months, whereas philosophy might be able to provide more immediate and possibly long-lasting guidance, as it has done for myself. While CBT has no doubt helped a vast number of struggling men, the improvement within biomedical structures is often temporary and tragically, lives are lost due to a lack of access to medical help. Whilst there is the urgent need to vastly improve the funding to NHS mental health services, other platforms exist to discuss issues and can become mechanisms for self-care.

'Seek not to have things happen as you choose them, but rather choose that they should happen as they do; and you shall live prosperously.' - Epictetus.

'The happiness of your life depends upon the quality of your thoughts: therefore guard accordingly, and take care that you entertain no notions unsuitable to virtue and reasonable nature.' - Marcus Aurelius.

Philosophy can help shift attitudes towards a positive future by using reason rather than the dogma of religion to approach mental health. If helpful, it allows the sufferer to do the healing themselves, granting them autonomy in their own self-care. Epictetus recognised the importance of mental autonomy; we should dissect the sources of discontent ourselves by empowering the mind to recognise and re-evaluate what we have rather than striving to acquire more. The concept that 'man' should - and could - be master of his mental wellbeing sends a positive message to sufferers today from more than 2,000 years ago.

It seems vitally important that we diversify our methods of treatment and sources of guidance away from the provisional nature of therapy and the dependency provided by medication. The popularity and wide-spread adoption of mindfulness is an example of the diversification of mental healthcare methods and how there has been a redirection of emphasis towards Eastern philosophies – for Stoicism, too, was an elaboration of Taoist values. Although CBT is derivative of ancient stoicism, it is inseparable from the eagerness of the western health provision to medicate – so as to boost the profits of Big Pharma and to covertly supply them with data on an individual's mental illness. The role of philosophy in mental health care could also topple the power of the medical establishment and democratise therapy, diverting the circle of treatment away from exploitative capitalist values and towards human well-being.

Moreover, instead of pathologising mental illness, philosophy brings mental self-care to a comprehensible level of awareness and acceptance, taking it as a normality of life. The Stoics believed that failure was an unexceptional and essential part of being alive and as such nothing to fear. Notions such as these open an essential dialogue for men when it comes to mental health issues. It creates a large network of conversation rather than being restricted to one-on-one treatment relationships. Modern men need this support network more than ever, particularly considering that 76 percent of suicides in the UK are committed by men. The lack of understanding around men's mental health is creating a rapidly deteriorating situation, one which further normalises a culture of stigma and ridicule. Modern western men, often under the belief that showing emotion is a sign of weakness, have disastrously become culturally conditioned to suppress their feelings. This male evasion of exhibiting emotional weakness may derive from the common misinterpretation of stoicism itself, that man should embrace the 'stiff upper lip' attitude. Conversely, these thinkers were preaching that men should consider and share their negative emotions, but not fall victim to them. Ultimately, it is imperative that male mental health is discussed in a much wider forum, and that all the possible practices for alleviation and healing are brought to light.

Illustrations on following page, by Aiden Duffy

'fat man on a fat horse'
'man pissing on rhino'
'man eating a subway at night'
'selfie' , Ranald Macdonald

-

I work in the same room that I sleep in every night and wake up in every morning. By keeping my walls full and working on multiple pieces at the same time it allows me to have a dialogue with myself and externalize feelings I would otherwise struggle to put into words.

Schizophrenia is a general term for a group of psychotic disorders characterized by long term disturbances in perception, affect, behaviour, and communication. Bipolar disorder (previously known as manic-depression) is a psychiatric diagnosis that describes the category of mood disorders defined by the presence of episodes of high energy (mania) and extreme depressive states. Psychosis often occurs during the manic phase.

-

'A View From Inside ',
Published by White-Card, 2012 , ALEXA WRIGHT

-

How do we define 'reality'? In order to explore this intriguing question, I have re-appropriated a set of pictorial conventions to represent some of the experiences of people whose sense of reality does not always coincide with that of others. The ten portrait photographs that make up 'A View From Inside' draw on the principals of eighteenth century portrait painting to give form to some of the unique realities encountered by different people during psychotic episodes. Whilst the people I have photographed here all appear entirely 'normal', their ability to function within society has, to varying degrees, been affected by the experience of a psychotic 'disorder' such as Bipolar or Schizophrenia. The visual, auditory and other sensory phenomena that occur during a psychotic episode contradict accepted notions of what constitutes 'reality', and yet for one person they are absolutely real. The disorder and disruption arising out of even a temporary detachment from consensual reality can be immense, as the first-hand accounts that accompany the images in this book demonstrate.

In making 'A View from Inside', I was interested in the challenge of creating believable, realistic pictures that reveal some of the chaotic and sometimes incomprehensible phenomena that are present for an individual during psychosis, but are not accessible to anyone else. In each photograph the external appearance and the internal experiences of the subject are depicted within a single, formally structured portrait. The aim is not to exoticise the 'unreal' or bizarre perceptual experiences of the people portrayed, but to find a visual language that will provoke discussion and add to our understanding of the experience of mental illness, and of psychosis in particular.

Historically, portraits have been constructed as a celebration of the uniqueness of an individual and his or her accomplishments. Based on the physiognomic belief that a person's appearance mirrors his or her subjectivity or 'inner' identity, a traditional concern of portraiture has been to create an external 'likeness' of someone. In these photographs, however, the physical expression of the subject reveals nothing of his or her inner world. It is the (highly constructed) setting - which in each case incorporates a view through a window and an array of significant objects - that gives some clue to each person's private world.

Having visited many potential locations for these portraits, I felt most drawn to sumptuous but faded eighteenth century interiors because of their elegant symmetry and sense of order. Each of the chosen sites seemed to offer a suitable setting for the unusual array of objects it was to host, and at the same time to characterize the atmosphere of a particular psychotic episode, or series of episodes. Although I have digitally reconstructed most of the rooms depicted to create places that don't quite exist in the 'real' world, the components of each space were all derived from the same location. Having viewed a number of different venues, the decision to restrict the choice of settings to those created in the eighteenth century was primarily a visual one. However, it is also perhaps worth mentioning that the late eighteenth century marks the very beginning of a long, slow, and as yet far from complete, move towards the social acceptance and integration of people with mental health issues.

Everyone involved in the project volunteered to participate, most in response to a call put out by the forward thinking charity, 'Rethink Mental Illness', which elicited nearly a hundred responses. Each participant has contributed a short written statement to this book. All of these reflect both rationally and creatively on a time when reality has taken on a very different, often confusing and sometimes terrifying form. In the words of one of the project participants, Julia Chambers:

"Standing up, feeling pretty raw, signing a consent form that allows my image and admission of having experienced an excruciating and mostly misunderstood mental state to be made public was quite nerve-wracking. But it has also been liberating. Taking my ego out of this, I think that unless people stand up and allow their histories to be seen in this way, things will never change. Hopefully work like this will pave the way for a more general understanding of mental illness and will help to break down the culture of fear and mockery that surrounds people who have done nothing wrong."

On a personal level, I have been impressed by the courage and generosity of all the people who have worked with me on this project. The images have, by necessity, been arrived at collaboratively. In each case my visual interpretations were discussed with the person depicted, and then modified to arrive at a final image that characterizes his or her recollected experiences. The aim has been to find a form for the seemingly irrational events that people described, whilst retaining some sort of pictorial logic.

I hope that this book and the photographs it accompanies will help people to think again when treating someone with a mental illness differently out of fear, misunderstanding or simply ill-considered prejudice. By giving form to some of the fascinating psychotic experiences of a small group of randomly selected people, the portraits also aim to provide a stimulus for questioning our established, consensual understanding of what constitutes reality.

Chas

Since first coming into contact with the mental health service in 1993 I have had several bouts of being in 'non-consensual reality' or 'psychotic and delusional', depending on your preference of terms. Some of these episodes have been pretty close to each other and almost continuous, whilst others have been separated by many years. I have experienced these states in psychiatric hospitals, on the streets, in hospitals, abroad - pretty much everywhere, really.

Over the years, the general trend has been that when I lose touch with 'normal' reality the spaces I go into become darker and nastier. Initially these realities were quite interesting and almost a bit of a high, especially when accompanied by 'delusions of grandeur'. I felt I was a very important person. As the years progressed the experiences felt more painful, harder to endure and I sought a way back more urgently.

Perhaps as a result of this, my attitude towards mainstream psychiatry has softened over time. I was once radically against any medical intervention, but now I have become resigned to taking medication to maintain my quality of life and that of those around me.

During the last episode I ended up in hospital, almost sectioned again, with several extreme realities running concurrently. The ingenuity of the mind can be extraordinary in its ability to conjoin fantasy with concrete reality. What people are actually saying and what is presented in the media, especially TV and radio, is mixed up with auditory, visual and tactile hallucinations. I have had the experience of living in a post-apocalyptic anarchic society, with a fear of aliens and a sense that I was living through archetypes. A feeling of persecution was linked to the sense of being in a video game. For me this demonstrates the pervasive nature of contemporary media and information technology.

Luckily I came out of that state fairly quickly through a resolution with my partner, the re-introduction of medication, some outstanding occupational therapy and a return to the discipline of work. Although I wouldn't give

these experiences to my worst enemy, I am still glad that I have had them. Being 'mentally ill' has taken me to amazing places, given me rare insights, introduced me to fantastic people and helped shape a very interesting life. I have learnt to value the dark, which balances out the light.

Dennis

My reality is based on the fact that I was incarcerated for most of my adult life. I was in a very real world, waking up every morning being scrutinized by those in authority and by my peers. So I isolated myself. I wanted to keep away from the other inmates and the officers, to distance myself from rumours and hearsay.

I was there longer than I should have been because of mis-communication. I wasn't easy to get on with. You have to keep a barrier. They said that I was saying and doing awkward things, but I was with a bunch of people that I didn't like and didn't find interesting. I didn't want to be influenced by them, so I became more anti-social as the prison sentence went on.

I was in prison for seventeen years before I was diagnosed with schizophrenia. Then I was released, but sectioned. I am at loggerheads with the label, I don't agree with it. I am a cool, calm, collected and down to earth person. Without medication I do speak in a fast and erratic way, but only because I am trying to get my point of view over. The anti-psychotic drugs are supposed to make you more laid back, but I like to keep fit. I don't want to be lazy.

I thought I would never get out of prison. I was unable to express myself in there. People perceived me as an empty individual - wasting time and daydreaming. Sometimes I want a private life with the door shut, but in prison people were always intruding because they wanted to search the room or something. Now it's better, my world is very musical and the door is half open.

'Communicating the Experience of Psychosis',
Edited from 'A View From Inside', GRAHAM THORNICROFT

Stigma and discrimination are common, often severe, and can profoundly jeopardise the social inclusion of people with mental health problems.[1] The expectation of disgrace, dishonour and reputational damage leads many, not unreasonably, to refuse the offer of treatment in hospital on a voluntary basis. Ironically though, in the longer term, if someone were treated on a compulsory basis in hospital, then the stigmatizing consequences may be even more severe for her. Such 'Catch 22' situations are indeed common. For a service user, the offer of psychiatric help can be seen as a mixed blessing where the harm may outweigh the benefits. Indeed, stigma also raises challenges for health professionals, who can often feel caught in a dilemma about how best to provide treatment and care.

Recent research, carried out by interviewing people with a diagnosis of schizophrenia in 27 countries worldwide, has shown that 95% report experiences of discrimination, for example in applying for a job. Stigma was present and damaging in all the countries assessed.[2] One toxic aspect of stigmatisation is that over half the people interviewed said that they had not applied for a job, or had not tried to initiate a close personal relationship because they expected to encounter a stigmatising reaction - because they expected to fail.

If we consider schizophrenia, one of the family of conditions that are called 'psychotic disorders', what does this diagnosis mean? To debunk common myths: it does not mean a split mind, or 'Jekyll and Hyde' split personality.

---

1 G. Thornicroft, *Shunned: Discrimination against People with Mental Illness.* Oxford, Oxford University Press, 2006.

2 G. Thornicroft, E. Brohan, D. Rose, N. Sartorius, M. Leese, 'Global pattern of experienced and anticipated discrimination against people with schizophrenia: a cross-sectional survey', Lancet, 2009, 373, pp.408-415.

Nor does it mean that the person is 'mad' in terms of a traditional stereotype of someone who is incompetent and out of control. What it does mean is that the person has unusual experiences in thinking or in perceptions, for example beliefs that they may have special powers (such as being close to God), or may be under some threat (such as being followed or persecuted), or can hear voices that other people cannot hear.[3] These experiences are as real as any other, and they are relatively common. About 5 people in 1000 have a diagnosis of schizophrenia, but some of these individual symptoms or experiences affect many more of us. For example, hearing the voice of a recently deceased family member during bereavement is relatively common. So, whilst such experiences are not completely alien to many of us, it is their intensity, persistence and distress which are such challenges for people with a diagnosis of schizophrenia.

The promotion of greater public understanding of psychotic disorders is one of the most important and pressing issues standing in the way of better mental health care and preventing social inclusion. This is why this work of Alexa Wright is so important. She has succeeded in something very difficult - conveying to others in the outside world the inner turmoil (and sometimes delights) of having psychotic experiences. In these compelling images Alexa inverts our expectations. We see individuals of great dignity portrayed in a respectful way, indicating the strengths needed to cope day by day with these conditions. Alexa's portraits are both sensitive and unsentimental. They depict complex individuals coping with the challenges of having psychotic symptoms. They show us, in clear and revealing terms, one aspect of an exaggerated state of being that is a part of the human condition.

Graham Thornicroft
Professor of Community Psychiatry at King's College London, Institute of Psychiatry

3   J. de Jesus Mari, D. Razzouk, R. Thara, J. Eaton, G. Thornicroft, 'Packages of Care for Schizophrenia in Low- and Middle- Income Countries', *PLoS Medicine*, 2009, 6 [10].

"I am a visual artist living in Gloucestershire. On three separate occasions, between November 2014 and July 2015, I found myself in a local psychiatric unit. In that period, I produced a great number of drawings. Depending on my symptoms and access to drawing materials I was able to make simple drawings using pencil and felt tip pens. The basis of these drawings were sketched out quickly on a communal white noticeboard and later drawn onto paper.

I started creating to escape the deep depression I was in, as well as circumvent the shards of psychotic ideas that I was experiencing. I was very ambivalent about my being alive. The drawings were, at times, to be my last interaction with the world, and at other points they felt not of me, of something other: sometimes benevolent, sometimes sinister. Instead of being my undoing, these drawings saved me from myself.

These three drawings have come to symbolise my struggle with both self and with a seemingly harsh clinical system. The drawings took me a wide range of time to complete. 'Unravelling I' took me about an hour to sketch; 'The forbidden shrine' took me about three weeks to finish; 'Unravelling II' took me a whole day.

Liam Whelan

July 2018"

-

'

'Unravelling I, EPISODE 1: DAY 27', LIAM GRAHAM-WHELAN

If illness has been caused by injury, then there are almost always bandages. With psychotic illness I try to figure what lies behind the layers of bandages; is it the head, body or both? So, with an unravelling (through recovery from illness in the community), what is exposed, and how vulnerable do I become?

'The forbidden shrine, EPISODE 2: DAY 73'

This is what the hospital felt like to me. We, as patients are thrown to the margins. All four wards are to be found in the corners. The spaces are vested with strong significance, as transgressing the boundaries often has repercussions for us. In the centre is the psychiatric shrine. The doctors, devoted to their diagnostic manuals, seem aloof and have offices upstairs from us. We have no access to that area. It is forbidden.

'Unravelling II, EPISODE 3: DAY 20'

With ideas of justice playing in my mind to an extent where I expected excision on my body, I remembered my drawing entitled 'Unravelling' from 2014. It was now the end of July 2015 and the bandages seemed old and torn. I was being held by a system that only sees what it wants to see.

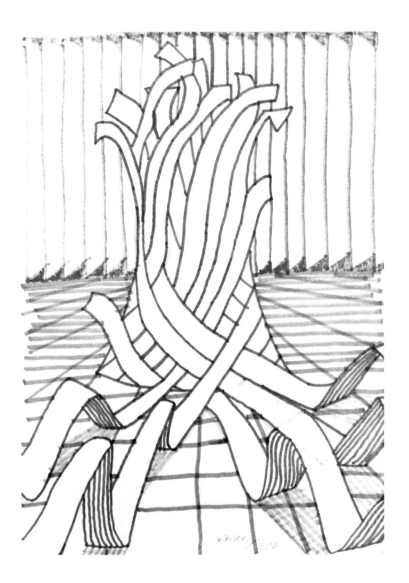

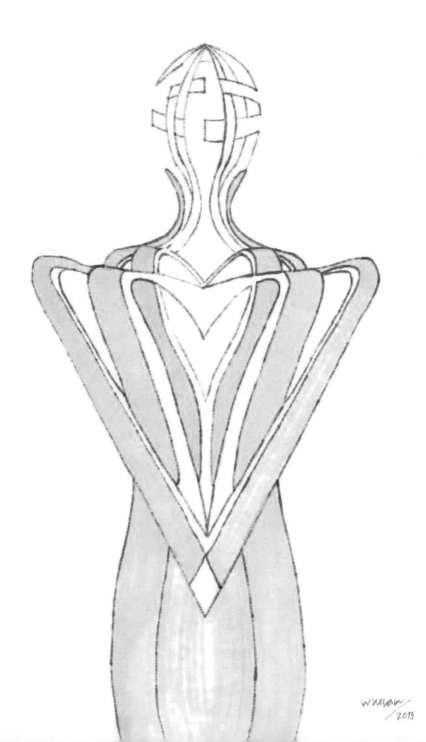

-

MDMA is currently a hot topic in the circles of pharma and tech, from the trend of bio-hacking and microdosing in Silicon Valley, to the "cryptocurrency philanthropist" who has donated $4 million (£2.9 million) in the form of Bitcoin, funding a scheme supporting the medical use of MDMA to PTSD patients. But could your party drug be the answer to people suffering from PTSD? Apparently science says yes.

Your brain on MDMA

MDMA (3,4-methylenedioxy-N-methylamphetamine) commonly known as ecstasy causes a major increase of several neurotransmitters in the brain, particularly serotonin. Serotonin is associated with the feeling of being happy, and cognitive functions such as learning and memory. The Class-A drug also increases the levels of hormones such as oxytocin and prolactin with oxytocin, allowing someone to appear more trusting and with prolactin causing a "post-orgasmic state" by leaving the intaker more relaxed with an increased sense of satisfaction. Probably this is the reason why MDMA seems to be a popular party drug.

Your brain on PTSD

On the other end, we have PTSD (Post-traumatic stress disorder); a severe anxiety disorder that is closely associated with war survivors (refugees, military veterans, war reporters), sexual assault survivors - a disorder, generally associated with patients who have already been victims - but it can also be passed to children whose parents are suffering from it. At the moment, psychotherapy seems to be the most effective method of treatment, especially when practiced with approved drugs that could be prescribed to compliment the patients' general therapy. But the main issue is that those drugs are only targeting the symptoms, as psychotherapist and clinical research for MDMA/PTSD studies, Dr. Mithoefer asserts.

While many patients who have tried MDMA to cure their disorder, mentioned that the drug actually helped them, it's not the specific actions of MDMA that appear to treat PTSD. Rather it seems that MDMA makes the psychotherapy more effective, allowing the patient to confront and openly talk about hers/his feelings. So while there is no clear correlation, the use of MDMA mainly enhances the subject's ability to talk openly and accept help from psychotherapists - a skill that could be worked on without any use of drugs.

Rick Doblin, founder and executive director of the *Multidisciplinary Association for Psychedelic Studies (Maps)*, a non-profit group based in California said to the Financial Times recently that: "MDMA brings back memories in a way [users] can deal with them... We know that it reduces activity in the amygdala in the brain, where fear is processed, and enhances the prefrontal cortex, where we put things in context. When somebody is recalling a trauma while using the drug, their fear-reaction is muted."

In other words, there is a 'frieze response', in order to help the brain neutralise the pain, and thus, be less vulnerable to extreme stress caused by suffering. In contrast MDMA releases the 'feel good' chemicals balancing out the anxiety that PTSD patients feel or patients who are at the terminal stage of cancer. Hence, people with PTSD when on MDMA are less likely to feel high while this is not the case for subjects who don't suffer from any stress disorders.

But MDMA, like every drug, has negative side effects too, the drug can cause symptoms such as jaw clenching and decreased appetite, while in some cases increased blood pressure and pulse. And adding into the equation that MDMA may come from the black market may mean that it is far more harmful than beneficial if not in a pure format and cut properly, as for instance 'Molly' that you usually find in the black market has less than 13% MDMA or sometimes none at all, according to DEA (Drug Enforcement Administration based in US) - making the use of it in a club environment a high risk to health, even causing overheating, seizure, hemorrhagic stroke and organ failure. Part of the MDMA experience also includes the symptoms of comedown: paranoia, depression, anxiety and insomnia. A natural consequence when the supply of serotonin to the brain is depleted and an experience that may last up to three to four days, the time needed for your body to recover completely from the use of MDMA.

Evidently, the side-effects of MDMA may endanger lives, a reason why it has the toughest classification in the UK, even stricter than heroin. The positive side-effects are yet to be seen, and whilst the medical use of MDMA to PTSD patients is useful, the drug should not be instrumental to psychotherapy and long-term healing.

This writing was an examination, an analysis,
and should not be taken as an advice.

-

Spoken word artist, Potent Whisper's poetry workshop with participants at CoolTan Arts, 14/April/18

'The piece was a group effort with different lines being written by different people at the workshop.'

CoolTan Arts is a Southwark-based charity run for adults with experience of mental distress. With 25 years' experience, *CoolTan Arts* have provided creative outlets for self-expression through workshops, self-advocacy, volunteering, guided walks, exhibitions and public art projects. In the last year they have worked face-to-face with 2288 people across London and reached out to 9 million more. 88% of participants said that attending *CoolTan* keeps them well and out of hospital, with one third of participants and volunteers moving on to employment, education or training. *CoolTan Arts* bears a founding belief in the power of art and that mental health needn't be a barrier to this.

"It has given me a sense of worth...I have reconnected with my artistic skills. I have met a lot of nice people with similar health problems. It gives you the chance to discuss issues with people who understand what you are experiencing".
"The environment in the workshops is encouraging and supportive. It is a perfect atmosphere in which to learn".
"It would be an understatement to say that my attendance at CoolTan has played a key part in my recovery. Its role in helping me stay well has been (and continues to be) absolutely fundamental".
"CoolTan provides a firm focus in my life".
"It has given me hope and purpose".
"Doing art is very therapeutic...it raises my self-esteem".

CoolTan Arts ceased trading in June this year because of issues with funding and financial sustainability.

My mental health is...

~~Oil~~

Olive oil, deep green and slow moving,
Pouring thickly out of the nozzle of a bottle
hitting salad leaves and a plate.
Its plasma, a mixture of all my emotions together
It's the sunshine, joining hands with a heavy dark cloud,
uncertain if it wants to rain, shine or shout
It's sun. No, it's rain. Wo! It's choo choo choo choo
No! Sun. No! Rain. Choo hoo choo choo.
It's Tenerife, and a lovely beach
My mental health tastes like Aloe Vera, learn
Strong and bitter, but good because I learn
and purge from it, ripping through me and I'm left
Stronger.
It tastes like Mash potatoe
that I mashed myself
that I am in control of.
It's my mental health!

'Aaron's Poetic Autobiography : Living with Schizophrenia' ,
A. W. J. PILGRIM

-

Hi. I'm Aaron W. J. Pilgrim. Of course, you will learn all about me, as this is my autobiography, but I thought I'd include this section anyway. I grew up & live in South East London. I have studied art at Addey & Stanhope Secondary School, Morley College & CoolTan Arts. Currently I attend CoolTan Arts, that is an arts based charity for people that have suffered mental distress at some time in their life. At CoolTan Arts I have been part of the poetry group for just over two years, it's where I wrote most of the poetry that is in this book. I have had five great poetry teachers at CoolTan Arts that are Ed Mayhew, Olivia Furber, Isley Lynne, Chase Lynne, and Karis Halsall. My poetry usually rhymes & is normally written in an easy to understand way. People have commented that not all the poems rhyme, but I'll let you know that they don't have to.

Lots of my poetry is autobiographical & about my life experiences. After two years of writing poetry in the CoolTan Arts poetry group, I had the idea of publishing my work, then of putting my poems into chronological order. And then I realized that if I wrote another forty poems that it would be a good autobiography. As you can imagine when you read this, I envied people who left school & learned a trade, & had stability as a result. However, I think that perhaps if I had learned a regular trade at a young age, I might not be happy today as an artist, & after all being an artist is a trade in its self.

Let's set the record straight, 'even though I have been diagnosed Schizophrenic, I'm not violent.' In actual fact, I like to think I'm quite nice natured. I realized, that if I was truthful about how many jobs I have failed at, & about my illness, that this might help others who have gone through similar experiences, & also it might help people that care for such people. But as you read this you will note that this is not a life story without joy and hope, and I feel that I have had some good luck too. I was born into a loving family, have many good friends, and a loving girlfriend and a beautiful daughter. I feel that maybe this book might impart some wisdom, and encourage others to not stop dreaming, as I really believe that if you try many things you will eventually find something that you're good at. I found art, music and writing. But above all, I hope that you read this book with a sense of humour, & that you have a little chuckle too. I don't think that you're laughing 'at me' but rather 'with me.' Having a good sense of humour is definitely really important for coping with schizophrenia.

I hope that this book helps others with the diagnosis of Schizophrenia, and those that care for such people. It is a really hard illness to live with. But I guess, I am proof that it is possible to live a good productive life, even if you suffer with the decease. At the end of the day, I definitely don't expect others with schizophrenia, after reading this, to all of a sudden feel that they have to be creative. I've realised that the most important thing is to try to be kind, and people like me with schizophrenia just do well to stay well every day. Some days can be a real struggle. But I will say that being creative is a great form of therapy, and a great form of positive escapism. When I am painting I'm always thinking about the work at hand. Like 'is that line straight enough?' Or 'is that colour right?' & when I'm writing a fiction book, I imagine I'm with the characters in a fictitious alien planet, in the past or future etc. This really takes my mind off my illness and all my worries. So you see, I don't create to earn money or be successful, rather I'm creative because it helps my illness, and I just also find it fun.

Also, if people 'like my work' it makes me feel proud of myself. This is really important for me, because with my illness of schizophrenia, people were not always proud of me. This was definitely the case when I was first mentally ill in my adolescence. But remember, it's not about how good you are at painting etc. but it's about the pure fun of being creative. But of course, if you are good that's a great thing. Perhaps this book might encourage others to write such a poetic book. I really hope that you enjoy reading my poetry as much as I enjoyed writing it, & say "happy reading".

A list Poem Titled 'I Am Aaron Pilgrim.'

I am called Aaron William James Pilgrim.
I am a middle aged man.
I am a dad to beautiful Grace, & the best I can.
I am a boyfriend to beautiful Michelle, she's a really nice girl.
I am a brother to Jason & Heidi, they're both great, & she's very tidy.
I am an uncle to three beautiful kids, Nyiah, Sarah & James.
I am a son to Keith & my late mum Stella, I miss her, and I wish I could tell her.
I am a passionate artist, & also very creative.
I am a painter, I'm good but I want to be really good. A few of my pictures are.
I am a poet, since joining a poetry group. It was the start of a beautiful thing.
I am a writer, with twenty e-books on the way.
I am a sculptor, I don't do it much now, I really must say.
I am a South East Londoner, & lived there all of my life.
I am half English & half Irish decent, to Ireland I often went.
I am a former racing cyclist, I was seldom any good,
but did have a good sprint.
I am a former mobile DJ, & have sung with the odd open mike band.
I am a music lover, & I am a Madonna fan.
I am a car driver, although I've only ever had small cars.
I am a quick typist, glad I learnt at college.
I recommend anyone to gain Pitmans knowledge.
I was a freemason, they are a nice bunch of men,
it's improved my memory greatly.
I am a Cooltan Artist, they are very supportive, & great for learning new skills.
I am paranoid schizophrenic, it's a hard illness, but I deal with it very well.
I am all of these things, & as my poetry teacher said,
"we all play different roles."

My Life Experiences

I come from English & Irish decent, sitting on farm tractors in Ireland.
I copied a lot with coloured felt tips, whilst in Ivydale School.
Grew up in a Victorian Terraced house, playing tip & run against the wall.
Learning cockney rhyming slang, with a little posh talk, thrown in as well.
I luckily got into Addey, & tried with great effort to learn.
With the hot sun beating down on me, in France with the cycling club.
Avoiding fights in Old Kent Road clubs, but did once get a beating.
Caught the 184 bus to Maudsley Hospital, what shame I really felt.
But drew some daffodils given to me, & regained my passion for art.
My mum said, 'now you've got help, I know you'll be OK.'
Whilst dancing I met the beautiful Michelle.
Blessed by God, my beautiful Grace was born.

Old Fashioned Religion

I was not in a very religious family,
But was taught the importance of Jesus.
So I could live much more happily.
As a baby I was christened,
& I sung in a choir where the congregation listened.

My mum took us to church, for midnight mass on Christmas day.
It was rejoicing, I must say.
I was inspired to paint a portrait of Jesus.
By the way, the painting is great, may I say.

P.T.K.O. (Put the Kettle on)

P.T.K.O. put the kettle on & I'll make the tea,
That way we won't miss much snooker you see.
Phillip may be the best at blockbusters,
But then again, he is a pea brain hairy carrot,
Go on, "throw your nationals against the wall."

"Oh you cheeky monkey, we made do with a farthing carrot."
"Oh you cheeky monkey, we make do with a farthing carrot."

Shall we 40/40 over the cemo, tip & run, black jack, a game of cannon,
Or maybe make spas bikes, they're all good fun in the street.
Headers & volleys with an, "on me head, yop, bent foot" & an "Andrew special...............S..H..A..M..E!!!"

"6 & out, you hit the window."
"6 & out, you hit the window."

"He's been inside he has, he's been inside."
I say, "He's been inside he has, he's been inside."
Mr. Lear has called the Old Bill, but we haven't hit his window yet.
Lilly says, "It's a nice day," even if it's pouring with rain.

Stretch man's playing on the Spectrum, listening to Queen & drinking Red Stripe.
Bleach is recovering from a crash, he really did get smashed.

With a, "tea up," Brian brings in the tea.
This is all part of my childhood you see.

The Warriors Gang

Steven started The Warriors Gang.
To join, you had to climb up the drainpipe, & through the upstairs window.
Lois Jeans with frayed edges, & body warmers was the dress code.
Yes, it was good being in The Warriors,
As Steven often said, "S.H.A.M.E......Never!"

I Am a Madonna Fan

I've had a crush on Madonna, since I saw her on Top of the Pops,
She was wearing a pink wig.
I love her many looks, I never dreamed she would be so big.
I had a poster of her on my bedroom wall.
I was heartbroken when she married, I love her after all.
I was jealous when my brother chatted to her, at The London Boat Show.
Maybe I'll see her one day, you never know.

Just use my imagination, & I always have good recall.

What Career to Choose?

My school suggested I get a trade.
At 16, I didn't feel suited to anything.
Didn't feel bright enough, for a top job.
Bricklayer? The wall would fall down.
Roofer? I suffer with bad vertigo.
Mechanic? The brakes would fail.
Electrician? I would cause an electric shock.
Driving jobs? I'd get lost.
Gas fitter? I'd blow up a house.
Carpenter? I didn't feel safe with power tools.
Shop work? Well I knew this was badly paid.
Factory Jobs? Too boring.
A Plumber? No I hate toilets.
Bin man? Road Sweeper? Cleaner? Well I hate dirty jobs.

A Parking Warden? Don't like confrontation.
Jobs Abroad? Not confident in traveling far.
Armed Forces? Don't like violence.
Security Guard? Not tough enough.
This left The Sixth Form and Office Work, so I decided to pursue this.
Not a good start at all...
Years later my dad told me, "But you learnt how to be safe."

My Disastrous Job

My mum saw a job advert, in The Daily Mail.
It had a picture of a rough stone, for the job of a diamond sorter,
The sort of job that raised a brow.
I had two long interviews, & I got the job,
Along with a certain kudos, with also very good pay.

So I started intensive training, before I worked on the floors,
& was soon checking diamonds, looking for all their flaws.
I was aware that I was developing slight tunnel vision,
Had great trouble concentrating, I hummed to concentrate more.

A fellow worker who sat next to me, was a guy whose name was Ashley,
Who laughed at my immature world views, that he obviously saw.
"Do you think Buddhists agree with cycle shorts?" was one ridiculous
question he asked.
But I answered seriously, which they all found hilariously daft.
Then at break time, some of the workers dressed up in orange Buddhist
robes,
& stood in front of me laughing, praying, humming.
Of course it was all just a school boy joke, but my mental health was broke.

Then when it was time to go home, I made a massive mistake,
Of course with all this going on, I wasn't thinking straight.
I decided to take a small diamond home, just to show my mum what an uncut
diamond looked like,
I thought, after all my mum told me about the job,

I'll bring it back tomorrow, this was really dumb.
I showed it to a work colleague, waiting for a train at Farringdon Station.
I'll bring it back tomorrow, I told him, for his information.
He looked at it & replied, "of course, but it's small & not worth much."
So I set off to my mum's work, which was in the middle of Rye Lane Peckham.
In the street I took the diamond out of my pocket, ready to show my mum.
Then I was pushed & I looked in my hand, the diamond was gone,
It all happened in a second.
Immediately I thought, "I can't return it back, oh no now I feel like a thief."
The company somehow found out, maybe by a camera, I came to know they knew.
As you would rightly expect, I was ostracized in every way they could do.
Shunned, placed in the corner, given wrong information for a trip, locked out of the sports ground, no cakes from a bun run,
Treating me badly of which they had great fun.
Then finally being paraded around the company, exposed as a thief, before being given the sack. The kudos certainly shattered.

The whole sorry experience, contributed to me being mentally ill.
Being reminded of this job, sometimes made me unwell.

I know what I did was stupid, but boy did I pay the price.
Now I know Buddhism is great, love diamonds once again,
That it was all just a joke gone wrong,
& Ashley & the others are probably quite nice.

Old Kent Road Night Clubs

In the 90's, the lads went to the Old Kent Road.
The Frog & Nightgown, The Gin Palace, The Thomas A. Becket,
The Green Man, Drovers & Caesar's Funhouse.

There were always fights over the ladies, but not so many in The Frog.
I once did get a beating, ending up in a King's hospital bed.
I met two girlfriends there, Helen & Lucy were their names.

Usually first to The Royal Albert pub, that was in Blackheath Hill,
Get the bus to The Frog where we were "on the pull,"
After go to Mayur Tandoori for a curry.
So we weren't jostling for a cab in a hurry.

All the clubs closed down, it's completely different now.
I painted a picture of The Frog, to a former clubber I might make a sale.

I needed help

I really thought I was autistic.
I wanted to be hypnotised, so I wasn't so sick.
All I knew, was I needed help, & quick.

Being diagnosed

I knew I wasn't normal, for a long time.
Being diagnosed Schizophrenic, was a relief of mine.
I welcomed the help I'd get, with the illness spelt on a dotted line.
This would make me more normal, & hopefully shine.

The Doctor

The doctor looked at his brain scan, as through a microscope.
& labelled the patient with a number.
He was out of his tree, he wrote with a pencil.

You Can Believe What's Not True

It can be so hard being mentally ill.
You can believe what's not true.
Every day you need to take a pill.
They can have side effects, such as making you tired.
Sometimes every day is an uphill battle.
In scary hospital, you take so many pills you rattle.

But most of the people in the system care,
Providing you're nice, they are there.
I count myself lucky, that at present I'm well.
Of course that is swell.

The 184 Bus

When we were young the lads joked,
"You need to catch the 184,"
You see it goes to the Maudsley Mental Hospital.
I thought, "I've caught the 184."

David

My school friend David liked a drink or two, especially a Whisky Mac.
He would laugh, "I'm maaassshhheedd."
We'd go to, 'The Gin Palace,' that I called, 'The Bash Palace,'
he'd look around saying, "Loads of Birds."
His catchphrase was, "Yeah man bad man."
He loved his Sky TV, & he was a mad Liverpool FC fan.

He was a proud worker at a lighting factory, he loved The Working Man's Clubs.
In the middle of the day, he criticised me for not drinking, in his Working Man's Club.

He was a really good friend, but after I became ill, he'd mock me.
I really wanted to tell him, that I got upset, that I wasn't a psycho.
But I just couldn't talk about my illness, as I felt so embarrassed.
I envy my friends, that don't live the stigma of Schizophrenia.
David is more grown up now, and lives in Australia.

The York Clinic and A Vision

My mums battle with cancer, made me mentally ill as I saw her suffer.
I was taken to The York Clinic to get well.
In my dormitory a patient played loud music, making me more unwell.
An Irishman opposite me had long scruffy hair & a beard,
You're Jesus I declared.
He played up to this, & I believed.
When ill I often have Hallucinations, & in the morning I had another vision.
It was of Jesus and some angels, they drifted through the window.
He said he was real and not the Irishman, & if I live by his teachings I'll be OK.
Then he flew back out of the window, this was profound I'll tell you so.
I'm not a true Christian, but I live by his teachings though.

View from CoolTan's Kitchen Window

The nice thing about CoolTan's new building, is it has windows.
Natural daylight really cheers you up,
& is good for creating art.
It's always nice to look at the sky,
The type of clouds & the weather.
It's good for depression, indeed any problem.
You can see The Houses of Parliament, with its flag flying,
The Oval Gasworks & The Battersea Power Station chimneys.
As Gary said, "the world's your oyster."

'Creative Marks' (Inspired by a Poem Called, 'A Brief History of Those....' by Kevin Higgins)

I often make points in my poetry,
Read them to the group, & leave politely.
Creatively most at CoolTan, leave their mark on society.
I suppose some don't, work nine to five, don't live lively.
As long as the mark is good,
That's the main thing, that I've understood.

Expression Poem

Poetry is the expression of the words of life.
Art is a fabricated view of expression.
Writing transcribes expression.
Acting is a demonstration of expression.
The camera & microphone capture these truths.

-

'I think this meeting was most upsetting when I realised what a huge amount of time I had wasted. At this stage about two years had passed since being diagnosed with bipolar disorder, and I started a search for my current psychotherapist.

During all this time, feeling that I was fighting an endless battle, I retreated to my art where I found something priceless and urgent, expression and understanding. I realised that I had little vocabulary or even understanding of the emotions and feelings I was experiencing during manic and depressive attacks and a reason why I found it very difficult to explain my state of mind to doctors or therapists. By creating collages with my own photography to unravel and explore all these suppressed and dark feelings, I discovered art therapy. In art therapy I found a way to communicate with myself that was compassionate and understanding, opening a gateway to complex emotions and feelings by giving them colour, shape and a voice through interpretation. During the creative process I reconciled emotional conflicts, fostering self-awareness, personal growth and eventually in combination with psychotherapy that started 14 months ago, art therapy became a big part of my continuous rehabilitation and healing process.'

Seasons of the Mind is a self-portrait series and project about Mental Health.
There is nothing subtle in theme or in colour; the images are bright, colourful, quirky and even fun, hoping to close the gap between the audience and the stigma towards mental health.
Each project consists of research, a planned model, props and landscape photo shoots from which I gather chosen images to create the final image in Adobe Photoshop. My images are strongly influenced by my many years in the theatre world, the whole process can be very rewarding.
Each image expresses a multitude of emotions and feelings with surreal representations of illusions, paranoia, depression, manic attacks and much more.

The head open and exposed with fantastical explosions of extreme happiness and sadness, shows a vulnerable and personal experience with these life crippling emotional mood swings.

What's most extraordinary for me about this series is among the chaos, busyness, detail and drowning figure, there is something very controlled and theatrical about the expression of the character, considering the emotional distress. This shows me how important it is to protect people around me from my personal turmoil even when most vulnerable.

The images are quite beautiful in contrast with the insanity and dark thoughts of depression, paranoia and suicide, easing the viewer into my pain and then also looking for acceptance and approval.

Spring (top opposite)

Expressing a visual image with emotions and feelings that are translated into words to understand the first stage of a Manic attack.

euphoria, euphoric, extreme elation, extreme optimism, strong, impulsive, grandiosity, racing thoughts, insomniac, extreme focus, comedian, happy, exciting ideas, reckless, uninhibited, sharp

Spring represents awakening and energy. The exploding flower arrangement shows the ability to entertain many creative ideas and simultaneously feeling connected to the world around, perceived in vivid colours. The character shows confidence and even the fool with this new found optimism. There is a sense of grandiosity with the angelic seen rising above and an overall sense of euphoria.

Summer (bottom opposite)

Expressing a visual image with emotions and feelings that are translated into words to understand the second stage of a Manic attack.

grandiose, very active, hearing voices, irritable, illusions, paranoia, impulsive, impatient, restless, reckless, agitated, heart palpitations, grinding teeth, insomnia, self-harm, losing touch with reality, suicidal tendencies

Summer represents the unravelling. The Russian doll effect with different expressions, shows discomfort, distrust and creates a sinister feeling. Many forms of the same clown, seducing and luring into chaos represents

paranoid illusions. The seagulls disappearing into space creates a sense of disintegrating as a reaction to exhaustion and the overload of all senses.

Autumn (top opposite)

Expressing a visual image with emotions and feelings that are translated into words to understand the first stage of depression.

feeling sad, tearful, hopeless, falling, want to escape, feeling down, alone, despair, pessimistic, self-doubt, lacking energy, isolation, social phobia, anxiety
Autumn represents falling into darkness. While sinking into water there is a feeling of becoming airborne, representing melancholia, a familiar and safe place to retreat to, since childhood. The mind is telling a story of a man flying away, escaping into a fantastical daydream. The single tear amplifies the deep sadness that is growing, with the swans, soothing and reassuring that this is the best place to be at this moment.

Winter (bottom opposite)

Expressing a visual image with emotions and feelings that are translated into words to understand the second stage of depression.

Feeling fatigued, feelings of despair, inability to experience pleasure, loss of appetite, physical and mental sluggishness, speaking slowly, irritable, sleeping too much, difficulty in starting or completing everyday tasks, isolation, thoughts of death and suicide
Winter represents the abyss. The mind becomes a graveyard and like the asylum in the background, a prison, incapable of escaping to fantasy worlds. The expression is painful and the character is stuck outside in the snow and the freezing water. The black ravens and the staircase into heaven represents the overwhelming and involuntary thoughts of death and suicide. The image is bleak with what feels like endless suffering.

Summer Madness (opposite)

I reworked Summer Madness for HIM + HIS. It is a tribute to some/all artists and musicians that have suffered/suffer from mental health problems. With sinking instruments and an ear that has been cut off like Van Gogh's, I am trying to show the creative energy during episodes and also the emotional pain involved in creation.

Thank you for giving me the opportunity to share my story and the series *Seasons of the Mind.*

Currently I am still in therapy, working with visualisation to try and contain manic and depressive attacks. I have covered so much ground in the last 14 months, feeling confident that I am getting good results and the best support from my psychotherapist.

The road with the national health system is still very rocky and difficult. Having to return to work in the near future is bringing up a lot of pressure and anxiety, and although I am in a programme that supports people with mental health, there is no place for artists. I am being pushed towards cleaning, retail and security jobs which will give me little or no time for my photographic art. We will see what life brings...

Best wishes, Marius

'No Knight'
'Shore Unsure' , **KYLESS BLUE**

-

"No Knight"

A song made in the shroud of a broken relationships future and insomnia. Sampling "Eternal Sunshine for A Spotless Mind" - An ode to the importance of memory and sleep in order to heal self-deprecation and inhale light. Healing trauma that most men choose to ignore.

"Shore Unsure"

A rhythmic groove to acknowledge the beauty and growth in pain. A repetition of vocals spewing "my latest and greatest", it's an homage to the empathic self, to love you, like you love. An acceptance message to men declaring that is okay to demonstrate and feel love, Something the male gaze takes for granted.

Photographer: Eva-Grace Bor

'*An Album A Day*', JOEL McCORMACK

-

I started creating 'An Album a Day' at a time that was incredibly
complicated. I decided to leave from being a Jehovah's Witness, the faith
system I had been part of for 22 years. I was and continue to be shunned
by all in the community, including my parents and the friends I had. At the
start of the process of leaving, I didn't think I had the strength to continue
and entered a very dark headspace. I felt so lost and alone.

A constant anchor for me has always been music. Finding artists that
resonate with my feelings, or songs that allow me to work through whatever
emotion I'm feeling give me an opportunity to process and to reflect.
'An Album a Day' gave me a personal space for meditation. When I felt
overwhelmed I would stick on a full album, and allow the artist to share
with me their thoughts and vision. Sometimes the music let me fester in the
anger of my grief, sometimes the softness of my emotions.

I would pick up my sketchbook, draw the album cover, and write down a
reflection on the music. It was my own form of therapy, and helped me to
keep checking in on my feelings.

My life continues to be complicated, but my situation changed drastically.
To look back and read of my experiences continues to give me hope that life
has new routes and opportunities that will continue to be open to me if I
just keep going.

DRAWING OF THE Vg ALBUM
COVER ON THE TRAIN TO WAKE-
FIELD TO MEET AITOR. MY
BRAIN IS BUZZING, I FEEL
SO TIGHT AND SENSORY. I'M
NOT THINKING WHEN I'M
DRAWING, I CHOOSE THE
COLOURS WITHOUT CARE. A
BOY, YOUNG AND ARAB, WATCHES
MY HANDS SCRIBBLE AND
MAKE MARKS. I'VE NEVER
FELT LIKE THIS, MY WHOLE
BRAIN IS ALIVE. I AM
THINKING OF EVERYTHING AT
ONCE BUT NOT CONFUSED.
I THINK IT'S THE NEW MEDS,
IT'S NOT BAD, JUST STRANGE.

THINGS ARE BECOMING MORE CLEAR,
I AM ALOT CALMER TODAY. DIDN'T
TAKE MY MEDS LAST NIGHT BECAUSE
I DON'T HAVE ENOUGH. I'M ON THE
TRAIN TO MANCHESTER AIRPORT TO
SEE SHIREEN FOR TWO WEEKS. I'M
THINKING OF LOVE, BOYS, MY FUTURE.
I'M AN ILLUSTRATOR AND THAT FEELS
(MANN LIKE THE GREEN JUMPER I'M
WEARING. I FEEL LIKE I'M
BECOMING MYSELF. I LOVE HIM FOR
IT. I'M THINKING OF DUBLIN, OF
A9491 OF AN THE COMAGES THAT
LINE HER WALLS. THERE IS HOPE
HERE.

DRAWING OF YOUNG FATHEAS, TAPE ONE.

I'M FINALLY HAVING THE EXPERIENCES MY MIND AND SOUL WOULD OFTEN LONG FOR. AS I SIT AND LISTEN TO KID CUDIS MASTERPIECE – PASSION, PAIN & DEMON SLAYING, I AM REMINDED TO LOVE LIFE. I CONNECT TO KIDIS MENTAL STATE, THE SUICIDAL NATURE BUT THE WANT TO BE FREE AND TO LOVE ETERNALLY. I AM SEEING THE VALUE IN MY LIFE MORE AND MORE. I AM HAPPY + BLESSED WITH THE DEVIL'S EXIST AS IN THIS LIFETIME I HOPE TO BRING MY SWEETNESS AND SOFTNESS TO THE NEXT. MAY I NEVER BECOME TOO HARD. I'M EXCITED FOR A NEW CHAPTER, OUT OF NEW JUDGEMENT AND SUPPORT. I AM BEAUTIFUL, I AM EXOTIC. MY BODY 18 ME, IT IS MY VESSEL FOR THIS SOUL NOW SO MAY I LOVE AND CARE FOR IT. YALLAH BYE.

(ITAY, BERLIN, MY FIRST)

AS I WALK AROUND KREUZBERG TAKING
I PHONE PHOTOS OF RUBBISH AND OLD
FURNITURE I SING 'ALL IS FULL OF
LOVE'. THINKING ABOUT LAST NIGHT,
ABOUT THE FUTURE OF ME, ABOUT MY
PAST OF WHICH I WILL LEARN TO LIVE
TOO. ONE DAY, BJÖRKS WORDS

"YOU'LL BE GIVEN LOVE,
YOU'LL BE TAKEN CARE OF,
YOU'LL BE GIVEN LOVE,
YOU HAVE TO TRUST IT,

MAYBE NOT FROM THE SOURCES,
YOU HAVE POURED YOURS
MAYBE NOT FROM THE DIRECTIONS
YOU ARE STARING AT,

TWIST YOUR HEAD AROUND
IT'S ALL AROUND YOU
ALL IS FULL OF LOVE
ALL IS FULL OF LOVE"

IN HONOUR A DRAWING OF THE
AMAZING 'HOMOGENIC' BY MY
GODDESS BJÖRK XX

blond

𝍤 𝍫

BLONDE / BLOND WAS AND IS SO IMPORTANT
TO ME. IT HELPED ME RELATE TO AND
UNDERSTAND THE SADNESS AND EXSTACY THAT
COMES WITH QUEERNESS. I SIT HERE TONIGHT,
A LITTLE SAD AND TIRED, FEELING LONELY.
I WONDER IF I'M DELIRABLE ENOUGH, IF
I'LL EVER BELONG. BUT IN MY HEART
I KNOW IT WILL GET BETTER AND
BE BETTER. THIS IS JUST THE START.
I HAVE SO MUCH AHEAD OF ME MAYBE
I'LL GO OUT TONIGHT, ALTHOUGH I
FEEL PRETTY DOWN. TRYING NOT TO DRINK
IS HARD WHEN YOU'RE YOUNG AND
ALONE IN BERLIN. LET'S SEE
WHAT HAPPENS. HOPEFULLY I WILL
BE KIND AND GOOD TO MYSELF
TONIGHT IS TO FRANK O'CONN TO BEING
QUEER. TO BEING SAD. TO BEING
HONEST.

COMPOSED TO MOTEL SUNSET, ARGANTINIA

GENTLE BOY,
PLEASE BE GENTLE BOY,
TAKE IT EASY ON MY HEART,
I'M TOO GENTLE BOY,
MAY YOU UNDERSTAND MY PAIN,
AND BE GENTLE BOY,
IT'S A HARD FOR ME TO EXPLAIN,
HOW I'M GENTLE BOY,

I ENJOYED THE PAIN,
NOT TOO GENTLE NOW,
TRACED YOU WITH MY TOUNGE,
STOP THE GENTLE NOW,
DOMINATE MY SHELL,
FUCK GENTLE AWAY
HELP ME TO BE TOUGH,
I'M YOUR GENTLE BOY

IF ONE DAY YOU FIND,
I'M TOO MUCH TO TAKE,
IF YOU REALISE MY PAIN,
AND ALL OF MY MISTAKES,
IF THIS WAS ALL TOO FAST
TOO NAIVE TO WAIT
MAY WE EMBRACE OUR GENTLE HEARTS,
REMEMBER ME,
GENTLE BOY

TO BENJAMIN

IT'S BEEN A WHILE SINCE I WROTE HERE.

I'VE BEEN DISTRACTED WITH LIFE.

I'M PISSED MOST OF THE TIME. REALLY FUCKING ANGRY AND AGRESSIVE. MUM AND DAD ARE BOTH TOYING WITH MY EMOTIONS, THEY SAID THEY'D KEEP IN CONTACT WITH ME WHILST I FELT 'DEPRESSED'. MUM SENT ME A MESSAGE ABOUT KEEPING IN CONTACT, ABOUT BEING THERE FOR ME. I FEEL ABANDONED.

I HAVE NEVER FELT MORE ALONE.

I'M PISSED AT EVERY MOTHER FUCKER THAT HAS CUT ME OFF FUCK YOUR BULLSHIT CULT WORSHIP. FUCK YOUR OPINION OF ME.

I AM NOT YOUR GOSSIP.

I'M ANGRY AND HURTING. I WANT TO CRY BUT I CAN'T BECAUSE OF THESE FUCKING MEDS. I'M SCARED, I'M CONFUSED.

I'M STILL IN CONFLICT ABOUT MY SEXUALITY I CAN STILL FEEL THE OPINIONS, THE VIOLENT HATEFUL WORDS THAT THE WITNESSES USE, CLOGGING EVERY PORE IN MY SKIN.

I'M FUCKED UP WITH BEN. SOMETIMES I HATE HIM, BUT I LIKE WHEN HE FUCKS ME MAD. IT NUMBS THE PAIN FOR A WHILE. FUCK.

(QUAY DASH — TRANSPHOBIC)

I CHOSE DEAR ANNIE BY BESSIE SMITH MAINLY
BECAUSE HE'S A DUBLIN BOY AND I'M
CURRENTLY IN DUBLIN. BUT ITS ALSO RESONATING
WITH ME TODAY. IT'S LIGHT HEARTED BUT
STILL DEALS WITH DEEP PAIN. IT ALSO
CENTRES AROUND HIS EARLY TWENTIES.

TODAY I FEEL CALM AND GENERALLY
HAPPY WITH AN GENTLE UNDERTONE OF
ANXIETY. I LIKE DUBLIN. (I'M HAPPY THIS
COULD BE AN OPTION FOR ME.
ITS BEEN NICE TO CONNECT WITH AUNTY
MAGGI AND HAVE A MOTHERLY FIGURE
AROUND WHO DOESN'T JUDGE ME.
THIS PROJECT IS SHOWING AND REMINDING
ME THAT MY MOOD AND EMOTIONS ARE
SO VARIED RIGHT NOW. IN MY LAST
ENTRY I WAS SO ANGRY.
HAS MY BRAIN CHANGED SINCE? HAVE I
DEALT WITH IT MORE? IS IT MY
MEDS? DOES IT MATTER IF I'M
HAPPY AND POSITIVE RIGHT NOW? NO.

'*Oboe*', TOM DUNN

-

When I was eight I broke my oboe, and something in my head broke with it.

If that sounds absurd, bizarre or just plain stupid, all I can say is that things are going to get a whole lot more ridiculous as this story goes on.

Some months prior, I had begged my parents to let me enrol in oboe lessons through the local council. For the low, low fee of £5 a week, I got to rent an instrument of my very own and attend sessions during break time with my assigned teacher. She had a flower in her hair and a voice that gave me goosebumps.

I still remember her opening the black plastic case, clasps unfolding to reveal a soft, velvety interior. Inside sat the oboe in its constituent parts, and as she guided me through the assembly I was rapt with attention. A beautifully complex array of silver buttons and levers revealed themselves as a mechanical language I was eager to learn, all wrapped around dark, lacquered wood (this is how I choose to remember it, rather than as - the far more likely reality of - cheap, cast black resin. This was a council-owned instrument, after all). Real wood or not though, there was one thing keenly impressed onto me by my new tutor: treat the oboe with the utmost care. And in that first lesson, as I listened to her play, I fully felt the weight of that command.

For weeks I would sit at home, hurriedly finishing up whatever the latest practice was, just to sit there and play, filling the house with what could charitably be described as the giddy quacking of a duck on LSD. But I genuinely loved the sensation of my fingers running along the network of rivets and dimples in my hands, the warmth of the reed in my mouth, the initial forceful breath giving way to a free flow of loud, bright sound. It reminded me of my grandad, a committed pianist. I now had a bullish, uncompromising voice of my own. And so I kept playing, incorporating each lesson's newly minted note and chord into the sounds of my dissonant jazz sessions.

This continued until the first week of the summer holidays, where my usual routine - swiftly assembling the three parts of the oboe, watching the quicksilver-like keys light up as they came out of the box - ended in a different way. I felt the oboe fall out of my hands.

There was a sad little click and rattle as the instrument hit the floor, and then something like the sound of white noise made physical ran across my forehead - just for a second - leaving me blank. I bent down and picked up the oboe. The splintered reed could easily be replaced, but when I worked my way through the keys, try as I might - and I really did try - I couldn't find anything else wrong with the oboe. Life could carry on as before.

But something had broken, some delicate part of that metal network irreversibly changed. I had heard it.

I hadn't taken care.

And if I thought about it for too long, that horrible blankness cut through my head again.
And I did think about it for too long.
And I started to think about a lot of things for too long.
Silly things, like needing to tell a friend something as soon as I saw them at school in four weeks' time. Something minor, like what I thought of the new Transformers episode. And that need to talk about it would sit at the back of my head all day, until it didn't feel like my thought at all, but something separate that I was being compelled to do.

As the holiday rolled along, I spent my days alternately ignoring and submitting to the whims of this separate thing. Whether it dressed itself up as that desperate need to talk about a cartoon, to correct a perceived mistake, or simply articulating myself more clearly, at the heart of all these banal activities sat something utterly alien. The white noise had become shrouded in the everyday preoccupations of a child; softening itself, blending in. But it was still there, like a violation.

The separateness would tell me to apologise with every step I took outside -

any number of insects could have been crushed, after all - and so I did. And if anyone heard me, I made sure to whisper more quietly next time. Eventually, I realised that merely thinking 'sorry' was enough to satisfy the thing inside. I started to wash my hands like soap was going out of fashion. If they didn't feel clean enough, I would wash them again - until the sensation of the suds took on a new quality, and my hands gained a certain numbness that made towels feel hard.

The separate thing inside would become increasingly more imaginative in its requests over those six weeks, culminating in the great card reading saga of my ninth birthday. Whilst sat alone in the living room watching TV, it had decreed that I was to read each of my birthday cards in turn, out loud. If I made a mistake in my reading, I was to make the sound of a tape rewinding and begin again. Along the way, new rules were added; I had to read the cards cover to cover - simply reading the individual greetings inside wasn't enough.

In the quiet moment between my eighth and ninth attempts, I was interrupted by my mum gently asking me what I was doing. There was something in her voice I hadn't heard before, something in the eyes of my dad, stood next to her, that left me with a new kind of sadness.

But the truth was out now; my sad parody of time travel had an audience.

During the long conversation that followed, I learned something important between cute little stories of my uncle's own infant germaphobia, and more veiled allusions to a family history of feeding something separate inside. It was a lesson that I still live by, for better and for worse. It's a lesson that's seen me through later, thornier conversations with partners and therapists, when my rituals became internalised and my obsessions more troubling: nothing drives the separateness away like a good confession.

A few weeks later, I quit playing the oboe.

'Inside Out', OLIVERBIZHAN AZARMI

-

I wasn't able to talk properly till I was around six years old, so drawing from the start was always the easiest way to communicate how I was feeling when I was younger and I am pretty sure my parents have those drawings somewhere.. As I grew up I learned new mediums that excited me more at the time than drawing such as poetry and video, but I'm noticing now that it has come back to me like a very slow boomerang, and that I mostly draw when I have run out of things to say, or cannot find the right words, it has worked as almost like an extension to my language.
I am a Cancer and for those who don't know, we are pretty much like an emotional sponge.

This past year I have had regurgitating hiccups from someone who likes to come make a mess and leave. It almost felt like I was continuously sewing up holes in a blanket that kept ripping. As I kept keeping things in I felt isolated from the ones around me and started finding myself absolutely exhausted. Recently that person has come again.. it turns me inside out every time. To show this I have been drawing and writing backwards and using the traces from the other side of the paper as the end result. As I look back at my drawings it makes me a little sad... there is this almost utopian but also dystopian island's full of abandonment and betrayal which has been a map of my head recently, but at the same time, the things I went through have taught me a lot of what I need and don't, what I am worth and what I am not standing for any more. So I guess in that respect even though things get hard you really learn more about yourself from the inside out too.

I DONT KNOW WHY I GO

IN THE GARDEN TO PLAY
WITH THE SNAKES

IF THEY
BITE ME
OVER AND
OVER

FOR
MORE
THAN
ONE
YEAR

SHOCKED HE
IN YOUR BE
SO IN DOUBT OF US
I FELL DOWN THE
STAIRS

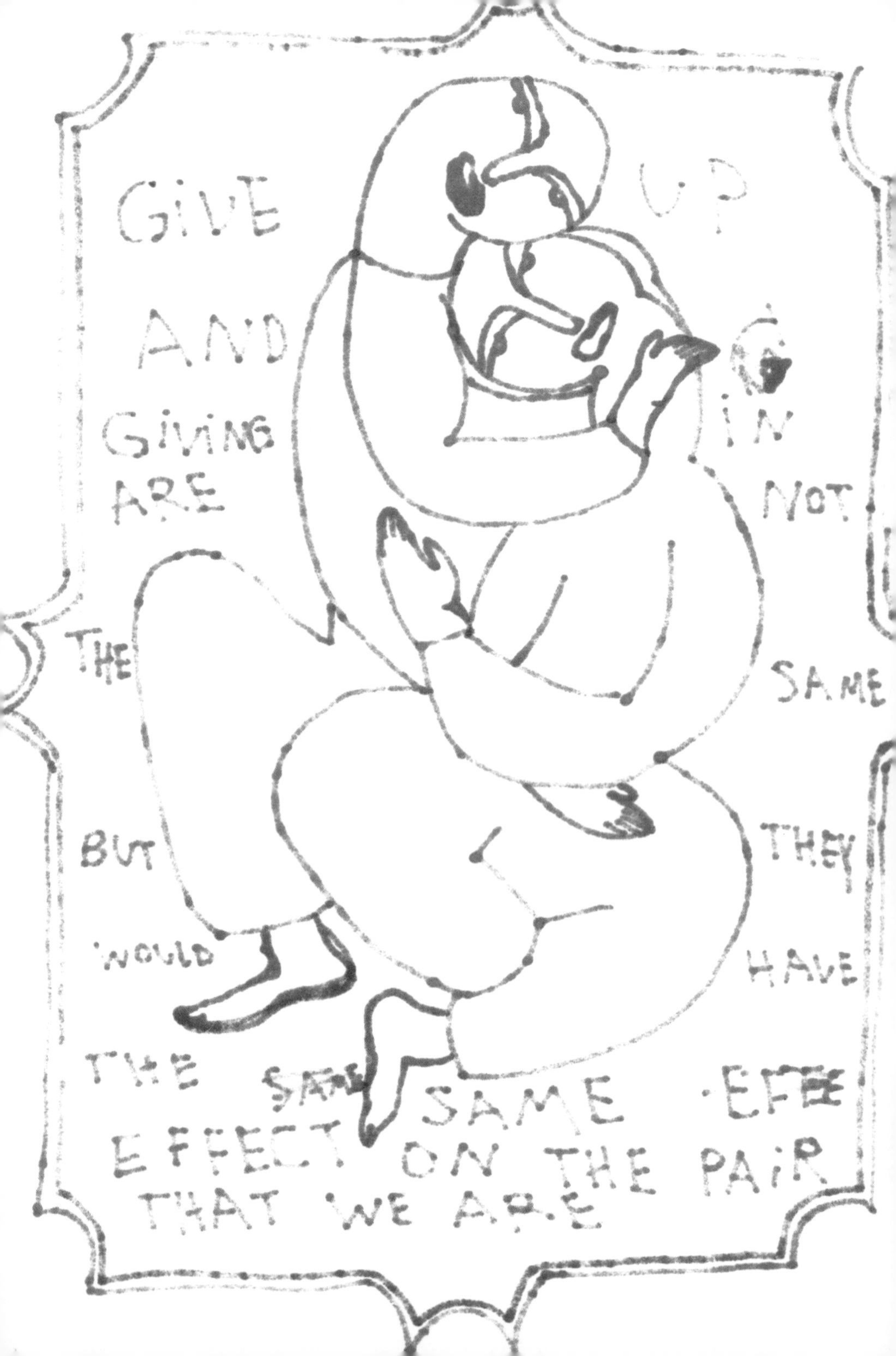

GIVE UP
AND G
GIVING IN
ARE NOT

THE SAME

BUT THEY

WOULD HAVE

THE SAME SAME EFFE
EFFECT ON THE PAIR
THAT WE ARE

'Untitled', HARALD SMART

-

Like the glass of coconut milk
I drank
and held in my mouth
after too many chilli flakes
went in at once

reprieve came late
from the pre-invented world
of hetero-
norm
thanks for nothing (fuckers)

pain
inflicted
by the space suit
crafted thin
woven diamond
(benefits: affability
a placid demeanour)

with imperceptible
spiked and compressing lining
my price for breathing in the world
for excursions beyond the tower
and walking down corridors
unnoticed
homo normalis

like some Shalott
her brother, maybe
growing up
vision distorted

on a silent isle
long, longing looks
disrupted

I dragged my tower with me

I remember crying in
the office
of that slight and slanting
fisherman's cottage-
cum-clinic
about
the way i see sex everywhere
even in that hill
I climbed first at two
its crag and ruin
are places i
could...

cried more
when i realised
that most of the tears i'd held in
for eight years
had not evaporated
that the tower i'd designed
had diamond walls
thick
high
had held them in
like a silo
kept them fresh

so that looking out from the top
distant
dragging around with me
this diamond tower
and wearing the diamond suit
to live
to breathe
the problem
the issue really
was that everyone looked
and saw diamonds
and saw nothing
and saw through

'Untitled', CURTIS DEAN OCHAN ASHOK

-

I   struggle   to   express   my   feelings   using   words/
language   -   it   makes   me   feel   lost   in   myself.

Addictions   -   I've   been   struggling   with   one   for
many   years   but   I   keep   try   try   trying   again.

It's just the words, the images and everything else is only a visual aid.

Only some images best describe the feeling of the words for me.

For me, something that makes me feel less alone is sharing how I feel
on Instagram. It used to be my platform because then I would feel like
someone was listening even if I had no followers, but I don't do that
anymore. Maybe because I'm scared about the internet holding all of
this deep personal information about me which makes me feel uneasy.

Sometimes I wake up and I'm still asleep my mind wanders my head hurts is my brain still with me?

I don't always feel because I don't always feel, I don't always love because I don't always feel. I stop to feel and often I'm left alone.

Next jahr ist just two weeks away: a conversation is happening in the car. We're (we are) on a journey to mi hermano's neu place, his future is beginning. What about mine?

Oh I'm lost again. Stuck in a cycle of deconstructive reconstruction. Where language fails me. So at what point will it all make sense?

And **WHY** MUST I EXIST IN A WAY I CANT EVEN UNDERSTAND WHERE IS MY BEGINNING WHAT IS THE END WHY SHOULDI CARE AND WILL I EVER be satisfied with the in-between?

Maybe she's right… it is what I choose to accept and everything I choose to expect.

Next time I'll Scream until I feel it again

Open your eyes sun
Forgive me for what I have
done
Believe that soon I will be bet-
ter
Stronger and Smarter and
humble
Whether I can cry or smile i'll
always be honest
I love my love my life and all
else
Thank you
It's okay you will be fine
One day

'Sanctuary' , **DANIEL CHAMBERLAIN**

...they always think medication is the answer but it's not... I'm fed up!

Don't shout please.

I'm not gonna take the medication anymore I've had enough. Then they did the procedure to inject me... this and that... I don't get the system... the system is messed up.

People injected you? When was that? Was there an incident or something?

I can't remember. I was angry. I was upset. This place is not suitable for me because it's far away from you guys, you have to commute, which I feel bad about and... I just want to do a tailored apprenticeship on tourism... there's a Danish company...it's an agency who help companies find autistic people work. I felt safe at home, I've learnt my lesson from the past... and you guys think that i'll do in the future the things I used to do in the past and I won't because I've learnt my lesson.

It's not your fault... when you say "I've learnt my lesson" it sounds like you did it purposefully. You didn't do it purposefully because you were not remembering all these hallucinations... it's not the fault of the person, it just comes. It just comes. Maybe it's stress levels or-

I don't know! They asked me "did you take a drug or something?" and I said no!

I don't want to talk about it.

I'm sure when you feel calmer they will let you out just continue to make an effort-

I'm trying as hard as I can mum what can I do... I'm a human being for crying out loud

We'll make sure they don't keep you here long. The main thing is you remain calm so they have reasons to say "now you feel calm you can go home there is no danger". They want to know you are not going to endanger yourself.

But you can tell them this - I forget to tell them these things on Tuesdays.

Instead of me telling them, your actions will tell them

They won't listen to me that's why

Don't talk. Your actions will tell them - brushing teeth, washing... it's those basic things they want to see... "now he's become calm, his mental health is mastered, now he can go out". Unless your actions show that you're calm-

I wish they didn't assess me when I was on that ward! I wish they didn't assess me at that time!

Let's not talk about the past. If we keep going back to the past we will get stuck in the past. Now we are here. What you've got to do is you remain relaxed, when you become angry use other techniques.

They just do it for the money that's it. They're sick in the head!

If-

They do it for the money that's it!

When you are blocked like this it means we can't even engage in conversation and they will keep you. The moment you internalise this: "I have to remain calm. I have to keep myself calm" then we will go home. You do your best you are doing a lot... keep on doing... don't lose your... don't show them your anger.

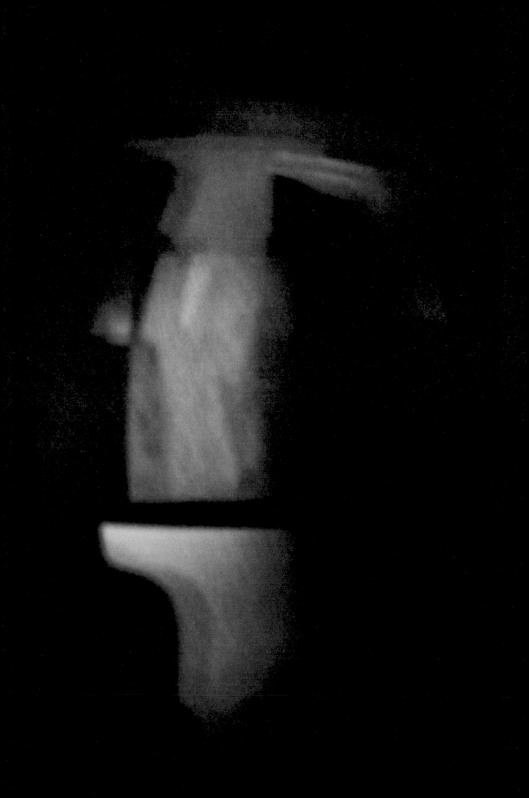

What do they want from me?

What they want is... they want to see you calm and not shouting. If you don't shout then it means you have recovered - they will let you out. They will have no reason to keep you if you are calm.

Why did they transfer me here in the first place? It would have been better if I went to an NHS hospital...

Because this place is a rehabilitation place between hospital and home. In this place you are not going to stay long...

They have no reason to keep me here, I've been here since the eighth of March...

The programme with the psychologist hasn't even started. Remember we had the meeting with the manager-

I don't trust the staff! I don't trust anyone here I-

Ok, without trust we are not going to go anywhere. If you don't trust you get stuck here forever.

A minimum sense of trust has to be there to solve the problem because we can't solve the problem by ourselves by being angry...

This place is not safe for me I've seen so many incidents happening... there's already one patient getting on my nerves and I don't want to fight... when I see these things it scares me, mum. If you were here to see what I do during the day when I'm awake... then you'll see how scared I feel when incidents happen here...

The same thing at the other ward happened. You were scared at some points, you hated it. It will always be the same everywhere you go. I didn't see anything here that shocked me more than you were. I have seen worse than that at the other ward. All the screams I used to hear on your ward without stopping...

Yeah they always scream and they fight when you guys are not here that's why I'm telling it to you!

Okay. Those things... try to be in your bedroom... and simply say... "every hospital where you go it will be like this". They are not going to construct a special hospital just for you. People are here because they are ill. They will make a lot of noise. I don't expect it to be like a church because it is a mental institution whether we like it or not, but considering that it's a mental institution I find it quieter than some we have seen. Since three o'clock we have been here in a quiet place - sometimes you don't even find a quiet place in some institutions. What time is it?

It's five to five.

Shall we go? Its dinner now. So tomorrow first thing at nine o'clock I will call the doctors to find out about the meeting... about the plan that they are making and I will see if one of the ladies can help me {cover at work}. If she can help me I will come to the meeting, ok?

'Untitled', LETITIA MOHABIR

-

I got a phone call in the early hours of the morning. It was my brother. He was talking in the phone. He was having a conversation. But he was not having a conversation with me. He was laughing. But he was not laughing with me. I did not hear anyone else speaking. Only him. I spoke one, two three, four words. "Brother, what is it?" He did not respond. But continued his conversation. Words, phrases, names, situations. Talking, laughing, pausing. Him and him alone. One, one and a half, two, two and a half hours passed. And then I knew. Something was not right. He phoned me. He phoned me in the middle of the night. He was talking, but not with me and yet he did not put the phone down. He was communicating something, but I did not understand. He was communicating. HELP?

My brother was diagnosed
with schizophrenia later that
year. He was 21 years old. He
was in his second year of university.

-

Young men get to a certain age where they begin to experiment with drugs. Little do they know that the abuse of certain types can seriously have an effect on how your brain operates. This was unfortunately the case with my younger brother. He started to get paranoid, felt unsafe and was hearing voices.

Without touching on subjects too personal, he was in a very dark place and needed some serious help. His friends did not understand or support him, doctors did not take him seriously.

It was hard to find information on how to refer someone but I researched and researched and found that therapy, or medication could help. When he refused both of these it rang alarm bells. He didn't think anything was 'wrong' with him, but in fact that the paranoid thoughts and voices in his mind were true. He did not want help because he thought he didn't need help. People say you can only help yourself, but how is it possible in this situation? If a loved one or family member has enough evidence that the person in question needs help, this should be enough.

He did not know he was ill. Unlike when I experienced severe anxiety and depression a few years back - I knew something wasn't quite right. When someone is seriously mentally ill, it can take a long time to realise and understand what they're going through. Similar to other illnesses for example Alcoholism. If a patient is asked if they are addicted to alcohol, the first stage is often denial. Denial is one of the main roadblocks that can keep the person from enrolling in treatment and moving forward with their life. Fortunately, there are ways around it. With mental illness it can be quite difficult and in my brother's case, this is something we're still struggling with, as it's not something that can be diagnosed with a blood test.

Things began to worsen and I didn't even recognise my own brother. He stopped taking care of himself, every day was a massive struggle for him. I felt pain for him, my chest ached with sympathy and my heart was breaking seeing him like that. He'd only open up to me when he felt like it, just in case it was true and I actually was against him - like his racing mind told him so. Later that year he was eventually diagnosed with psychosis. He was sectioned and released two weeks later not because the doctors told him he was on the road to recovery, but rather because the decision was put in his own hands. I was disappointed, unsatisfied and disgusted at the fact that this was the case, we were back to square one but now he was angry that he'd been hospitalised against his will. To him, it gave another reason to why everyone was 'against him'.

My brother is extremely clever. He knows exactly what to say to the doctors to make it sound like absolutely everything is fine in order to avoid being labelled as 'mad', or even worse in his eyes, sectioned again. In my experience, the most important thing is that young men like my brother are given options when they are taken to the doctor with mental health problems and educated on these options. For example, enrolling in therapy, self-help or medication. GP's may not particularly specialise in mental health, but I do feel in severe cases like my brother's, you should be referred to a specialist. You should be analysed not only by yourself, but with and by your family where possible. We had provided more information about his case than he did, of course because he didn't want to open up.

Luckily, two years later after finally agreeing to take medication and share his feelings and problems more to our family, his mental health has improved. This improvement has happened solely down to himself and us. He still struggles with a lot of things daily, and I do think that he could be helped a whole lot more.

It's been a very tough journey and I hope that he eventually gets the right help that he needs to live a happy life. I've seen many men struggle with mental health issues, bottle them up and turn to alcohol, my brother being one of them. I think this is often the case when someone doesn't get the help they need; they turn to substance to numb the pain. People in his situation deserve professional help to stop the things snowballing from problem to problem.

Having suffered from mental illness myself, I can empathise with the fact that it can be something you don't want to exactly shout about. At first I thought it was a really bad thing, that no one would take me seriously, that there was something 'wrong' with me and that people wouldn't look at me the same. People see mental illness as something to be ashamed of, a sign of weakness. I can totally see why men would not want to make themselves vulnerable in such a situation and could be afraid of being labelled 'weak'.

I found it difficult to open up to anyone about my feelings at first, because I was scared that I might be the only person going through it and it wasn't normal. I eventually reached out to a parent who then told me I should see a doctor. I ended up on medication and started cognitive behavioural therapy, which I researched myself and asked to be referred to - I wasn't given any other options by my doctor other than anti-depressants. I was on the waiting list for weeks, nonetheless it did help me in the end and I was lucky to receive this kind of help.

Relating back to my brother's story, I think that young men, especially at the age when they become more experimental with drugs, need to be educated on mental health problems related to what they are taking. I remember in primary school, charities and organisations would come in and teach pupils about fire safety, dental hygiene and such. I think it would be very beneficial to teach kids in secondary school about mental health and also the mental health issues that drugs can cause. They should also be given advice on what to do if they experience, or know someone experiencing mental health problems, by being taught the signs and symptoms i.e. change in behaviour, isolating themselves out of friendship groups. Every single one of my brother's friends at university completely cut all contact with him when he began to act differently - little did they know that he was suffering. If we are taught at a younger age how to deal with people who have mental health problems, or at least given more information on sources of support, this could benefit many lives.

To me, I think it's important that we also educate men at a young age about feminism. Feminism by definition, is the belief that men and women should have equal rights. This applies to the equal right that men should be able to express their feelings. We need gender equality ambassadors to teach kids that men should be able to ask for help when suffering with mental illness, that this does not make them less of a man if they do so. We don't often talk about men being labelled and gender stereotyped. Both men and women should feel free to be sensitive, vulnerable and 'in touch' with their emotions. They should not be labelled as 'weak' if they open up about their feelings / problems and it should not be a privilege that only women have access to. All genders should reap the benefits of equality, and we should be fighting for that equal right of expression for men too.

'*Cry Tear*', **JESSICA CANJE**

"I am slow to notice when someone mistreats me, it's always so surprising: evil is somehow unreal." I am slow to notice when someone mistreats me, it's always so surprising: evil is somehow unreal." "I am slow to notice when someone mistreats me, it's always so surprising: evil is somehow unreal." "I am slow to notice when someone mistreats me, it's always so surprising: evil is somehow unreal." Édouard Levé, Autoportrait- You were my first role model and taught me all things cool. I was happy to share the weight of the world on someones shoulders that I could call my blood. I watched you go through many different phases but you were never afraid to show emotion and your depth of love for others. I told amma you were smoking gravity bongs, I googled what that meant, basically a water bottle bong. I was scared you were getting into the bad crowd and terrible things. I bought you a Casey Veggies concert ticket for your birthday haha did you go? Thanks for looking out for me. one halloween I wore your blue Supreme sweater the same one Tyler had in the 'She' music video, i got cool points for that. Thanks for picking me up from lunch and co op because I had no one to eat with. I want mothers to raise their daughters and sons the same way, I want the same emotional expectations and obviously I know there's layers to this shit but why can't he cry too? CRY TEAR - JESS

"Today I speak up..... for those battling any type of mental illness: depression, anxiety, manic depression, multiple personality disorder, etc. You're not alone. Together, and most importantly within..... We shall keep fighting. Every day is a battle, but it's a battle for everyone in this world not knowing which day will be their last. Mental health is just as important as physical health. You cannot survive without one or the other, eventually one will eat up the other, leaving you stuck. Let's all be aware. Let's all understand one another, even ourselves. Let's all do our research... this is something that can't be ignored. So please, let's rise together and share love.... pay it forward, because you may have no idea, what you have done for the better. You could be saving someone's life...... My life." , FARUQ OLAMIJI SARUMI

-

My brother and I grew up side by side for 18 years until I went away to college. Our childhood was nowhere near sweet, but at times far from bitter. Together we set course to experience the same trauma, adventures, episodes, and events during those years. Surviving long Chicago winters whether alone or at our aunts' homes, we clung to each other for assistance and navigation through the system. As two years my junior, my little brother was considered spoiled in my eyes; many times I felt things were handed to him, whereas I fought for acceptance. One moment we were best friends, the next moment we were our worst enemies, but at the end of the day we had no choice but to look after one another, especially when our parents traveled away for some periods at a time.

As we got older their absence put us in situations many would consider beyond our years, and this unfortunately became our norm. By the time we were 8-10 years old, as black males in an oppressed urban community, we were gang affiliated and treacherous. Run-ins with the police, petty theft, playing basketball and cigarette smoking was how we defined our masculinity and identity. Bad ass kids is what we inspired to be, I even picked up the habit of smoking marijuana and stealing our favorite Pokémon card sets or music CDs from the corner store. Finally, our parents mustered up the courage and funds to implement some change in our lives and pulled us out of the inner city public education system of Chicago to join the Catholic school system.

Suddenly the dynamics of our acquaintances changed. We went from having Puerto Rican, Black, and Eastern European (Assyrian, Albanian, Bosnian) friends, to being one of two black kids in an all-white system (school). There was no room to talk about our sudden change or what it did to our identity, but as first-generation children of African immigrants in America, it altered our concept of community and masculinity. Street credit did nothing in the classroom of St. Gertrude, or St. Henry, privilege dominated this space, and we were strangers to it. My reluctance to this change was apparent, but my younger brother felt finally at peace. He felt the freedom of no longer relying on the crazy antics of previous friends to be accepted into the state of "manhood". He was in a space where his masculinity was not challenged or based on drug usage, theft, or dangerous behaviors. All my little brother wanted to do was dance, play basketball, and be happy... and he was finally given this opportunity when he met Jeremy.

At 12 years old, my 10-year-old brother and I experienced the death of a loved one for the first time. Our close cousin was the only one pronounced dead at the scene of a highway accident whilst on their way home from Disneyland, he was only six years old. Forced to "man-up" by our own father, the same person who we had never seen cry until hearing the news, we were not allowed to attend the funeral or have an open discussion about what had just occurred. After the event I became more secluded and fought solace with the nature of novels, music and writing. My little brother had Jeremy though, and they spent day and night consoling each other as true friends.

Jeremy came from a half black and half white family. Goofy, entertaining, and always in trouble or dancing, him and my little brother became partners in crime at St. Gertrude. They even had a small clique in their grade, and all their peers wanted to be close them. At the beginning of 7th grade for my brother and Jeremy, Jeremy's father was released from prison after a lengthy sentence. With Jeremy's emotions as mixed and complicated as his ancestry, he sought solace in my brother on all terms. Occasionally in the past I would tease the two about their relationship, but in all honesty, I was jealous and happy that my brother finally found a true friend. Despite them being brought up in a culture where it's hard for men to find validation in their feelings, my brother and Jeremy confirmed theirs without anyone else's consent. They spent long hours on the phone, but only after 9 o'clock when our cell phone minutes were free. Our home life was nowhere near steady or stable, and there was no air in the room to talk about it either.

It was the summer of 2007, I had just finished my first year of high school, and my little brother was on his way to his final year of grade school. Jeremy and him had plans set for their high school dreams of playing basketball and staying popular, as usual.

June came quickly, and school was finally out for the summer. Jeremy's family had planned a road trip the weekend of my brother's 13th birthday. It was their first family trip since their father's release, and they were taking the family's new silver dodge Durango to Colorado. As per usual, Jeremy and my little brother stayed in contact that whole week talking about plans for the birthday party upon his return to Chicago.

Jeremy never made it back to Chicago to celebrate my little brother's birthday with him. In fact, I don't even think we ever continued on with his birthday plans that weekend. The whole summer became a blur and a shift occurred in not only my brother but everyone who understood their relationship. On the 16th of June, 2007 on the way to Colorado, Jeremy's family car fell into a ditch. The accident killed Jeremy, his mother, and his younger sister. Only Jeremy's father and two other brothers survived the incident. Intoxication of the driver was the noted cause. Jeremy's father was the driver.

My brother's world has changed ever since. Since we didn't talk about our emotions or feelings to begin with in our household, the implication of consoling my little brother was impractical. None of us had the tools to deal with the trauma or pain he felt at the time. No one thought to seek therapy or professional attention. Losing your best friend at 13 years old was the norm from where we came from. Death, trauma, depression and systematic oppression was our recipe for a mental health disaster.

As high school rolled in for both of us, we went our separate but conjoined paths. Once my brother, always my brother. The only thing we shared in common was our constant demand of social and mental support from our peers. Our social circles expanded, and we were the brothers to know. By the time I was 17, and he was 15, we were throwing some of the craziest parties in high school. I was heavy in drug dealing, and my little brother was popular to the point that he had a senior in my grade as a girlfriend. My ways eventually led me to getting expelled from high school, but my brother took reign and became Prom King in his senior year.

Around 2015 our aloof attention to our mental health was catching up to us, mainly for my little brother. Our drug usage increased once we began university. Substance abuse became our coping mechanism within our social circles. At the same time, I got expelled from another school for my ways, and my little brother got diagnosed with depersonalization disorder that progressed to agoraphobia. It was hard to imagine that my little brother who I grew up side by side with was going through so much. I was going through a lot with my own life path, but we didn't know how to talk about mental health still even if we wanted to. With the help of friends, some still here and some gone, my little brother was able to seek continuous mental health care. Something that probably would have never occurred if he had looked towards our parents or I for help. Despite the lack of mental or emotional support we had growing up, we always had a knack of choosing the right friends. Friends that you could drink with and cry with, together. Friends that aren't too scared to ask if you're ok.

Two years after his diagnosis, my little brother and I finally started to feel like a real family. During a night where I felt suicidal and desolate, he came to my rescue. No one had the right tools like he did, and I was even so more shocked at how I undermined the importance of my mental health, and how it was my own brother who had aided me through it all. It was the same year he released his music project Vanilla Sky DSM to the world, talking about his journey with mental health, family, friends, and most importantly himself. His mixtape was a call to action that reminded me how sensitive life can be, and how important it is to help each other during the downs. I could riddle you with statistics on the importance of mental health but instead I leave you with a final message from my little brother, Fawaz:

"Today I speak up..... for those battling any type of mental illness: depression, anxiety, manic depression, multiple personality disorder, etc. You're not alone. Together, and most importantly within..... We shall keep fighting. Every day is a battle, but it's a battle for everyone in this world not knowing which day will be their last. Mental health is just as important as physical health. You cannot survive without one or the other, eventually one will eat up the other, leaving you stuck. Let's all be aware. Let's all understand one another, even ourselves. Let's all do our research... this is something that can't be ignored. So please, let's rise together and share love.... pay it forward, because you may have no idea, what you have done for the better. You could be saving someone's life...... My life."

'*Amor Maníaco (Vasco)*' , **IZZY CLIFFORD**

-

Slowly
gradually,
bit by bit

The places we laughed in
together
are becoming

Places
I have cried in
alone

Your losing
yourself
has left me
lost

And alone

-

In times of need, you were there.
To offer support, you were there.
To offer affirmation, guidance, and patience, you were there.
A quiet companion.
An unerring silence.
A get out, an alibi,
A foil, a shield.
You were there.
Comfort, respite,
A moment's solace.
You were there.

I have been aware of the presence of my own personal depression for at least fifteen years. It comes in waves and cycles, sometimes I wouldn't even know it was there but eventually it would rear its head. Simultaneously, I would sometimes welcome its presence in my life. It offers an escape from social anxieties, validating 'negative' personality traits and behaviours, and gives me the perfect excuse not to confront potentially difficult situations.

The presence of this depression has held me captive at times, prevented me from pushing myself towards reaching my potential. It can stop me from being able to make the simplest of decisions, spurning opportunities for self-growth due to an inability to act. I find myself in a state of flux, governed by the fear of making the wrong decision instead of seeing what one can reap from a situation, or the wisdom that can be taken from any failures that may come of it. The cyclic nature of this merely deepens those depressive thoughts.

Having grown up in an environment where an accepted but untreated form of depression and anxiety seems to have had a constant presence meant that I went on to develop a set of unhealthy coping mechanisms. When thinking and discussing my early experiences with my depression, it evokes a feeling of boding silence, a serene place to where I could retreat. Over time, this place would become increasingly fortified, a place where I would go and initiate my own internal conversations and try to put those anxieties at ease. Only once the dust had settled would I re-emerge, my deflecting merely adding to the emotional weight that I would then bear, rather than confronting my issues directly.

It is now that I have arrived at a point where I can no longer cope in this manner. The inability to confront my depression and the anxieties that it brings with it has caused my life to take a meandering path. I have lost the most important relationship in my life due to this. This loss has put into focus the toll such a long interaction with my depression has taken on my life. This loss will teach me more than I know. It has given me a new lens, of which I am the subject; and caused me to reconsider the tools at my disposal to prevent myself arriving at a similar point in the future.

I am no longer allowing my depression to define me. Merely outwardly speaking of it has lifted the bulk of its weight from my shoulders. Simply being open to my feelings, remaining in the light, rather than ducking into the shadows has enabled me to function more freely, even in some of the darker moments that I may encounter. Though I am just starting out on this section of my journey, it has allowed me to connect and reconnect with others that I may have clouded out. I have realised that I am lucky enough to have a support network out there for me, I simply had to interact with it in the right manner. It has also given others the strength to reach out to me and enquire about possible routes that they may take to confront some of their own issues.

One of the places that I have always been able to turn to in this journey is creativity, through my own work or that of others; there is something that everyone can take through this form of reflection. Through this, I conceived the idea for *Compos Mentis*, a venture showcasing the works of photographers that I admire, to raise money for MQ Mental Health, a charity that specialises in mental health research.

Compos Mentis

Mental health issues affect one in four us each year. These mental health issues take many shapes and forms, often heightened by many socioeconomic factors. Of those affected by any of these mental health issues, 75% of those individuals will receive no treatment.

Current statistics suggest that mental health research only receives 5.8% of total annual health research spending. A vastly disproportionate amount given the widespread effects that mental health issues can have on the population. Overstretched services are focused on coping with crisis, rather than prevention and operate with long waiting times and a complete lack of specialised services in some regions of the UK.

Continued cuts to public spending and the increasing levels of poverty feed into the cyclic nature of the many causes of mental health issues. The most common mental health problems include depression and anxiety, both which are distributed according to a gradient of economic disadvantage across society.

Compos Mentis has worked alongside Carhartt WIP and a series of photographers that have donated their images to be used on t- shirts, to raise money for MQ Mental Health, a charity that provides funding for worthy projects and collates the findings of independent research to paint a more detailed landscape of how we deal with mental health issues.

With a greater understanding of mental health, we can be better equipped to help treat it.

'Him : Then & Now' , ANONYMOUS

-

My mum has always said that you don't truly understand what happiness is until it's taken away. Now I believe her.

It's hard to remember a time before now; a time before the worry, the stress and the not understanding. The eleven years that went before us seem so simple now, naïve almost, as we didn't know what was coming.

Like a noiseless change in seasons you gently moved from light to dark. The things that mattered, no longer do. The people you cared for, don't have the same worth.

To try and make sense of it all, my brain has divided you into two people. A heartbreaking vison of you then and now. I remember that person so clearly though, the text messages still remain, so unthinking and easy.

But we must keep going. We will only really be defeated when we stop trying; when we lose hope. I know you're in there somewhere.

-

These are photographs of a man.

This man showed me his strength, and his vulnerability. He helped me to learn respect and compassion for men, after years of fearing and resenting them. I learnt that we all suffer under the restrictions that this society places on us, and it's up to all of us to support each other in breaking free from them.

A SMALL COLLECTION OF THINGS I CAN'T SAY WITH WORDS

LAYOUT	AJ HORTON & JOSIANE MH POZI
CONCEPT	JOSIANE MH POZI & AJ HORTON
STYLING	AJ HORTON & JOSIANE MH POZI
PHOTOG	JOSIANE MH POZI & AJ HORTON
CASTING	AJ HORTON & JOSIANE MH POZI
MUA	JOSIANE MH POZI & AJ HORTON
HAIR	AJ HORTON & JOSIANE MH POZI
PRODUCTION	JOSIANE MH POZI & AJ HORTON
CATERING	AJ HORTON & JOSIANE MH POZI
MORALE	JOSIANE MH POZI & AJ HORTON
PHOTO ASSISTANT	AJ HORTON & JOSIANE MH POZI
DRIVING	JOSIANE MH POZI & AJ HORTON
ART DIRECTION	AJ HORTON & JOSIANE MH POZI
LOCATION	JOSIANE MH POZI & AJ HORTON
SCRIPT	AJ HORTON & JOSIANE MH POZI
ON-SET MASSEUSE	JOSIANE MH POZI & AJ HORTON
MANICURE	AJ HORTON & JOSIANE MH POZI

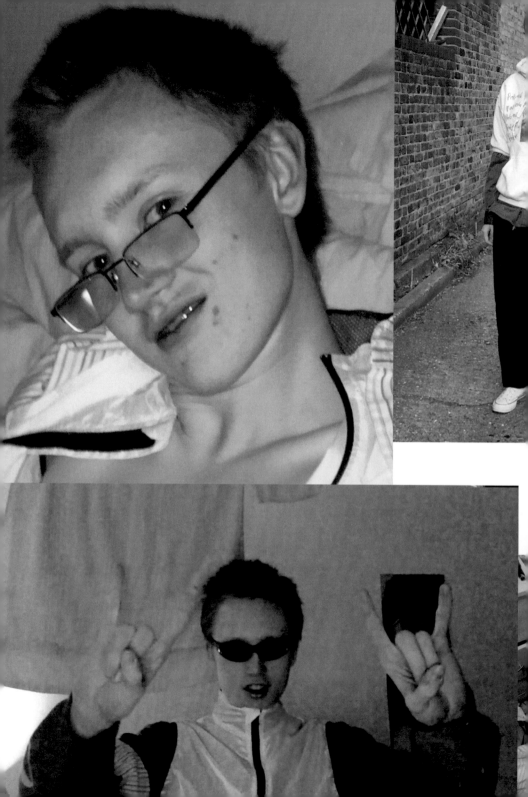

'A Small Collection of Things I Can't Say With Words' ,
ARRAN HORTON

-

Conversation - Arran with Josi, December 2016

I'm not saying anything I don't mean
It's not like I'm just saying shit for the sake of it
fuck I don't really know what I mean
I'm just getting kinda depressed over the holidays
I'm trying to tell you when something is on my mind
I think what I've learnt from counselling is I need to share things with people
I never ever share my worries or issues with anyone
I keep them in my head
I'm sorry if it's a bit too much though
you can tell me to stop
in my experience though talking about it always makes it infinitely worse and
blows it way out of proportion
well we can talk about it if you want but just know that it almost gets ugly
when I talk about this shit
this is why I say I always fuck things up
I never seem to be able to rationally talk about it
I work myself into a state

We all have moments in our lives that help to define us. Personal milestones, significant dates and experiences that burn themselves into our memories, so we carry them with us.

For me, one of those moments came on November the 8th 2017. Having been stuck in a deep depression for several months leading up to this date, I finally decided that it was going to be the day I ended my life.

Being 40 and having suffered from depression since my early teens, suicide was a concept that I had become intimately familiar with over the years. But as bad as things had been previously, it had always been a somewhat abstract concept. Something I'd thought about often but never believed I'd act on.

Nov 8th was different though. I found myself in a state of such overwhelming despair and utter hopelessness that I would literally do anything to end my pain.

I'll always remember lying in bed with my laptop researching how to kill myself. Trying to find the most painless way possible. It was a task that ultimately didn't take very long.

A simple Google search revealed pages and pages of websites devoted to the art of suicide.

At the time I was morbidly fascinated by the wealth of information that you could find online. From chatrooms to forums discussing methods, right down to how you could compose your own suicide note. Not only was there no end of people telling you how to do it but they were also actively encouraging people to do so.

At the time I couldn't comprehend just how appalling this was. All I cared about was dealing with my own suffering. These online ghouls placed absolutely no value on human life and that only served to reinforce how worthless I was feeling.

An hour was all it took to plan my own death. Meticulously down to the last detail, from where I was going to do it, how I was going to do it, and when.

I was just about to order everything I'd need to put my plan into action, but something stopped me. It took me a while to realise what, but it was fear.

Plain and simple. I was terrified to die.

I didn't know what to do, I was in so much emotional pain that I didn't want to go on living, but at the same time I was too afraid to die.

And in that moment I did the only thing I could do; I sent my wife a message telling her I was scared that I was about to do something insane.

And she did the only thing she could do; she came straight home and saved my life.

The next 48 hours were a blur for me. I was rushed in to see my psychiatrist who immediately recommended that I be admitted to a hospital for my own safety.

Initially I was very reluctant to take that step. At the mere mention of a psychiatric hospital, I instantly began conjuring up memories of One Flew Over The Cuckoo's Nest. A bunch of broken people in white pyjamas shuffling aimlessly around a broken down hospital ward; a Nurse Ratched in a starched white uniform looking on disapprovingly from the corner, and, if you don't behave yourself, off you go to have gruesome electro shock therapy to turn you into a mindless vegetable.

I can honestly say it was one of the hardest decisions of my life, but one look at my wife with tears streaming down her face was enough to convince me. Even if I didn't have enough will to live for myself, she had more than enough for the both of us.

It's a choice that probably saved my life.

Lots of people have asked me what it was like to be an inpatient. I think there are a lot of misconceptions out there. Some of my friends jokingly assumed that they had straightjackets and padded rooms. And I think a lot of people (I used to include myself), are afraid to ask exactly what it's like in a mental health facility.

For me, the overall experience really challenged my perceptions and fears of what a psychiatric hospital is actually like. Admittedly I was admitted to a private facility which was better funded and resourced than a humble NHS psych ward.

I was expecting an overcrowded, sterile and cheerless environment.

Instead it was more like a Travel Lodge with nursing staff. It was safe and non-threatening, exactly what I needed at the time.

After settling in, I was given a timetable of classes and therapy that I could attend. It was all voluntary but the staff did a great job of gently encouraging your participation.

Having that structure and support in place was vital. Rather than spending all my time alone and brooding, I was interacting with therapists and other patients. The daily classes provided much needed education and support. I found the lessons on the various therapies, Cognitive behavioural therapy (CBT) and Dialectical behaviour therapy (DBT), fascinating. We also learned about the importance of simple things like sleep and nutrition and how they can affect your mood.

I had previously found dealing with my own depression to be a very isolating experience. I pushed people away and tried to deal with it on my own. My reasoning being that I was protecting people from my negativity. I also assumed that no one could possibly understand what it felt like to be me.

But after my first group therapy session all of those misconceptions were blown away.

I found that opening up and sharing how I felt with others was incredibly therapeutic. The sessions gave me a safe, non-judgemental space to explore my issues and gave me the opportunity to expand my perspective and increase my empathy by listening to other people's stories.

I discovered I wasn't as unique as I thought I was. The other patients had remarkably similar stories and lived under incredibly similar circumstances as me.

The understanding and support I received, and gave, during those sessions amazed me.

As reluctant as I was to be admitted, I can look back now and see just how important it was for my recovery.

The hospital provided me with a safe and secure space. It also gave me much needed structure and routine. I also received a really good education in the fundamentals of mental health and how to focus that towards understanding and dealing with my own problems.

It also taught be what I consider to be a vital lesson. You should never be afraid to ask for help. Suffering alone can only ever lead to more suffering. Whether it's seeking professional help, going to see your GP or even just talking to your friends and family. It can make such a big difference.

Overall my time as a psychiatric patient was life changing. And definitely not scary. No dingy cells. No creepy, seemingly endless, dark corridors. No nutty professors. And not a single straightjacket in sight!

In the two months since I was discharged I've made amazing progress even if sometimes I can't see it. Depression can really affect your perceptions in a negative way. I still have bad days, and to me these bad days make it hard for me to remember all the good days that came before. But I'm so much better at recognising that now, and in recognising it I can try and deal with it. I'm having continual weekly therapy and I still see my psychiatrist regularly. I think these are both essential tools in coping with my depression and going forward. In no way do I think I'm 'cured'. I still suffer from depression and I most likely always will, but now I have the tools and the knowledge to lessen its impact on my life.

I also started blogging about my journey. Not only has writing about my experiences been incredibly therapeutic I've also received amazing feedback from people. The fact that something I was writing for myself has actually helped others is incredibly rewarding.

And through it all, my amazing wife has been the lifeline I so desperately needed in the darkest days. One of my strongest fears is that my illness might destroy our marriage but I believe that going to hell and back has only made us stronger. She continues to inspire me to embrace the life I know I deserve.

And that brings me to another significant moment in my life.

The 27th February 2018.

I've always wanted to be a comedian but the fear of failure and ridicule had always stopped me. So, after being through a breakdown and still suffering from pretty serious depression and anxiety issues I decided I wanted to prove to myself that maybe I could make people laugh after all. I signed myself up for a stand up slot at an open mic night and performed in front of 50 people. And it turns out, I could. I even came second out of 20 other comedians.

It's given me so much hope for the future. And the fact that I can actually imagine a future at all is proof that the darkness doesn't have to win. Life is a fight worth winning.

'*Self Portraits 1 & 2*', **JOSHUA OSBORN**

Time restricted drawings reconnecting the sitter with the present moment.

-

You are holding a cigarette packet that says in large writing "Smoking kills" with the image of a dead baby below it: you have been warned of the consequences; do you take the risk? Every risk - large or small - has its consequences, but at what point might we decide that the consequence outweighs the risk?

Risk and consequence are prevalent themes all around us, two main ones being law and religion, you know the consequence so are you willing to take the risk? And in these cases what is the moral decision to make?

Risk vs. Consequence was inspired by Hieronymus Bosch's *Garden of Earthly Delights*, a triptych that essentially represents the human choices faced in life in the middle panel, with the rewards for the good choices made on the left, and the punishment for bad choices on the right. My interpretation was the choices that a gay man makes in the middle of my image, with, like Hieronymus Bosch's, the rewards on the left and punishments on the right, using mainly renaissance symbolism, but also more contemporary references to create the still life.

That summer I had read *The Velvet Rage*, by Alan Downs, and *Straight Jacket*, by Mathew Todd. The former inspired the latter, and they are both books that address the issues that lie in the gay community (particularly male). They address depression, suicide, and the advance of mental health issues that are enforced by living in a heteronormative society as a gay man. One area they both address in detail is the use of drugs in the gay male community as escapism, which is something that I have not only experienced expansively, but also interests me hugely in my work.

The use or abuse of drugs in the gay community - what are the roots and the impact? What is the Risk and the Consequence?

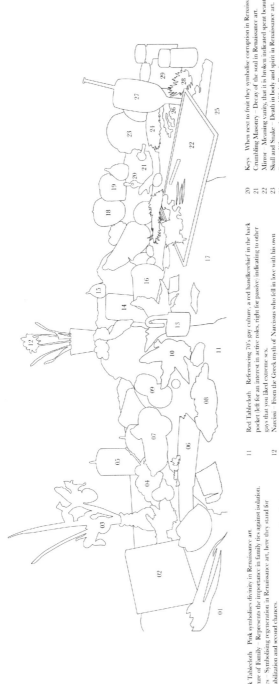

01 Pink Tablecloth – Pink symbolises divinity in Renaissance art.

02 Picture of Family – Represents the importance in family ties against isolation.

03 Irises – Symbolising regeneration in Renaissance art, here they stand for rehabilitation and second chances.

04 Grapes – Throughout the still life grapes are used to represent lust whether good or bad.

05 Lit Candle – Used here to symbolise life.

06 Open Book – The willingness and interest to learn more.

07 Aubergine – Taken from emoji language to mean a penis, placed next to no. 09 as a reference to gay sex.

08 Florentine Biscuits – In Renaissance Europe florentine was a slang word for gays, due to the high number of 'sodomites' in Florence at the time.

09 Peaches – Taken from emoji language to mean bottom see no. 07.

10 Lilies – Symbolising purity and virginity in Renaissance art, placed next to no. 13 as a reference to innocence when entering the gay scene.

11 Red Tablecloth – Referencing 70's gay culture, a red handkerchief in the back pocket left for an interest in active roles, right for passive; indicating to other gays that you liked extreme sex.

12 Narcissi – From the Greek myth of Narcissus who fell in love with his own reflection, used here to represent vanity.

13 Lock – Standing for free will in Renaissance art (see no. 10).

14 Grindr – Gay dating app, here it represents the eternal judgement of ones peers through social media.

15 Fig – Meaning a fall from grace in Renaissance art.

16 'Holy Water' – Represents GBL, a chemical drug commonly used by gays with corrosive properties, sometimes comically referred to as holy water.

17 Blue Tablecloth – Refer to no. 11, here the colour indicates an interest in normal sex.

18 Apple – Biblically meaning the fall of man, here it represents sin.

19 Spent Candle – Death and decay of the soul.

20 Keys – When next to fruit they symbolise corruption in Renaissance art.

21 Crumbling Masonry – Decay of the soul in Renaissance art.

22 Mirror – Meaning vanity, that it is broken indicated spent beauty.

23 Skull and Snake – Death in body and spirit in Renaissance art.

24 Strewn Wheat – A wasted life in Renaissance art.

25 Brown Tablecloth – Earthy hues represent the mind in renaissance art, the darker the hue the more irreversible the corruption.

26 Lavender – In Medieval times prostitutes signified their trade by wearing lavender, here it represents escorting prostitution for drugs.

27 Wineglass with Pipette – When alcohol is spiked with GBL (see no. 16), it can be used for subduing a potential sex victim, here it represents rape.

28 White Feather – Zeus, the Greek God, was said to turn himself into a swan and rape the maiden Leda. Here the feather stands for rape.

29 PEP – Medication taken when the patient has had exposure to HIV, here it reflects bad decisions made when not using a condom.

-

I really wanted to actually sit down and properly add something that I feel properly reflects myself, of some of the things I have been going through the last couple of years.

I have struggled with a porn addiction (which is now leaning towards a sex addiction) problem since the age of 11. Although the last year has seen me take measures to 'break free'. For me, breaking free starts with understanding why I developed the porn addiction in the first place. That was very tough, maybe the hardest part. Nevertheless, I feel like I've made peace with my past and I am trying to focus on my present. It hasn't been easy, but I never expected it to be. I know I still have a long way to go.

I PEP and GBL - I have started to take anti-HIV medicine because of previous experiences, it expresses how I feel now about my decisions (which to a certain extent I couldn't control).

II In Principle: Rules to live by - (I paraphrased a few), principles I try to live by, each bringing me a greater sense of peace and appreciation of life.

If it is possible, I would prefer for the submissions to be anonymous. Please let me know if this is a problem? I wrote as honestly as possible, I didn't pay much attention to usual things like grammar etc. just because when I was expressing the thoughts, the result that you see is the product of that expression. I just want people to be open with discussing the things they go through, both the good and the bad, there is no need to sugar-coat it or package it up so that it can be more digestible/approachable. I want everything to be raw and honest. Essex Hemphill was definitely a big inspiration.

I see my skin move closer to me, I wonder why. – I understand.

A knife twists slashes through my gut

graffiti cleared from its walls, semen glistens at the first exit,

a coated tablet protects my future, | You indestructible dream,

by destroying me now. | I don't blame me,

| not anymore.

I can't hear you

anymore

In Principle: Rules to live by

Dream Big

Chew the meat - spit out the bones!

Go at your own pace

To be okay with being the only one, the one who dies, and leaves no ambitious celebrity level legacy behind - to enjoy embrace and face learning - life as it is, for the short time that I am here, in the small scale of my nature.
I am and this is enough!

I am my own muse, the subject I know best, the subject I want to better

Reflect to avoid becoming overwhelmed

Patience

An unshakeable and unbreakable belief in self

Everything is impermanent

Tomorrow is not guaranteed only the present

You have to do something different to expect something different

Fantasy is what people want but reality is what people need

Everyone is trying to figure it out.

→ *No one has the answers.*

'Parker Posey' , 2017 , Rafaela de Ascanio

-

Mental health is an important aspect of my work as I focus on images that show strength and rebirth, overcoming challenges, often within the mind. Whilst generally concentrating on women, I have depicted males in images playing with masculinity/femininity, confronting imposed societal pressures. I painted these portraits of Samuel Douek and Fiontan Moran performing at a Queer CAMPerVan event (a transportable queer performance, and LGBTQ community event space built by Douek), during their Grindr tour. Part of a Triptych, these portraits play on traditional renaissance portraiture, with the 'coat of arms' in the background and their 'family mottos': Douek van DER Camp of the Travelling Kingdom, and Parker Posey of the Madonna Cult.

'Douke Van der Camp', 2017 , RAFAELA DE ASCANIO

-

Coming unglued. just as animals amputate a limb and leave it in the trap in order to survive, in order to get out, in order to continue breathing and continue. pulling the limb away, and having to disregard the feeling that it is needed, that it was ever needed or ever part of you, it wasn't useful, you must tell yourself this, otherwise you will not work, it will not continue -this life- unless the limb is unstitched and unglued from the body. the limb is the straitjacket, that garment that you kept around you for years in order to feel as though you were being protected from the gale that is constantly hewing crevasses into the landscape around you, and into you. you've grown up with this defence, this thick, harsh, scratchy jacket that has altered your body shape, and made it appear from the outside as something that it is not. it has malformed the body, it has mistreated it, has bound it. for the sake of others only. not for your existence has this hard piece of binding cloth been wrapped around you, warped around you, warping you.

the cloth has insidiously been knitting itself into your innards, through the skin and into the bloodstream and the brain, and the thoughts. the stitches and weave caressing and lulling and clutching -now grip- around those thoughts, moving through the body into every tiny bone and crevice.

your landscape has been utterly altered by this material, you do not believe it has though. it is difficult to believe that with every move you have been laced into this straitjacket, made to believe that without it that you cannot exist. and that it even exists! it cannot! years of presenting as straight in a homophobic society inevitably results in this claustrophobia and internalised self-hate, holding you like a straitjacket; a straight jacket if you will.

trying to unstick, unstitch the straight jacket? like gutting an animal and leaving its innards behind, trailing along, leaving a stink behind wherever it goes. is that too far? trailing the scraps of fabric behind, the small stitches that once held it all together. is that more digestible? either way, it has fallen apart, and with it you have too. and now you must try and move through this world without the crutch of the deforming but comforting fabric. it can seem carnivalesque, this movement that you take through the world, darting eyes away, crouched over, hidden like the injured animal, then high and long and noble, taking in those stares and the calls of faggot or looks of disgust. or those that find you so repulsive without your jacket that they need to touch that tender skin, that freshly untouched and unglued wound.

stick the fingers deeper in, a seemingly inconsequential and harmless gesture, a movement away or towards. a poke or a thud, a push, a nudge, a hit, a throw.

like a finger exploring the wound in the rib.

moving around and looking for the spot that is wrong that has to be cut out, that has to see the light of day, that has to be exposed to all those around. the shame has to come out. that feeling of hate that they have has to be manifest in their exposure of you. it makes them taller and nobler and more of who they are if you are exposed further. because once that jacket is off, the exposure is like UV rays without the ozone. it is anticipated and expected, but you long for the exposure not to occur. either to still feel as though the insidious cloth remains, in the form of a ruse, a changeling jacket, or that you can move around shielded from their gaze somehow, away from their eyes and the rip and tear of who you are. but you are exposed to the harsh rays of the world around you that despite that small circle that you have placed yourself in where you feel safe, is not safe, it's not safe out there. there's no SPF that will cover up gay. there is no shade in this world unless from the protection of a straight jacket. and yours isn't yours, it's not real; a fake.

it had to be taken away, ripped away, like ripping a toy from the grasp of a child, or the mouth of an infant from the mother's breast.

your protection has vanished. and you should feel free, but it's somehow worse, being out here without that claustrophobic material. you have been gagged by this thick cloth, it was stuffed deep down into your gullet, but it was somehow better that way? was it better that way? the material was like a dummy. it was the fake nipple, it wasn't real, and it wasn't what you truly wanted or needed, but it provided a distraction, from the reality, and now all you are left with is your own naked form, you don't even have the mothers breast to comfort you now with the dummy removed. both have been removed. you are alone. and now you will feel exposed for ever, and you will have to fight forever, and there feels like there are traps and landmines scattered in your path as soon as you open your front door and step onto the street. moving into the world and from the safety of your home can be the bravest thing that you do. but you have to do it everyday, and everyday there is a possibility -maybe even a certainty- that you will get stuck in one of those traps. and like the animal in the wilderness whose habitat is decimated by the humans that are moving in on it, you too will have to rip that limb off.

everyday a piece may be taken from you by the outside world. and without that straight jacket there is very little healing that can be achieved anymore. it is an exposed wound that only you can begin to repair, because no one else will want to go near it. but the scar will remain, it always will. everyday you will come unglued, your body will come unglued, not the jacket anymore that sheltered you -your body itself will come unglued. and it will be painful. it can be excruciating, moving in this world with your queer body exposed. but there is a relief in being unpinned from that jacket. unstick, unstitch.

When I was growing up I often felt trapped in the house. Didn't have much friends, was unsure of myself, had high anxiety, I didn't like the body I was in. My mom was very protective of us, but it was smothering and unhealthy for me. A lot of times getting up to go to school or any function was heavy. I wanted to be out the house, but I also felt lifeless and disconnected from my body. Going out into the world was in many ways foreign to me.

These movements represent the 'will to be'.

Photographer: Marija Marc

'My Forsaken Bed' , SHAQUILLE-AARON KEITH

-

Forsaken health, forsaken, hope forsaken me, forsaken bed

This cage that I'm stuck in
This maze that I'm lost in,
Honestly,
The circles I make
Going round and round
Make me feel disgusting...
It's my mind!
 that's the thing
 I'm discussing...
My thoughts move like the workers of New York City;
Hustling and bustling.
The dark thoughts make their presence known,
In the bushes of my garden,
Constantly rustling.
I seek help
But no one offers me any,
I know my answers don't lie
At the bottom of this 6th glass
Of Coke and Henny...
What more can be said, I'm broken, I'm torn...
Resembling my stained t-shirt
I'm constantly outworn.
My weary heart and damaged mind allow me to be misled.
This is a plea for help,
Not just something pretty I said...
Text Messages sent out
Text Messages remain unread...
I wait patiently for my hero to save me
From the comfort of my tear stained pillows
And my sheets that are now red

I wish to be free
But my hunger for hope remains unfed.
I am Reluctant to draw back the curtains
Because One thing I know is for certain...
  I am chained to this forsaken bed...

'*My men: here and there*', **ABDOURAHMAN NJIE**

-

My men : London, Senegal, Gambia - 2017/ 2018

I just felt myself start to derail, I saw myself opening up to too many people,
Since I've had my place... It's good to have a base, and just sit down and
breathe.
Stabilize yourself - Have a place of comfort. For yourself only.

These are my men: here and there.

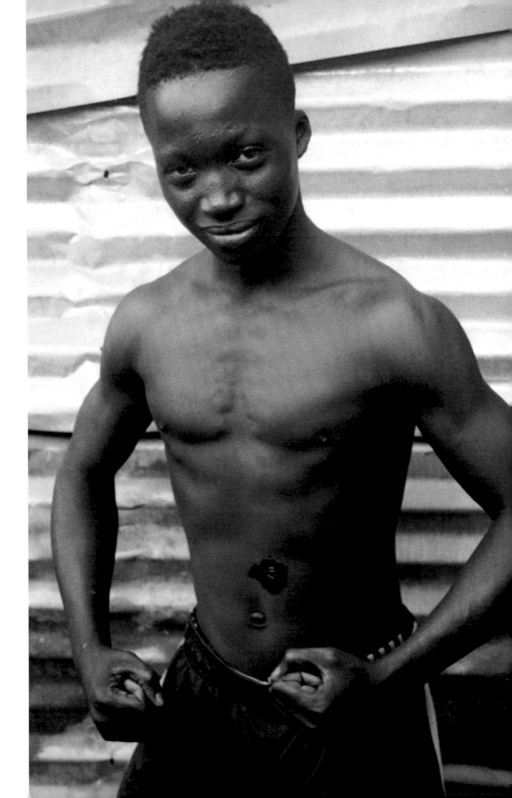

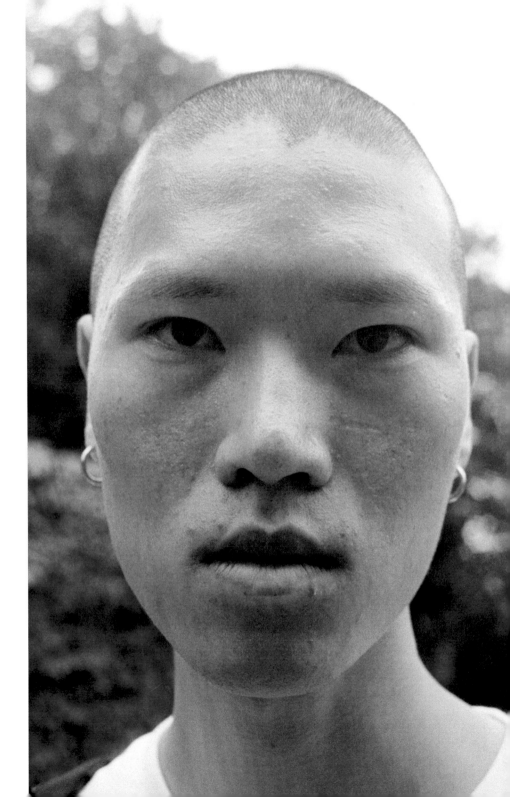

'Untitled', **PERWANA NAZIF**

-

I

"I don't want to see it," she said without looking me in the eye. "But why?" I persisted wondering why she wouldn't want to, I loved trips to 717, admiring the pink green home on Anita Street and happily remembering my mid-day routine of picking up marshmullow rocks in the backyard, fingers sensitive to the sun's generous gaze upon them. Years later, I would receive a text message from my mother with a photo of an apparition of a house with nothing but dirt around it. "This is Kabul now." it said.

II

AFGANISTAN uff GHHHH ani stahn af gah neestan

has been long gone, as Farida remarked on the phone last week. Like letters to forgotten lovers, stories about her bring up false hope and a deluded sense of dreaminess. Deluuusional, I think she says, rolling her eyes and rolling her tongue as she whacks the onions on the cutting board. Southern trees bear strange fruit Blood on the leaves and blood at the root croons Billie Holiday. How strange to think that Southern trees can also grow on Afghan (-American) soil!

III

I'm in a car with the windows down as it rushes past windmills. I pull around my sweater, attempting to cover the recently emerged goosebumps. It's cold work, I think to myself, cleansing stale air of pretzels, semi-eaten granola bars, and rest area soap-scented hands. You shudder too, but it's the sight of the massive, looming windmills that frighten and excite you. I'd like to stay in this car forever protecting you only letting the outside in when we need fresh air. At night, I watch the moon, with it the reflection of my gaze upon my brother superimposed.

IV

Fourismyluckynumber! 4ismyluckynumber! 4IsMyLuckyNumber! Does luck change when used as a password? Peeling off clothes only to remember that the curtains have yet to be drawn and there's never been an ashtray in the room wrapping my bare body in mauve drapes and flicking off the cigarette ends and ends out the window.

V

There are instances where I can't and one day will come to peace with failing to understand you. As your, I admit, porous, shield, I relay this feeling with eloquent hand gestures and decorative words at so many other times and so many other places to so many others, to strangers. At traffic stops you change the song as routine as the elderly lady listens to the watermelon against the beat of the palm of her hand at the supermarket, with respect and unquestionable authority.

Always, however, you look to me for a nod.

Afterthought

When I wrote this piece, I was thinking of home. Home, it seemed, and seems, will always be inextricably linked to my little brother, who has autism. Perhaps the guilt of leaving home, leaving him. I've always wondered what home really means, what home could mean to him. Him who needs home to be stable and unchanged, stability the only thing that can bring peace and conventional sanity. Could home be what brings him happiness, strings of wind turbines, his "windmills", whizzing away as he watches out of the window of a fast car, or could home be where our family is from, an unknown land to both you and, now, them. What is home if not stability and understanding? Can I understand you by knowing what home is to you? Can I attempt to access you? Access and understanding, I find, are not synonymous and do not go hand-in-hand. Many things have changed with you, with how you deal with frustrations and how you communicate. For the worse, I think, but temporarily, I hope.

Maybe home for me is you. I admit I can't write from your perspective when I can't fully say I know it. All I know is myself and all I can hope for is for you to know I want to understand you. And be there. - Perwana

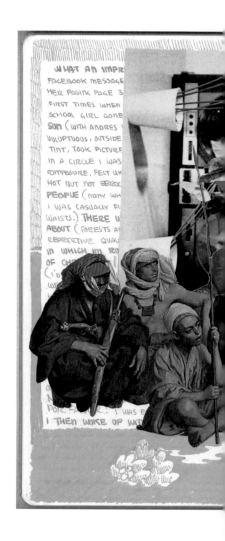

-

Alpha Tools looks at the effect of policing behaviours in order to fit in with restrictive ideas of masculinity. Playing with the fine line between hyper-masculinity ('acceptable') and homoeroticism ('unacceptable'), the pace of the film itself highlights the exhaustive effect this has on men's mental health.

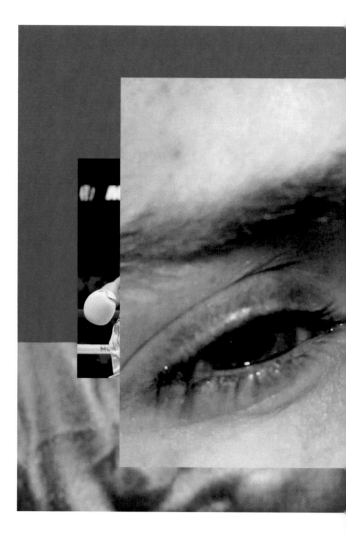

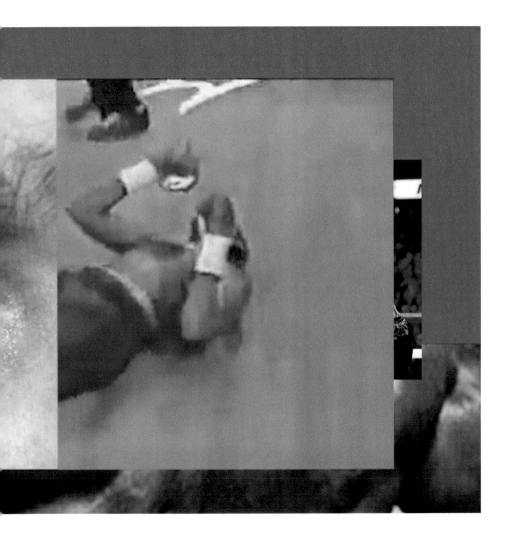

'Ask Don't Assume', FARUQ OLAMIJI SARUMI, MPH (C)
HEALTH PROMOTION SPECIALIST, ADOLESCENT TRIALS NETWORK
DEPARTMENT OF PEDIATRICS/ADOLESCENT MEDICINE

-

Please lets not make assumptions or be presumptuous about the next person

Born in Chicago in 1992, Nigerian-American, Taurus, its my multiple intersections of my personality that define Rooq as Rooq

If you ask about Rooqs on 79th and Ashland
I am that nigga with a bag, hustling with the kutthoarts from the land
10, 20, 30k, bitch I was the mans without any plans
Riding in a rental, five niggas deep with half a brick of crack cocaine and half a key of Mary

You see, I see

Im letting you see who I be, pose a question I will answer back in details and maybe with a receipt or a recipe

Receipts of that Chanel purse and Gucci watch I bought Queen Elizabeth from my first key

THEREFORE

Mind the gap as I position my mouth on this pussy as I have done for the previous seventy something odd women
"
"
PO
Mind the stare when I look into your eyes, as I ask about your intentions, your goals, ambitions, or sexual fetishes

Mind the blackness when I ask about social issues, such as urban development, human rights, poverty, systematic oppressions of marginalized populations, gender equality or public health

BUT
//

If you ask Chicago Police who I is, I am inmate number: 16837516

CAUSE

Six times I was arrested between 2015-2017
One time a day after my bday I fucked Nina the sex worker off of coke and patron without a jimmy
Five times I have contemplated suicide
Seven times I ever done anal
Three times my cousin and I plans a home robbery
Eight times I have loaded that pistol with intent to kill
Six times I cried about my father's ten year prison bid

And only one time did I ask myself what did I assume about life

I assume I was heteronormative
I assume I wouldn't live past 25
I assume I would work for the mans
I assume that I can trust a phat ass with some good head
I assume the white man's education would define me
I assume that others struggles wasn't my struggle
I assume that they defined my happiness
I assume you would judge me,

SO FROM HEREON,

I will ask life Herself, not presume. So when you see me ask about me

Faruq, Rooqie, Rooq, or Ruku DeNiro

Still Fuck 12

'Men Act, Women Appear', **CELIA DELANEY**

-

This project was a personal response to an internal frustration of watching the people closest to me struggle with their masculinity and mental health. It was an attempt to express what I couldn't put into words, to talk through photographs.

Men Act, Women Appear aims to present and celebrate the importance of acceptance, and as Grayson Perry described men's rights, "The right to be vulnerable, the right to be weak, the right to be wrong, the right to be intuitive, the right not to know, the right to be uncertain, the right to be flexible, the right to not be ashamed of any of these."

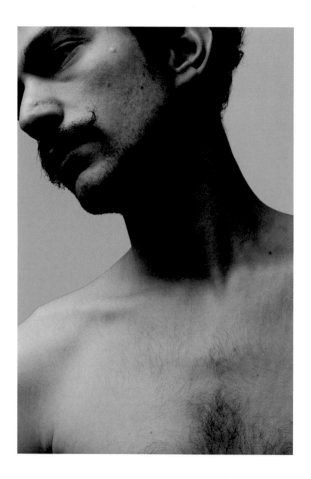

The images in the series are based on historical Greek feminine sculpture. Throughout history, artists depicted women in similar poses, using subtle body language to communicate the desired traits in a female - vulnerability, fragility and empathy.

By repurposing these poses with male subjects, the project aims to question how our understanding of gender roles have changed over time, and presents a new, proudly vulnerable version of masculinity.

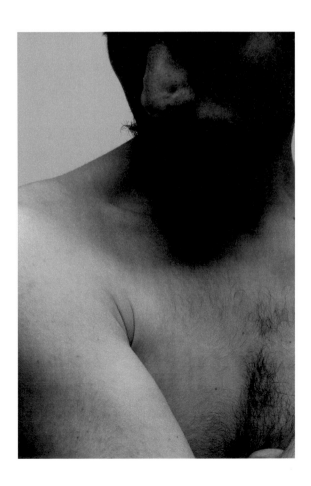

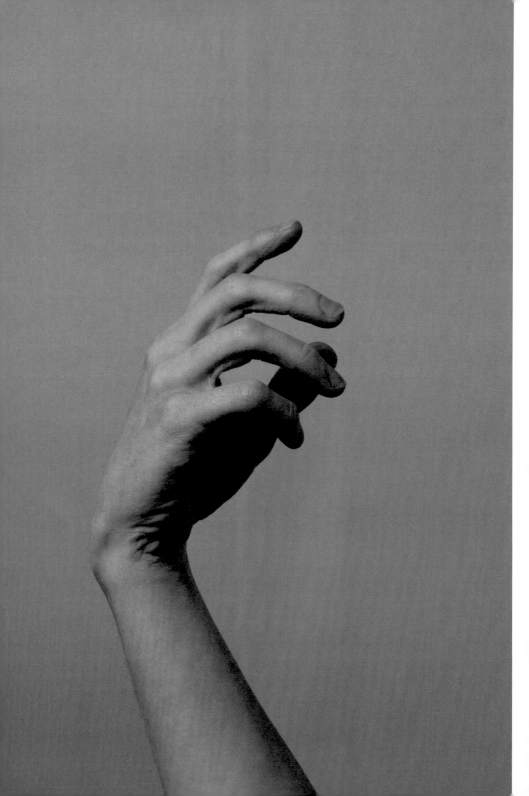

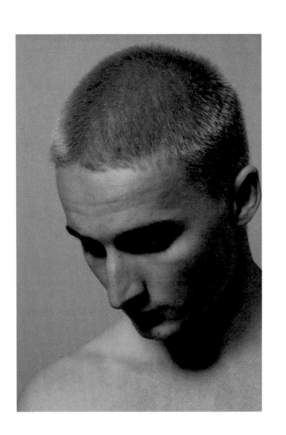

-

Never eat steak rare.

Trust in a God that was force fed to your ancestors.

A God that has countless homes - some filled to the brim with gold furnishings and stunning architecture (don't use words like stunning?), all with paintings of angels that do not look like you.

Don't be too confident, that's threatening, instead dilute yourself, be less, be obedient.

Worry about stacking money not self-worth.

Money cash hoes, well except your mother, shit if someone talks about your mother - throw hands, knives and bullets.

Forget your mother, your first home, her skin tone that looks like yours.

Find yourself unattractive.

No gay shit, no explorations of sexuality or gender.

Boys wear blue girls wear pink.

Spirituality is a myth.

Fuck practicing emotional intelligence, stunt on the 'Gram instead.

Number one rule above all others - do not talk about your feelings or how these rules affect your mental health.

Never let go, never forgive, never look weak.

Dear Oliver,

It's Daisy, your biggest (and best) cousin writing to you from November 2017. I'm 23 years old right now and you're 8, but when you open this I'll be 31 (ahh!) and you'll be turning 16! I'm sure the way we look, sound and act will be so different, but I hope some things about us are still the same.

I'm sending this letter to offer you what I can about the way the world works and to check up on how you might be feeling. I don't know what it's like to be a man, but I do know how society will try to mould you into their version of one. It's not fair, it's not fun and it ultimately makes things harder for everyone.

I want you to think about the last time you hugged your male friends.

The last time you told your Dad you loved him.

The last time you asked someone to help you.

The last time you cried.

Did these moments happen recently?

How do they make you feel?

Are you struggling to pinpoint some of them?

Why do you think that is?

For the first eight years of your life you've been kind, thoughtful and full of advice for us all. You've shown genuine emotion, cried when things have hurt you and shared with us why that is. You've apologised when you've needed to and you've acknowledged the importance of sharing, being honest and helping others. These are positive traits. Never mistake them for weakness. They are a part of you and the foundations of your personality.

You've also shown that attitudes based on the construction of a gendered hierarchy have worked their way into your belief system. You've told me that activities that require strength and logic can only be done by you and your dad. You've said that boys can't wear dresses and you've refused to play with toys that you think are "too girly".

You are not faster, stronger or more able to do certain things than me or our cousin Summer just because the world sees you as a boy. Although it might seem like these words are only oppressing and belittling the capabilities of women, remember that these attitudes hurt you too.

When people say that men are tougher and more rational because they don't add emotion into their work, our society is saying that emotions weaken you. They will tell you that the only valid emotion to express is anger, but holding your true feelings in will cause you to erupt later on and you will struggle to process why this is, but there are always places and people you can go to help you. And *spoiler alert* I'm one of them!

I love you Olly, you are my first born cousin and we are the most similar out of everyone. We have the same alopecia patch on our heads, we are the only ones with brown eyes and (currently) we're both only children! I hope you continue to be loving and an example to everyone in the family. Be kind to your mother, she has done more for you than you realise.

Your Grandad told me this when I turned 18 and although I found it cheesy at the time, it does ring true:

"Be yourself, because everyone else is taken."

Love from,

Your big cuz Dais xxx

I grew up being raised by my nan, my mum, my auntie and my three cousins. It's a family that has been built and sustained by women and although men have come and gone, all blood relatives in my life were women. Until I turned 16, and my cousin had a little baby boy who has grown into an emotionally intelligent, sensitive, loving child. But as I watch the grown men around me struggle to process their emotions, be selfish with their time and take out their frustrations on their wives and girlfriends, I remember that that loving child is doing all his learning within that heteronormative, male dominated environment.

Writing this letter was a reminder to me that there is continual work to do. I cannot let him disregard his emotional intelligence. I cannot let him be fooled into thinking that the women in his life aren't the reason he is here. I cannot let him become those men.

I hope that this letter will find him at the right time.

Illustration on previous page, by Joey Yu

'Flip The Page' , LEMUEL JONES

-

Affirmations
I am allowed to feel

Angry
Sad
Lowliness
Discomfort
Confused
Hurt
Manipulated
Aroused
Curious
Weak
Low on energy
Strong
Excited
Love
Distress
Stress
Concern
Vivacious
Certain
Determined
Proud
Anguish
Nothing
Everything
Out of control
Silence
Conviction
Solitude
Satisfied
Uncertain

Anxious
Scared
Fear
Ethereal
Claustrophobic
Annoyed
Glad
Gracious
Rough
Fluid
Lost
Reincarnated
Deep
Ambitious
Nervous
Weary
Out of this world
Human
Compassion
Nourishing
Burned out
Hungry
High
Rich
Real
Old
Naïve
Basic

I acknowledge that the way I feel is ever changing and no one feeling or emotion shall consume me forever. I declare that as I continue to look inward and grow as a person so will my emotional state. I will evolve and will experience happiness. I will experience times of hurt and sadness but they will control the love I show myself. I will love myself even through suffering, to healing and beyond. Through my evolution.

-

To me, portrait photography is the way I mark an interaction, the beauty in having the chance to hear about other people's lives.

It was my father who spurred my love of photography, he was my inspiration for both of my photographic series' in North Philadelphia, Dear Philadelphia and Capturing MIracles. In 2016, I received news that he had a stage 4 brain tumour. This news would then lead to so many changes in my life in London. The title 'Dear Philadelphia,' aims to project to others this importance of vulnerability in my work. I was missing stability and embracing the laughter, carelessness and youth in Philadelphia; these photographs, this shared humanity, were my respite.

I want my audience to know me, to understand the perspective and experiences I come from when creating. Not to destroy their interpretation but instead not limit their chance to comprehend my work. My dad passed away last October.

Something I am very attracted to in my work on Philly is brotherhood. I think that is something that is very similar to my love of London. I have always been drawn to the visualisation of brotherhood. The importance of it, the tenderness of brotherhood and most of all the inclusive factor behind brotherhood. It knows no boundary of age or race. It was something I could identify in a basketball court in a predominately Hispanic area of Philly and I would see in a barbers in Tottenham.

In Case You Were Wandering my current and ongoing series, highlights the need to have open conversations within your relationships. I had some very vulnerable conversations with some very strong guys the day these images were taken. You realize it's not often a lot of men get asked, "how are you doing?" about the tough moments they go through.

They are often carrying so much, they take their load to school, to work and at times into relationships, because too often they are made to feel they have nowhere to put their load down.

In Case You Were Wandering was previously in the studio, now taken to the basketball courts, because that is where, for a lot of these boys and men, they get to be free with no emotional expectations.

To the men and boys who shared their lives with me, their pain, their victories and their dreams, thank you for proving that there is immense strength in weakness.

I wish you would cry like you used to. Before injustice and pain were regular, before society taught you about manhood.

'Khalid is Tired', **LIZ WARD**

-

*The central character represents several young men I've worked with who have
regularly been missing from their care placements.
All the details/speech in it are true and verbatim.*

Khalid is tired
Tired of this shit
Tired of this life
And quite literally
Tired.

He walked into his placement five minutes ago and lucky for him, I was
standing there.

Khalid is tired.

Stuck in a kid's home
With 4 other losers
And a communal
Kitchen
In Croydon
This isn't quite what Khalid imagined
When his mother said they had to leave
Croydon wasn't in his dream of
safety
& Britain
& England
& London
& Croydon?
A kid's home in Croydon?
Croydon. isn't. London.
(No offence to Croydon)

Khalid is tired

I greet him and meet him and try to act friendly
'Hiya mate sorry to have to do this I know you must be proper busy but I was wondering if you'd talk to me?
I'll make you a cuppa tea?
look mate - I promise I'm not the police.'
He stares at me
'aiight cool'
I sigh in relief and we take our seats in the sitting room.

Khalid is tired.

The room is an oppressive deep blood red,
with black plastic sofas
and a shelf of donated dvds.
There's this attempt at family familiarity,
but the council issued fire doors
and CCTV
Are anything but homely

Although I do see one of the films they have is Jumanji
Like, the one from the 90s
[insert thoughts on small kids escaping imaginary monsters]

Khalid is tired
He's been missing for four months
Tells me he's fine
Tells me he's a big man now
Tells me he don't need to stress coz life is stressful enough
and after a while ya just stop feelin'
and I start to wonder if he's drowning

Khalid is tired
Khalid is sleep-deprived
Love-deprived

Soul-deprived
Have you seen what that does to a boy?
A boy dragged through streets
& deserts
& forests
& motorway service stations
Each an iteration of what's supposed to be Heaven
To build a New Life
Only to find that his
Mum's repeated rape by the rebels
has left her mind like rubble
like the rubble they fled from
Like the rubble he was born in
Like the rubble he believes he is worth nothing more than

Khalid is tired
He is managed moved and sectioned
Khalid is tired
I look deep into his deep brown eyes and see only pain
Khalid is tired
his brand new air max 95s give him away;
not purchased with his £5-a-week allowance
they're an indication of a lifestyle
or a life choice
that every other black boy
is forced to make
whilst packing a 12-inch blade

Khalid is tired
stabbed 16 times and left to rot
He is not
Precious
So what makes life so special now, when death is so hard to keep a hold of?

He thought he was leaving hell.
But this doesn't feel like heaven

Khalid is tired
Khalid is tired
Khalid is tired

My job to ensure his safety
seems kind of pointless
He answers my questions with a duty-bound politeness
Never quite giving me enough to understand
but enough to know
Enough to know that

Life is shit and there's nothing you can do to change it
I'm stuck in this puzzle and you can't rearrange it
I'm dying anyway in these ends let's face it

so what they teach us in training
about building self-esteem?
With Khalid?
Seems a bit whack.
[Something tells me he isn't going to want to draw a sunflower
and name each petal an emotion he feels]

I throw compliments at him like pennies into the deep dark well of his soul

Tell him that
He is worthy
He is precious
He is human
He is eloquent
He is heaven sent
He is meant to succeed
And never to impede his own brilliance
He is better than he thinks
Even when he sinks
To a low
He isn't hollow

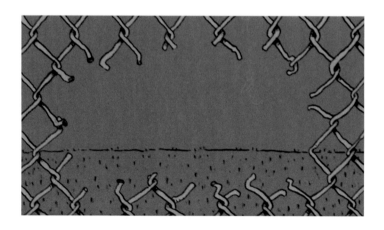

'Negro Child', EMMANUEL UNAJI

-

Negro Child is an artwork I created in 2017. I feel it's my most significant piece to date as it is so playful, yet holds so much weight.

A piece that conveys the duality of human nature and the mental turmoil faced by a disenfranchised human being internalising pain. The idea was to draw a person at breaking point, hiding behind a smile, whilst in fact the pain and frustration has become overbearing.

The silver lining - that it encourages the viewer not to be afraid of being vulnerable.

During recent discussions with assistant psychologist Obajide Alademerin, he has strongly urged that there needs to be more of an emphasis on early intervention support within ethnic minorities (BME). Reason for this being: BME groups make up the majority of the population who are in need of mental health care, but in reality they access and receive the least support in comparison to other ethnic groups.

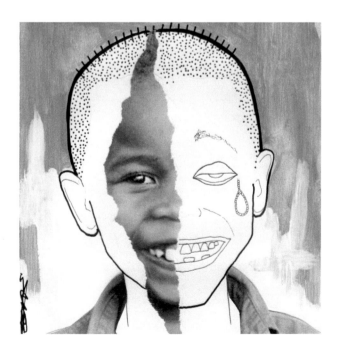

'Vomit of A Young Somali', HÉLÈNE SELAM KLEIH

-

For him and her, and the communities in between.

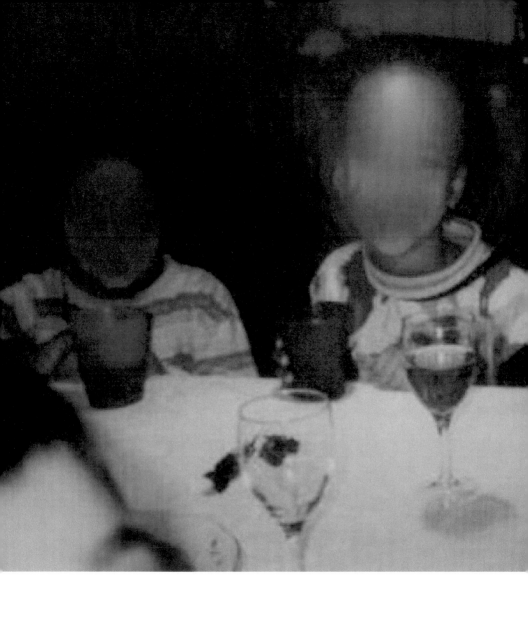

the vomit of a young somali

Physical , no language barrier, more real. Minorities are dehumanised. We are products of our histories.

she Writes down her life story. The drawing helped, but writing was the best.

\

Family portrait, a sad one she had to share.

With the writing she spoke about her life, civil war, having to migrate , the trauma of being a single mum. The breakdown of her marriage. Getting diagnosed, getting sectioned.

Just the struggle of raising us whilst having a mental illness.

Her and her art therapist. saddened by my mums st

She had to share it.

You don't do that in the S community. No one know mental health is. Writing' ? You're possessed. Ther attached to mental illness

386

But I'm just paraphrasing.

Well, "I'm not sure what I'm saying."

People need to talk

Make the stories about us more human.

S' - its not any different between me and my mum.

Working class and Somali

Im not trying to reinforce stereotypes. I used to work for my GP. 17- year old boy, almost 18, family really worried, demanding.

He was seen within 2 weeks.

st felt

I feel like with my brother it took him months to see a psychiatrist .

igma

17 - Repeat prescriptions of citalopram within seconds.

Undiagnosed or diagnosed, can I, yes. mental, yes.

But yes one that I'm trying to overcome on my own.

Nhs doesn't work. My mum yes ha

Im someone who recognises that I'm mental. Its lessons. I'm being slapped with lessons. Ephinanies. I appreciate the lessons. I laugh about it sometimes. I'm going to go back to watching René Descartes , they speak to me. Philosophers.

The underlying problems will always
~   be depression and anxiety

Direct cause of childhood, trauma. I
feel disgusted. Sick. I'm Muslim i
believe in god. not by chance I can
connect these dots.

Seeing her rely on drugs. And no
proper programme to rehabilitate her.
Scares me. I don't want to have to
rely on drugs. Drugs have had an
impact, not, maybe, yes on
intelligence.
She used to be so hard working. So
motivated. she is.

She cant even drive. There's a risk.

I'm not going down that Route of
mental assistance, she, did that
already.

brother is a victim of the system.
Terrorist. Muslim. Somali. No person.
No suffering. The newspapers, he
never chose to have that illness.

He was failed. He tried.

brother is a victim of the system. Terrorist. Muslim. Somali. No person. No suffering. The newspapers, he never chose to have that illness.

He was failed. He tried.

Its all fucked H~. Its all fucked. Actually fucked.

She won't even consider living in Somalia. Without drugs. I wish they gave her a plan without having to rely on the drugs.

Her mind is so used to the idea. These drugs make me feel sane so i need to keep taking them.

My brother couldn't get an appointment. No offense to the kid. My brother could hear voices .

There's institutional racism. Its intrinsic. All the way into our health care system.

PAin is immeasurable.

My brother was fine. The lawyer said you have to play the game.

Its all fucking in my head. I'll play the game.

Its all fucking in my head. I'll play the game.

I'm not gonna play it like you are.

We were a nomadic people. Before colonisation. The country got turned upside down on its head. Individuals need to be accountable. Institutions need to. I'm so physically. I can't.

My brother couldn't get an
appointment. No offense to the kid.
My brother could hear voices .
There's institutional racism. Its
intrinsic. All the way into our health
care system.

PAin is immeasurable.

My brother was fine. The lawyer said
you have to play the game.

'*Musibo (Tragedy)*' , SAGAL BULHAN

-

Young boy, Black.
With a shattered soul
Carrying a burden? A Secret...
He felt silenced
Ignored
Couldn't cope
Cried in his sleep
The echoed voices in his head wanted to feed.
Yet, the only thing they could eat,
was his rational stream
of conscious thought.
He slowly started to fade away,
into someone we barely recognized.
Panic
We tried to help
Take a deep breath they said.
He'll be okay they said.
Next thing,
Blood on the pavement floor.
came back to an empty home,
and a broken door.

'La Arki Karin (Invisible)' , SAGAL BULHAN

Lyon's 13th Biennale, *La vie moderne,* which ran up until January 2016, came at a fitting time for France. Comprised of work from 60 artists, the congregation addressed the fraught tensions between national identity, immigration and post colonialism in its relationship to modern day France and the world beyond.

With the terrorist attacks in Paris re-opening the debate around France's position towards its tainted colonial history - a history that has not been consolidated, but rather sealed and silenced - the curator Ralph Rugoff put it, these are all issues very much encompassed in the present.

"La vie moderne is acutely attuned to the ways in which contemporary culture constitutes a working through, and a response to prior events and traditions. Even as artists in the world explore current situations and images, they are also excavating the past."

Whether it be in France or elsewhere, the constant malleability of our social, cultural and economic landscapes cannot be restrained - despite the best efforts of far right political parties such as France's Front National and Britain's own UK Independence Party. While these viewpoints are being emboldened, in equal parts is the pushback. For many of the artists within Lyon's biennale, the exhibition became an ideal platform to utilise art as means of social change, commentary and consolidation of trauma.

An uncomfortable topic in France, French-Algerian artist Kader Attia focused on the relationship between mental illness and the lived reality of immigration, and ultimately the notion of reparation - of France accepting its position towards its previous colonies, specifically Algeria. 2001 saw Jacques Chirac introduce the first national day of homage to harkis, the Algerian veterans who fought against their countrymen to preserve French colonial rule in Algeria. Year after year (obviously always within a presidential campaign), the media has covered first Sarkozy and then Hollande's "well-intentioned" declaration that France must compensate the harkis for their strife.

Yet, these promises of repair are, more often than not, fleeting and unsubstantial, drowned out by racist, Islamophobic and xenophobic cries, and an environment of apathy. France, like many of its Western allies, continuously brushes off the institutional and systematic side-lining of its immigrant communities, even as their denial of economic and social prosperity bred the bitterness that fuelled the riots in Paris in 2005. Attia's site specific installation, *Traditional Repair, Immaterial Injury* aims to counteract France's blindness to these inequalities. Reconstruction and repair becomes a tangible, and somewhat haphazard act, as cracks in the floor of Le Sucrière are stapled together and restored. The floor of this structure, like skin and like the earth, is heavy with its wounds. Wounds if not fatal, turn to scars, but despite the 'repair' the abrasion, the damage remains visible. An impossibility of concealing such scars lends to an impossibility of denying and silencing such histories.

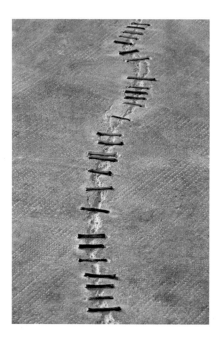

Traditional Repair, Immaterial Injury, 2014. In situ sculpture, metallic staples, concrete, view at the 13rd Lyon Biennale - 2015, courtesy of the artist, and Galleria Continua. Photo credit: Blaise Adilon

This concrete depiction of repair gives way to a more conceptual and theoretical understanding in the fittingly titled *Reasons Oxymoron*. The installation, which has also showed at the Galerie Nagel Draxler in Berlin, comprises of 18 videos featuring interviews with ethno-psychologists on the experience of immigrants adjusting and assimilating to different cultures and environments.

Thematically ordered into categories including "Reason and Politics", "Genocide" and "Totem and Fetish," the videos provide an expansive insight into how mental illness is treated by doctors and families alike, and the shifting balance between traditional and modern methods of healing. The comparison of Western psychiatry to the more physical stance that "healers" adopt in non-Western cultures generates debate of what is deemed 'rational' and 'irrational'. Through research and interviews with philosophers, ethnologists, historians, psychiatrists, psychoanalysts, musicologists, patients, healers, fetishists, and griots, Attia created a multi-faceted conversation on what should be and is currently regarded as a mental illness.

Reasons Oxymoron, 2015. Video installation, view at the 13th Lyon Biennale - 2015, courtesy of the artist, Galerie Nagel Draxler and Galerie Lehmann Maupin. Photo credit: Blaise Adilon

Rather than the textbook depiction of mental wards and patients that are all too familiar (not that mental illness can ever be textualized), Attia explores the complexities that surround mental illness and the foreigner. Whether it be first, second or third generation, immigration is intrinsically linked with the mental turmoil that comes with leaving a home, a land and a culture with which you have always been accustomed to. The videos bear witness to the onslaughts of depression, schizophrenia and paranoia that refugees face as a result of constant surveillance and daily social injustices inflicted by the lands which promised them prosperity.

As one ethnologist states, "[a]ll they see is white - and they then recoil within themselves," demonstrating that the acceptance of the receiving society and the ensuing social integration is vital to ensure the ability to cope sufficiently with new surroundings.

Despite this social commentary, Attia ultimately favours neither Western nor non-Western practices. The resounding phrase, **"Notion de l'être - on ne pas juste des véhicules"**, ("The notion of existence - we are not merely machines") also questions the pressures within immigrant communities to acquire social and economic status, where the struggle for money prevails over happiness. Money is an inevitable ruling factor over mobility and standard of life, thus non-Western communities, particularly among the older generation, often lack the lexicon in which to talk and understand mental health. Art is becoming far less exclusionary in the sense that it is more easily accessible - online, in galleries and museums - the abundance of art is not voiceless and vacuous. The Lyon biennale, and more recently Franco-Algerian Mohammed Bourouissa's *Urban Riders* at the Musée d'Art moderne in Paris, have proven art as an important medium in actively facilitating thought, reflection and discussion around mental health amongst the post-colonised community worldwide.

Through *Reasons Oxymoron*, Attia blurs the boundaries between modernity and tradition, showing that mental illness and reason alike cannot be defined. Instead, it is the responsibility of both families and welcoming societies to implicate and involve those mentally ill in society because "only then will they feel at one with themselves and have the purpose to live."

Rugoff's take on this year's Biennale was brave, as was Kader Attia's inclusion in the exhibition. In a country where secularism and patriotism continue to dominate political discourse, the subtleties of difference, within race, religion, culture, gender and mental states, are rarely given a voice.

Is it enough to foster a different mindset in France? Probably not. But, as Attia puts it, the question of reparation will always remain "omnipresent." Whether or not discussed, it's an unavoidable - perhaps even an irreparable part of our modern life.

-

Most of them left their country to find a place in which to work, to get some money for their future! In a way I feel they are all brave men!! And so interesting to hear their stories too.

These men come from Senegal - with cultures different from mine and Italy's. They have struggled to get here, in hope of finding a better situation.

They are already used to a struggle, but not this one. This state of being both ghosted and victimized.

People always talk about these men, these men with great hearts - all I see is their mental closure, as a superficial society pours out against them.

With   great   sadness.

It is sad to find yourself the scapegoat for any crime or national problem. Exclusion and imprisonment could bring someone to suffer a trauma mentally?

-

Mental health in Nigeria, as well as other countries in Africa, is known as the 'invisible illness'. Many of us, here in Britain, are not aware that our peers are suffering from mental illnesses. Nigeria is no different, and a lot of Nigerians do not seek mental health assistance due to ignorance, fear of stigma and discrimination, and a lack of access to mental health education. Some who are not educated on mental health issues believe that it can be cured by native doctors, an example of this is shown in 'The Stigma of Mental Illness in Nigeria' video by BattaBox show - a man was beaten and tortured to 'cure' himself of his mental illness.

Before I was educated about mental health, I assumed that a mentally ill person was someone who walked the streets naked, looking un-kept or a 'madman', as many others will describe the person as. This is not always the case, but if you have no real understanding of the various types of mental health issues, you would never know.

Mental health issues, similar to special needs, are seen as taboo. People do not want to talk about it due to fear of being judged or embarrassed. I'm sure there are mental health institutions in Nigeria, but these are not often spoken about and the discussion regarding this needs to increase.

-

How do u feel with ur mental health and being Nigerian?

Tbh this is quite a difficult one, the two don't really link with me,

When the two link - here is what I think:

1. What it's like being a man in Nigeria and having to provide for the family & be the head.

2. The stress of doing business and working in Lagos can really affect your mental health negatively. Traffic, power cut, nonsense on the street.

3. A Nigerian with a British accent and how local Nigerians treat me. They automatically look at you/speak to you a certain way if they know you don't live there.

4. What is considered the correct way to dress. My Dad doesn't like the way I roll up my jeans.

5. The clash between living in a secular society & having Christian home values.

6. The pressure put on me by my parents & myself to succeed in life and how I'm told I should be more successful than my rents! (Is that a Nigerian thing?)

7. Arguing with your Nigerian parents - you don't want to argue in a certain way because it may come across as rude?

I dunno this is just what comes to mind. The things that stress me.

'Karaye, Kano - August 2017', STEPHEN TAYO

-

'When it comes to mental health here: Men are pretty much under pressure all the time. Because there's so much that is expected from them. And they hardly share these parts of themselves to people at all, unlike women who share their feelings with friends and family. Perhaps women don't get much attention in terms of who they need to talk or rant to, but in general Men and Mental health is an issue for me that needs more attention.'

'Icarus', SAM WOOTTON

Masculine stoicism is often manufactured and fostered in the home. Playing on the classical figure of Icarus (influenced too heavily by his father), the central figure looks to the sky, daydreaming of a colourful outside world of self-expression, void of the desaturated and non-expressive.

The traditional family unit can inhibit the emotional growth of a young man in his formative years.

A plant can be seen dying in this vacuum: prolepsis?

-

My poet friend *Juillet* was probably the first person I was able to speak to about the problems of patriarchy from a male perspective.

I grew up in a strong patriarchal family. Whenever we go home it feels like we are back to the same reality - becoming a boy again without any possibility to act.

Living abroad freed us from this psychological state, this anxiety.

I'm turning 22 in October. Originally I'm from the south of Hungary, a city called Szeged. Juillet is older, he was born and grew up in France, and is of Gambian heritage.

I often participated in self-knowledge therapy in those years at home, but the real release from my "ghosts" was moving abroad and focusing my whole life on art.

Day by day I see people who are not aware of their own limits so they can't deal with it.

-

JUILLET: Do you have any experience of a mental condition?

KGT: There is an exercise that my psychologist advised me to do when I was 16. Write a letter to the person you recognize has restrained you, you don't have to send it to them, just write it out for yourself. In my case it was my father, I wrote that letter for 4 years. That marked the point when I could step over my anxieties which went back to my childhood. It's hard to separate a starting point of my first memories, during my juvenile years I was an extremely tempered person. Despite the fact that I was very social and made connections easily, I often felt isolated and angry about the world. You know I was just really not okay with myself. A sort of duality conflicted inside me about feelings - on one side my mother supported me to express and talk about my problems, on the other side my father who rather kept his issues inside. The final step was my complete self-destruction - this conflict eventually turned into panic attacks of deathly fear. I started visiting a psychologist who helped me to understand the core of the problem. However, I had to unchain myself from the burdens. The key was given by art and spending time with artists. The unlimited possibilities art can offer helped me to throw away my chains of anxiety - I became friends with myself.

This would not have been possible without all the conversations I had with people, not necessarily about psychological issues but rather art and life in general. Recently the artist Nathalie Du Pasquier recommended that I read about Carlo Rovelli, whose writings are on the boundary of philosophy and popular science. Carlo talks about relational quantum mechanics in his book like you would talk about walking with your uncle on the sea shore. Through science, he explains human interactions. How we can only measure electrons when they are in reaction with other objects, the same way we only exist in relation to others. This keeps me on my path - to not to be afraid to seek advice, or talk about my deepest feelings.

KGT: What is your personal journey to understand your feelings?

JUILLET: I have experienced mental distress from a very early age. Being exposed to violence as a kid has definitively impacted my psyche. As far as I can remember, those traumas translated into mutism or on the other end of the spectrum, into bursts of anger. I remember how my inner persona constantly fulminated, how oftentimes I was asked by my mother what was going wrong with me. The pain distorted my facial expression for years and turned me into an unwelcoming kid fearing strangers, which in turn I have tried to push everyone away from me in my life. And so you start to lock yourself into solitude. I have never really had moments of peace. This neurotic behaviour eventually alerted my mother who guided me towards a therapist when I was around 12 or 13 years old. I suspect that she was being advised by a friend or something at the time. Unfortunately, I never gave it a chance, after one or two sessions I would drop out, disheartened since that experience was only making me feel more estranged and emphasised the guilt in me. I was feeling even more out of space. When you take the world into account for it and you want it to burn into the ground, you go to therapy and you are leaving being diagnosed as "mentally ill", thinking "le monde marche sur la tête."

KGT: Do you think that where you are from, seeking help from a psychologist is a problem?

JUILLET: That question is at the heart of the problem. I grew up with my mother and never really got to know my dad, or at least the good sides of him. My mother was busy trying to provide for me and my siblings. She has tried her best to blend into this foreign country with no external help or resource. The only way for that to happen was to give precedence to French culture. So part of my history, part of my West African heritage was buried, or downcast. Where my family is from, therapy is not commonplace, not that there are no mental illnesses, but it is surely a taboo. And on the other hand social life is more present, your mental strength is a pre-condition to survival, and survival in those regions differs from the west, it overtakes you, it consumes your whole.

My point is that I have only inherited from the part of her history and personal struggles that she wanted me to see, the ones I could sense... A medical diagnosis can only help if it highlights the roots of your problem. When your identity is hidden from you by your own family who wish to protect you, it has consequences, leaving you with no other choice than to fight with years of structural oppressions layered in gender roles and societal myths, you end up being lost, without a position, in a somewhat antagonistic environment full of preconceptions. Here you are, eaten by the diagnosis that would emphasise how much of an outcast you already are.

KGT: Was there a particular turning point?

JUILLET: I had few turning points and I continue to have "aha" moments as I keep on learning and growing. But I guess in my teen years an important landmark was coming to the realisation that I had to shift my energy to get any better and so I have started to write. Writing was the healing process for me since I never really spoke about my pain to anyone at that stage. It was just pure expression. I am still relying on my writings to excavate the wrongs I have assimilated. I have released two poetry collections last year to recall my experience of travelling within a black hole, again. Some 15 years after the first therapy. Can you believe it!?

KGT: It is amazing that you have the strength now to openly show this to the world! So is it your creative output that allows you to express yourself and give you some sort of freedom?

JUILLET: Totally, now there is one thing. Creativity is soothing, but it is surely not healing what you are carrying deep inside. It allows me to experience more life, to isolate myself and overcome suicidal thoughts, to meet with people, talk with strong women around me, listen to music as my main therapy, to read, to practice daily spiritual and physical rituals – it is an endless journey.

Although I have just mentioned isolation, I do not mean to encourage anyone to rot in a den. When you experience mental distress I want those thoughts to stop judging the self as "ill". We are carrying centuries of disgrace and trying to fix it with poisonous treatments. That's my whole point. What is sanity anyway? Who is sane? What are the foolish standards we raised to define sanity?

But yes, enough of me. Thank you for your questions, they are so liberating. This is how one can and should help a brother to check himself, I believe. I remember a similar conversation we had a few months ago. One thing we both commented on was how males pass from teenage years to adulthood. How we can mix up power with the abuse of power which erases the possibility for feelings to socially exist. How oftentimes do you speak about the way you feel, how accepted is that?

KGT: Occasionally - I've only had a few deep conversations, and only very few of these were with men. Mainly, my close female friends who are more willing to engage in this topic, which only follows the pattern in my life. My emotional upbringing was through my close relationship with the female characters around me.

JUILLET: Why is that?

KGT: In my opinion a large percentage of men still live in denial of an existing power structure. While the ones who would be willing to discuss are still afraid to because of the lack of a safe space. The original macho idea about the male figure does not allow you to talk about feelings outside of your trusted circles or even inside them. The point is that this lack of conversation mostly has to do with education. A close friend of mine who opened up to me about his fears told me a personal experience growing up in a boarding school. As often happens in our teenage years he was fighting with his demons and when he felt he could not fight on his own any more, he approached the person in charge to seek advice. His best words to were to "get his shit together". You can imagine this piece of 'advice' only caused further damage. Eventually, my friend had to return to closed family circles for some weeks which helped him to overcome his distresses. He was lucky, two of his fellow classmates committed suicide in the last year. Certain schools are infamous for still promoting a conservative male figure which leads to isolation. Many schools either don't have the capability or their educational staff lack the pedagogical skills to deal with the students' mental health. These problematics are the core of the problem. Education should be just as much about teaching the mind, as supporting the soul.

JUILLET: Well, you are sadly right. It is true that as you get older everything becomes so clear, and it is abnormal to witness the imbalance you just revealed, but I am still hopeful about a shift in education. So what is your role and your responsibility to solve some of those issues?

KGT: Asking people these questions! In hope they are willing to open up. Talking openly about the issues of suicidal thoughts, depression, anxiety, the problem of power. I would like to highlight the importance of creating certain safe places for conversation, having a drink or just sitting down at a table together. It's our job to build a community of trust through our own personal tendencies to openly talk about our mental state and feelings. Our responsibility is connected with the journey we make, as we become capable of fighting our battles we must reach out to our closest friends and reassure that they too are not alone.

JUILLET: How do you do materialise this on a daily basis? Do you actually and actively do it?

KGT: Yes, my friend, who I previously mentioned is an example. He was constrained by everything happening around him in life, you sense that if you know someone, I think. So I try to have a supportive attitude so that when he needs to talk, he knows I'm there. There's a set of conversations that have to happen before people change. The best way to start with this is to engage with your closest circle of male friends. Ask them: "How are you feeling?" We don't usually ask how the other one feels. Don't let them shake you off with the cold answer - I'm fine. Our silence won't save us.

This conversation happened over the phone on August 28 2018, between *Juillet* and Krisztián Török.

"Coucher de Fenêtre / DE-FENESTRATED"
(*Juillet*, Lost in Time publishing, April 2017)

Note to self
Bad is good suspended
/

OCULAR WITNESS (II)
Rope around my neck
Laughter on hold
Not a red cent
Delirious
Holy hole of love for my fellow –
none
Sincere lack of will – I
Stand on the pavement to bear
witness
Am I insane
Born non-being
Border-aligned
Seeking a cave
Craving a sinkhole
Please find attached my tainted
statement:
Play, I'd rather not
Alienated by galleons of spirits
Less than a bowl of rice to eat
Shall I be crowned
Deaf
Sober
Hand me the piece
Seen too much
Not enough
Enough

To die old in my birthday suit - But still?
/

It's only when you get older that the childhood view you had of your "normal" family gets shattered. All of the family secrets seem to come out. At 18, I found out that numerous close family members were struggling with mental health issues - most commonly clinical depression. Before then, mental health had been treated as an "adults-only" discussion. It was spoken about in whispers, like a dirty little secret ready to be swept right back under the rug. The loudest thing said was, "I'll pray for them."

Dialogue surrounding mental health issues is often hushed in the black community, leaving little room for greater understanding of people's experiences, triggers, or treatments. Writer and radio host Keith Dube challenged this in January 2015 by blogging about his depression and sparked a discussion. More than a year later, in September 2016, his platform for conversation extended to a BBC Three documentary, Being Black, Going Crazy?, which explored the stigmas and causes of mental health issues in the black community; unfolding the stories of three people whose lives have been affected by it. Working from the staggering statistic that black men are six times more likely to be sectioned to a mental health hospital than white men, the documentary proved that the silence definitely needs to be broken.

The socio-economics of impoverished neighbourhoods is a factor that Dube touched on throughout the documentary - growing up in this environment is something that can impact the psyche negatively. Although this sheds light on people's surroundings playing a significant role in their mental health, the NHS, which costs around 4 percent of your salary, doesn't always provide suitable care. Dube discovered that racial inequality exists in mental health treatment, and in the documentary we see psychologist Malcolm Phillips talk about this on Radar Radio with Dube, claiming that black people are much "less likely to get any talking treatment" due to practitioners perceiving black people as "more dangerous". Unfortunately, biases are nothing new when diagnosing something as complex as the mind.

A well-known 1973 study by psychologist David L. Rosenhan, On Being Sane in Insane Places, investigated whether or not sane people can be diagnosed as insane and sectioned to a mental health hospital. Eight sane people approached hospitals claiming that they were hearing voices, saying the words "thud", "empty" and "hollow". Rosenhan specifically chose to use these words as they allow interpretation for an existential crisis to be the issue. Beyond this, the only other aspects professionals were judging them on was the pseudopatients' normal behaviour. It was found that completely sane pseudopatients were then diagnosed with schizophrenia and bipolar disorder.

In addition to biases being a general existing issue in diagnosis, the cherry on top is clear from Phillips' interview: blackness connotes madness to some medical professionals. People who work in a supposedly scientific, objective field are able to squeeze in preconceived, subjective notions about patients based on their skin colour.

Our voices should be loud and welcomed within our own families; isolation certainly doesn't ease the experience of living with mental disorders. As seen in the documentary, many people feel that their parents won't be supportive or understand that the mental battles they're fighting may need more than a prayer or time to heal. In 2014, The Guardian interviewed an evangelical musician, Carlos Whittaker, about this after his own pastor advised him to stay silent about his mental health issues and others encouraged him to turn to his faith: "I can pray 24 hours a day, seven days a week, and I'm still going to have to take that little white pill every single day," he said. As shown in Dube's documentary, in the black, religious community, mental health issues are sometimes dismissed as anxiety that can be overcome, or even perceived as demonic, causing even further isolation.

Rapper Kid Cudi's self-care choice - checking into rehab for depression back in October, 2016 - had also put black mental health in the spotlight via a Facebook post, "I am not at peace. I haven't been since you've known me. If I didn't come here, I [would've] done something to myself," he wrote.

It has encouraged people in the black community to start the discussion. It's raised questions about the pressure of masculinity, which seems to be a lingering issue for Kudi, as evidenced by a subsequent discussion of his depression with iamOTHER. If one man can manage to inspire people to open up with each other by displaying his vulnerability on a global platform imagine what we can do in our own homes.

Whilst religion and mental health treatments are both ways to help the mind handle and embrace reality, it must be remembered that one does not replace the other. For some people, spirituality can be a way to begin breaking the silence about personal battles and believing in a higher power can feel like a proactive way to keep us sane when we don't understand the dynamics of our minds or, even, this world. But for others, an appointment at the doctors might be needed.

Kid Cudi
5 October 2016 · 🌐

Its been difficult for me to find the words to what Im about to share with you because I feel ashamed. Ashamed to be a leader and hero to so many while admitting I've been living a lie. It took me a while to get to this place of commitment, but it is something I have to do for myself, my family, my best friend/daughter and all of you, my fans.

Yesterday I checked myself into rehab for depression and suicidal urges. I am not at peace. I haven't been since you've known me. If I didn't come here, I wouldve done something to myself. I simply am a damaged human swimming in a pool of emotions everyday of my life. Theres a ragin violent storm inside of my heart at all times. Idk what peace feels like. Idk how to relax. My anxiety and depression have ruled my life for as long as I can remember and I never leave the house because of it. I cant make new friends because of it. I dont trust anyone because of it and Im tired of being held back in my life. I deserve to have peace. I deserve to be happy and smiling. Why not me? I guess I give so much of myself to others I forgot that I need to show myself some love too. I think I never really knew how. Im scared, im sad, I feel like I let a lot of people down and again, Im sorry. Its time I fix me. Im nervous but ima get through this. I wont be around to promote much, but the good folks at Republic and my manager Dennis will inform you about upcoming releases. The music videos, album release date etc. The album is still on the way. Promise. I wanted to square away all the business before I got here so I could focus on my recovery.

If all goes well ill be out in time for Complexcon and ill be lookin forward to seeing you all there for high fives and hugs.

Love and light to everyone who has love for me and I am sorry if I let anyone down. I really am sorry. Ill be back, stronger, better. Reborn. I feel like shit, I feel so ashamed. Im sorry.

I love you,

Scott Mescudi

 589K   54K Comments 135K Shares

-

In March 2018 I lost my father to suicide at the hands of an acute psychotic episode. This is dedicated to him - Rest in Peace.

"*When definitions of abnormal cognition rely so heavily on cultural perspectives, we cannot expect to receive adequate psychiatric care without diversifying the psychiatric workforce... I feel that the relationship between ethnicity and treatment illustrates the vilification + fetishisation of the black male body, seen only in the realm of the physical and hollowed of a soul...*"

In a recent Instagram post I made on Instagram (@lauren.esjd), I touched upon the disproportionate rate of Black British (specifically Caribbean) men that are routinely diagnosed with psychotic illnesses in the UK. In fact, being in this group renders you S E V E N T E E N times more likely to be categorised in this way by health professionals.

Earlier this year I was exposed to the idea of viewing ethnicity as a "cognitive process". Rather than seeing it as a box to tick at the GP, I learnt to define ethnicity as a unique perspective of the world, shaped by our life experiences and expressed through "schemas". In psycho-social study, the term "Schema" is used to describe our mental frameworks and the routes we take to process our interactions and make decisions. These varying perspectives are typically shared within racial groups and govern our interracial interactions (apologies for the tongue twister). The ability to rationally interpret social situations in which the participants vary in perspective is necessary to exist healthily in a multi-ethnic community. Unfortunately, racial marginalisation warps these schemas leaving our heads...well... a little bit fucked.

I believe that racialised schemas are catalysts for the development of mental illness.

It is important to note that genetics can be firmly ruled out as being a factor for the above figure because the occurrence of such illnesses amongst Caribbean natives is no higher than that of native White Brits.

The internalisation of stereotypes has the potential to create self-fulfilling prophesies. This phenomenon occurs when we adopt the labels given to us, often as a subconscious act of self-defence. Marginalised communities in white countries and spaces are unfairly assigned a plethora of negative connotations. I believe that hyper-masculinity is the most detrimental internalised stereotype regarding the collective black male psyche. A few years back I came across a paper titled "Invisibility Syndrome: A Clinical Model of the Effects of Racism on African American Males" **. The paper linked the subconscious adoption of societal labels to feelings of invisibility which are then expressed through depression, addiction and other psychological ailments. This syndrome is believed to develop during the formative years.

This assumption of hyper-masculinity denies young black boys of a valuable privilege- vulnerability. It disarms them of healthy ways to express their emotions, normalising aggressive and self-destructive behaviours.

The obsessive racialisation of interpersonal interactions is a worryingly common behaviour amongst black people in white spaces - but can you blame us? Like many second gen immigrants I spent a good part of my formative years being fed self-hatred and digesting microaggressions. It's only natural that a hyper-defensive and self-conscious perspective shat all over my world - simple biology. There are undeniable similarities between commonly acknowledged symptoms of psychotic illnesses (e.g. feeling distrusted, scrutinised, watched and followed) and what it can feel like to be Black in the UK. There is scientific proof to suggest that these obvious parallels can act as catalysts for mental illnesses. This racial fixation can also be the root of nihilist worldviews making us feel helpless, convinced we are lacking the resources to better our circumstances.

Western cognitive frameworks influence psychiatric institutions almost exclusively which can make navigating through the system as a black patient extremely alienating. There is evidence to suggest that many Black Brits are being misdiagnosed and mistreated by mental health professionals.

"Western Schemas"

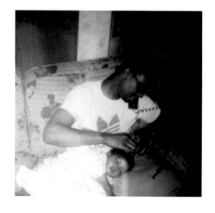

These occurrences are the consequence of neglecting the importance of cultural understanding and the presence of medical biases. In the process of making a diagnosis, a psychiatrist is given the responsibility of assessing a patient based on behaviours that deviate from the norm. Culture plays a huge role in one's ideas of what is normal and what isn't. When definitions of abnormal cognition rely so heavily on cultural perspectives, we cannot expect to receive adequate psychiatric care without diversifying the psychiatric workforce. Simple cultural disparities such as polarised views regardwing superstition or supernatural belief (this example is pretty relevant to African-Caribbean's) create gaps between the "specialist" and the patient. This and other medical biases including the perceived heightened threat of black men have been proven to lead to the overmedication of black male patients. In an inpatient survey (1991)*** surrounding the relationship between "psychotropic medications and ethnicity", black male patients were found more likely to be sectioned, receive electroconvulsive therapy and given antipsychotic medications. In addition to this they were more likely to receive these intramuscularly. I truly feel that this relationship between ethnicity and treatment illustrates the vilification and fetishisation of the black male body seen only in the realm of the physical and hollowed of a soul.

I have suffered from Depression for approximately six years. The delayed treatment of my illness stemmed from feeling unwelcome within spaces of psychological care - I have never been able to relate to professionals assigned to me. Desperately seeking someone who granted me comfort, I was stuck in a cycle of being referred and self-discharged for years (which might I add, is a pattern proven to be typical of black patients in outpatient care). Eventually, I found solace in medication. This felt like enough until the passing of my father... the collective mental health of my community is in a crisis and I want to demand more.

**Anderson J. Franklin Ph.D.,Nancy Boyd Franklin Ph.D.
*** Lloyd, K. & Moodley, P. Soc Psychiatry Psychiatr Epidemiol (1992) 27: 95.

-

(notes from me in London, a still angry Black woman seeking atonement, originally written for the Justice LA prison reform project)

I tried to write about my experience of what the system has done to my family...not quite sure I got it all out but it helped me cry while writing it, which is always a welcome release.

love & solidarity

How can I be so tongue tied, I should be stronger for all of us. I try. I'm writing this because I may never be able to do anything else. I lay a flower for you, for all of us. To release us from the weight of the crossing that follows us, heavy and weary, wherever we try to lay our head.

No.

Date.

a house with no door.

dandition

Soft people being tough.

They came to your home, to the top floor flat. Too w, I imagine you were scared, voices flickering in your head that are not your own, I don't know who called the doctor that time or what you had done. They were supposed to care for you. Ease the fear, quiet the voices. In ~~the lieu~~ ~~~~ as is protocol the police came. Why a pig when you need a nurse? You slashed them both, ~~one~~ in the throat. By the time we got to you they had beaten you so bloody your skull was cracked. You were lucky they said, doing what you did. The years that passed, ~~you~~ in prison I didn't know how to be. I was young, but old enough - I should have visited but I couldn't take it. I can barely write this now. I do love you. And I know its not your fault. I was scared too, I still am. I don't know. Fuck. But when we sit now and don't speak of this, we sit and pretend these few short years you have been free

I play that night over in my head
so often. I remember your flat somewhere
in Dalston I think. The last time I
remember being in there was when
your dad, Stanford was there. Is that
right? I saw a therapist who said your
time lines get fucked up when you experience
trauma. A kind of misty Amnesia.

I wonder how much blood there was.
~~It must have been~~

blood clouds

ok im going to sleep
now.
I'll think about you
more tomorrow.

blood tears.

would Jamaica
have been
kinder to you?

how did
you get
down
the
stairs?

did they drag?

-

'*To Bipolar*'

"Perspective is such a beautiful thing. The younger version of me wrote this. I remember writing 'To Bipolar' and being angry at the world for not understanding mental illness and the effects it had on families and lives. I look back at Bipolar Disorder with a lot of grace and gratitude for what it has brought and taught me. I wanted it to be heard by people who were going through the same thing and were torn between accepting fate but wanting change to start taking place within the mental health sector and in black communities. I no longer want to hide away from what was such an impactful and major part of my life but that also, affects many people within my community. This poem was my part of a larger testimony and sparked many of my future endeavours, it was definitely the start of something."

-

May we never meet again.
I saw you in him and ever since then, I hated you.
You came when I was supposed to be filled with love,
Rambling about his plans, impulsive spending, irritability and having loads of
energy without sleep - I thought he was invincible.
Flourished with gifts,
I thought I was special,
because we all love being showered with expensive things.
Little did I know there was such a thing as living within your means.
Bipolar was the root of everything.

Then the lowest mood of all came,
He didn't feel worthy of being in my presence
He would say things that made me fear he would end his life.
It was a different ball game.
Anger consumed him, violence and loneliness was his friend,

For the first time ever,
I saw something dark and scary in him.
The most fearless person I knew became fearful,
I distanced myself from him.
His anger towards others around me shattered my world,
Confused, not only because I didn't know what was going on
but as an eight-year-old the words 'mental' and 'ill' didn't quite register in my brain for too long.
I mixed up the person I knew with the person I thought he was,
Do you know how hard it is understanding that you've never quite known who someone really is?
The identity before this illness,
you were oblivious to all of it.

Bipolar deprived me and my world of someone we should've loved,
Even now society doesn't really understand it,
Quick to say
Are you sure you're not bipolar?
When someone has a change in attitude or isn't in the mood
They don't want be around it,
It is so much more than that.

To the world he was crazy,
They always fear the unknown.
Intellectually he was thriving,
Friends would predict his future as one of those who would go far.
So educated they said.
Why is it education didn't extend to the mental health sector?
And in the black culture, being private is the only thing we know,
We kept it within concealing it from our external world,
A chapter in our lives that we don't read out loud,
Like many other family embarrassments,
Bipolar became our dirty little secret.
Even seeking medical assistance from doctors who couldn't tell the difference,
Between bipolar and our culture,

Didn't provide much assistance.
It was so easy for them to prescribe medicine as a solution for everything.
I used to say, why don't they just talk to him?
Because to him the pill made him a zombie,
All emotions and heightened desires suppressed,
I just couldn't relate.

I didn't understand why God wanted my world and bipolar to integrate.
The disorder became part of him, it consumed him,
you know, I think I feared it more than him.
Thinking when those pills wear off he'll just be the victim again,
An ongoing cycle of a personified illness thinking it can take whoever it pleases,
I pleaded with bipolar to leave him,
It had a ripple effect.

When he gave up on treatment.
And a mother lost a son and a wife lost her husband.
The day bipolar became a part of his life,
A part of him died.
I hated my God for that,
Until I realised all things that are happening to me are happening for me.
The losses bipolar gave me were all lessons even blessings.
I've learnt that this man-made world sometimes is full of pressure and obstacles
We need to breakthrough.
As a community,
We act like mental health is something we deal with on the inside,
People don't feel comfortable telling us that their mind just isn't right,
they hold it in.
Until one day they reach a breaking point and can't take it anymore,
Pushing away everyone that could've helped,
This would've all been fixed if we checked up on ourselves and others from time to time.

Tomorrow's not promised,

Most people are even deceiving themselves in thinking hiding it is the only way,

Bipolar is the reason I'm here on this page.

Mental health affects us all.,

Maybe not at the same time in our lives,

we can't just say it's for them to deal with and be numb to it all.

Don't let society make you think you can't speak out on it,

And remember that your world doesn't just start and end with this bubble,

We call a United Kingdom now.

And I'd love it if this poem inspired you somehow.

Days You Missed

"For the majority of my life I felt like I missed out on having someone play the role of the Father, there were moments that I became bitter for not being able to experience certain moments with my Dad. This poem summarises this."

-

Welcome to the day of parents evening,

The time you never showed up,

Teachers weren't even surprised because they knew the stereotype,

Do you know what they say about the child you supposedly love?

Talks too much, doesn't do all of the work and has a future just needs to straighten up,

And she would always look at me with that stare that meant 'wait until we get home',

The time you weren't there,

Because she was the only discipliner that day.

Welcome to the day of my first heartbreak,

The time when I thought the only boy who could ever love me had betrayed my trust,

And though he did me wrong, he was the only man who showed me the right
kind of love,
The inner voice within that affirmed my beautiful existence
About a love I should've learnt from you a long time ago,
You broke my heart way before he did
Did you know I cried for you that day?

Forgiving my father

"When I wrote this, I remember watching Iyanla Vanzant's show on OWN
Network about 'Daddy-less daughters' and thinking for the first time that I
could relate. Although my situation was a unique one, being that my Father's
absence was not in his control, I did recognise that this shaped the woman I
was and who I was going to become. I am extremely grateful for the lessons
it taught me about forgiveness and removing expectations from those with
whom didn't ever get a manual on how to raise me and battled with their
mind. I wrote this for women, black women especially, whose lives became
dictated by the absence of a father and wanted more for themselves. This
wasn't to paint my father in a bad light, I am truly grateful for all he taught
me and I really wanted to pass on those lessons to other women and men. "

-

I told myself that if this is released then I will have fully moved on from
this subject, a subject that used to be such a personal burden on my life.
As a child, you always yearn for unconditional love and affection from your
parents or an influential figure; it's a natural form of understanding that you
want to make your presence known and an affirmation of love. When you're
a baby you cry because you want someone to pick you up and hold you, you
try and outdo your siblings through academics or various talents that you
have and for some children, they behave differently to get attention in the
form of discipline etc. As a child, you are programmed to equate the love you
are shown by your parents with how much you are loved in society (society
referring to the little bubble that you are in until adulthood). My experience
has been very similar to many young girls in society. I grew up with a single
mother that showed me exactly how an 'independent woman who doesn't

need a man' should be; the words resilience, honesty and integrity always spring to mind when I think of how I saw my mother. Parents separating can be hard on any child as this means the idea of two separate families, different celebrations, splitting bills and arguments about how the children should be raised and who should raise them. Amid all the confusion and heartache, I often reflect on how parents fail to realise how this affects their children.

Mainly spending time with my mother and the gradual decrease in time spent with my biological father meant that I became the dreaded 'fatherless daughter'. Although some of my father's absence was within reason due to health issues, a lot of it was down to, in my opinion, an inability to understand what a father was. It was not until I turned 18 that I realised this meant my outlook on what a man was and my relationships with men was affected. Someone once said: 'Anyone can be a father but it takes a real man to be a Dad'. The idea of a 'Dad' was more than just a phone call for Christmas and birthdays or the occasional and rare transfer of money; it was the proclamation of love that every daughter or son should hear about.

Sometimes I think maybe I expected too much from my father and in doing that, I failed to see how amazing of a job my mother, my stepfather and other father-figures in my life have done. When he was there he taught me about knowledge and learning, an incredibly educated man who had a real passion for changing things in the world. But as a child I needed more, and I expected more. Today I can say I am more confident in who I am than I have ever been. Forgiveness was key in moving on as a daughter who missed out on her Father playing the roles he should have. I remember a pastor in a youth Church a while ago preaching that 'forgiveness is the final form of love'. I forgive my Father for not being a constant in my life or not fulfilling the role that I thought he should have filled. The baggage of the past should not be carried into the present. Understand that forgiveness can be for your own peace of mind and it should be.

Did you know I cried for you that day?

-

'Anyway, I just wanted to say that I had a good weekend with you. Well we always do, don't we? You know, thinking about us going shopping, watching 'I'm a Celebrity'. Well, you're watching it, I'm sort of grimacing. It's the small things that really keep me going, alright.'

'Would you rather sweat porridge, or cry sawdust?'

'I'll always be proud of you. Alright, night-night sausage.'

-

A man leaves an affectionate message for his daughter while driving slowly through a carwash. As he recalls their weekend together and memories from her childhood, it becomes clear that this is more than just a catch-up.

'The Wall' was commissioned for Channel 4's Random Acts and Best 18-25's Film Nomination at BFI Future Film Festival.

The main idea for *The Wall* comes from an event in my life that I wanted to explore through film. Actually, it wasn't so much that I 'wanted to', but more that each time I tried to develop another story I kept returning to this one. It's a tricky subject to tackle in a three-minute short, but I was keen to attempt it, particularly because one of the main reasons there's so much stigma around mental health and suicide is because we find it so hard to talk about. So my aim was to present a character who's a loving father and is totally relatable and funny, but also suffers with severe depression.

I needed to be able to detach myself from the weight of the narrative, in order to go through the process of making the film, and fiction was very useful for that.

Making films (or any form of art) can be a useful way of processing what life throws at you, and I think the film medium lends itself particularly well to subjects that can't necessarily be explained, but can be embodied by fictional characters. You can also create visual metaphors and layer dialogue over music, which helps to create a sense of someone's mental state.

I hope that what people take from this film is a sense that there are many complex reasons why people take their own lives and while it can't necessarily be fully understood, we should at least acknowledge that it's a very real problem, and that those affected by it can be loving, funny, intelligent, multi-dimensional people.

-

Every year, on 24 November, we mark my brother's birthday. There is no cake or family dinner, but it usually arrives in the form of a hug, a reassuring touch on the back or another silent acknowledgement. Jonathan, my brother, died when I was five years old. I rarely speak about it, but have become better at being able to do so over the years. He was a few months shy of 21 when he died, two years younger than I am now. While I have left home, started a new job abroad and have made a life for myself, I am constantly aware that these are the things Jonathan was about to do before he was denied his right to embark upon his adult life. Sometimes I wonder what could have been, what he would be up to and if he might have had a family of his own at this point. But what has struck me, now more than ever, is the difficulty that my father has speaking about what happened to our family, and his reluctance to approach or mention the subject of my brother.

In the summer of 2016, after I graduated and moved home in that post-university daze, my father and I packed away the things in Jonathan's room, many of which had been left untouched for the last 16 years. We placed his ice skating trophies, ice hockey jerseys and his paintings, now all neatly organised, into those stackable clear plastic boxes, all the while only muttering minimal meaningless chit-chat to each other. I found a folder full of documents relating to the traumatic circumstances that surrounded Jonathan's death, and chose to stay quiet. I packed it away into the box with all his other things - this folder that had his death certificate in, newspaper cuttings about his death that my mother had saved, the police report. All these things that I so desperately wanted to speak to my father about but feared that I would be met with a one-word answer and a stony silence, as has traditionally been the case when it comes to Jonathan.

A couple of days after my brother's birthday that year, evoking such strong feelings in me and still barely an acknowledgement from my father, I attended the Southbank Centre's annual Being A Man Festival - it seemed like the timing was fate. Initially, I went along to try and do some research for an article on masculinity and mental health, a topic I'd been wanting to explore for a while, but didn't make the connection of how close to home it was. Male suicide is the biggest killer of men aged under 45 in the UK, and a 2016 study showed that while 67% of females who felt very depressed said they talked to someone about it, only 55% of males said the same.

While commemorative days and months can sometimes seem patronising and tokenistic, important campaigns around men's health, specifically male mental health, have traditionally taken place in November by organisations such as The Samaritans, Campaign Against Living Miserably(CALM) and Movember. The last few years have also seen a rise in high-profile men speaking out about their personal struggles with mental health. The frankness of Stormzy, Professor Green, Rio Ferdinand and Princes William and Harry to name a few, is truly refreshing to see and gives me hope that men across our society can recognise that they are not alone. These campaigns, like the Royal Family's Heads Together initiative, have done amazing work of highlighting issues that are nowhere near as well reported, researched or even simply talked about as they should be.

So I went to the festival, hoping to ask some probing questions about how feminist movements and male advocacy campaigns can work together, and to find out what International Men's Day was all about. Instead, I found myself attempting to control that familiar choking feeling in your throat when you're holding back tears, whilst attending a panel discussion that, of course, was called 'Boys Don't Cry'. And as I was listening to the panellists speak about their experiences with depression, grief and suicide, it dawned on me that their words had provoked my unexpectedly visceral reaction because I recognised that what they were describing was the behaviour of my own father. The shame they had felt in expressing their pain, the destructive reactions to triggering events in their own lives, the unbearable pressure to keep up appearances and "be a man" - it all sounded too familiar.

Jonathan was my father's golden boy, his "anchor" as my mum once put it. And after he died, my dad lost his way. In some ways, I don't think he's has been able to find it since. I recall my mother once telling me that she had encouraged him to seek help from a support group, but this suggestion was slapped down by a family friend, another man, who said to my dad "You don't need any of that therapy stuff, you're strong, you'll be fine.". My parents had just lost their son in an unexpected, tragic way, and my father's emotions were simply dismissed, as if it was something that could easily be brushed off. I feel a sting of anger even now as I write, thinking what that exchange must have been like to experience for my father, to feel like he couldn't talk about our insurmountable loss. No-one would really call my father a wallflower - in fact, in many ways, he's the opposite. When we're around most people, he's theatrical, embarrassing (as all dads are) and the life and soul of the party. I just want him to know that I understand why he does that, why he acts in this way - and that I understand why he does not want to acknowledge the reality of what happened.

Masculinity has traditionally been a societal stereotype directly opposing the negative stereotypes of women that we're all too familiar with. Men = strong, protector, provider, invulnerable. Women = fragile, emotional, delicate, weak. Yet as Jack Urwin so brilliantly put it in his 2014 article 'A Stiff Upper Lip Is Killing Men' and his follow-up book entitled Man Up: Surviving Modern Masculinity, the knock on effects of this tight-lipped, keep-your-emotions-under-lock-and-key expectation of men can quite literally be fatal. Comedian and CALM Ambassador Jack Rooke tells me that "my female support network worked better than ever trying to talk to my older brothers" after Jack's father died when he was 15. "For my granddad, the bereavement was really traumatic to the point of triggering dementia in him. The loss can accelerate the process, and he just suppressed his pain so much...eventually he started to think that I was my dad."

The *Being A Man* festival showed me just how heterogeneous masculinity can be, as I listened to men open up about the most personal, intimate details in their lives. Following this subject closely in the two years since, I am so heartened to see more and more men speaking out about their experiences with mental health. When gal-dem published an earlier version of this article in November 2016, I was unsure of how it would be received. Would people think I was oversharing? Would it change anyone's opinion, or just have no impact at all? Of course, these things are difficult to tell. But the private messages I received from male friends after I shared the article, some of whom were acquaintances I hadn't spoken to in a long time and all of whom from different circles of my past and present, showed me that this is a conversation that we often shy away from, but desperately need to have. Masculinity is such a multidimensional, diverse concept and means something different to every man - but only if we allow ourselves to see it that way.

My brother, all that he was and is, is an unspoken taboo between myself and my father. I don't think we have ever had one honest, meaningful conversation about Jonathan as a person, let alone his death. I have only seen my father cry on a handful of occasions throughout my lifetime. Grief for my father, as for many men, is so difficult to come to terms with precisely because it renders you vulnerable to emotional, agonising reactions that you cannot control. I can see the burden of grief he carries, and sometimes I simply wish that he would share it with me, to lighten the load. "Vulnerability is the absolute key to men having a better time in the future," the artist Grayson Perry says, and that resonates with me so much. To hear men speak so candidly and frankly about their experiences struggling with depression and grief is powerful, precisely because they are allowing themselves to be vulnerable in a way we might never associate with them. I hope that one day, as painful as I am certain it will be, my father will feel that he is able to do the same, and to hopefully share it with me.

-

Illustration, on following page, by Leyla Reynolds

449

It is incredibly problematic that Cisgender Men are forced to keep their emotions to themselves in fear of judgement and ridicule. Undoubtedly, this has a colossal impact on mental health, isolation and self-worth. I believe that I had quite an unconventional upbringing due to the fact that my Father had no boundaries with me, he was completely open about his vulnerabilities to the point where I see him as a friend as well as a parent. On the other hand, due to having a traumatic upbringing, where he experienced physical and mental abuse, he ended up inheriting destructive habits, which come out in the form of anger. He had to endure borstal (youth detention centre) and prison at various stages of his life. This has made him quite defensive, I had to deal with his anger issues, and we would argue quite a lot as a result.

On a positive note, now that time has moved on, we have learned how to communicate in more of a diplomatic way. I love how courageous my Dad is; we cry together and work through issues through having long and deep conversations about life. I feel privileged to be able to share this process, and encourage others to do the same with their Fathers to heal, and move away from intergenerational trauma. Men are sensitive beings too, they need to open up, talking can act as a means of reflection. By exploring trauma and it's ripple effects, I hope to move forward with My Dad and think about how we can get to know each other more.

My Mum had me at eighteen and you were nineteen, do you have any advice for young Dad's?

Gregory Hill: Yeah! To not be in Prison when your girlfriend is pregnant would be a good start.

Was that quite stressful?

G.H: STRESSFUL!!? It was an impossible situation, I had one year left to go, I was not there, as a Dad and I felt absolutely useless in every way. That is why I took it upon myself to get out of there and escape. It is intense, but you wouldn't be on the phone if it weren't for that. Although we were young, abortion wasn't really the done thing at that time to be honest with you, when your Mum said that was what she was going to do I couldn't handle it. I had loads of teenage friends who had children; they just dealt with it you know? Now it's a lot more different isn't it?

Some Dad's find it hard to nurture their kids, it's as if they find it hard to connect.

G.H: I see it all the time. When Debra (Mother of my step-sister & step-brother, Molly and JJ) and I were still together, her parents and grandparents would come and visit. Neither of them knew how to get on their knees, play cars with them and interact, they would just sit on the sofa and watch sports. They would talk a good bit about being granddad but if I left JJ or Molly with them - they would be screaming for me. That is the bottom line, they don't know them because they haven't put in the time to take them anywhere, or do stuff with them. Then they can't get to see who you are, or even get comfortable around you, which is horrible. If I was a Granddad or Dad and my kids didn't know me properly I would feel like a total failure, because my Kids would want nothing to do with me. You need to make an effort. They want the glamour, the representation of being a Dad, but they don't want to put the hard work in. The hard work is playing with them, even though you're tired.

I suppose the main thing that people need to do is get onto their kid's wavelength and enjoy life with them. What would you say to Dad's who are finding it hard to make that connection?

G.H: Get amongst it, get the playdough out - don't worry about having to clean it up for hours because that is what they want and you have to put them first. Also, because I don't see them all the time, I have had a break so I can deal with it better and I can do a lot more with them. If I didn't have that break, I don't know how I could deal with it, I would have a break down. I genuinely don't know how single Mum's and Dad's can do it. It's like trying to have three jobs at once, or one part time job, it's another world - it can be so hard.

In consideration of your parents distant and abusive tendencies... What do you want to do differently as a Dad, in comparison to how they brought you up?

G.H: I still feel like I have a bit of my Dad in me. I am not saying that I am a rapist, or that I would ever beat my children up. But I feel his rage, and it comes out of me in different ways, like if I am training or get into a fight - I turn into a crazy bastard. That's just genetics, he was into what he was into and it has had an effect on me.

This is really significant, we ingest our trauma - and it can be hard to escape what has been handed to you by your parents... With you, you are good at expressing your emotions but anger is one of them that comes up a lot.

G.H: Rage is rage, and I need to find ways to get rid of it. My way of getting rid of that rage is smoking weed, training and lifting weights, and keeping myself distracted. Otherwise, it is the wrong person who is on the end of it and receives that rage. It is never the right person who has to deal with it; I should be taking it out on my Mum and Dad rather than some poor sod on a Morrison's counter.

How do you relax?

G.H: I have this thing where I watch films that I am familiar with, if I watch something new it can be too overstimulating for me because of my illness. I suffer from functional tremors and central syndrome seizures. I can't watch a new show like most people, like if I were to watch EastEnders or something about shooting I would get overwhelmed. I would get too emotional if there was anything sad about kids, I wouldn't be able to deal with it - I know it sounds funny.

You have been through quite a lot, how has that affected you and your outlook?

G.H: The life experience that I have had has been negative; it has made me very hard and suspicious, hyper vigilant, suspicious of the government and generally a paranoid person to be honest. Not with my kids, but in general I don't trust a fucking thing. I wanted to prepare you for the big bad world; I think that is why I was so honest with you.

What are your views on social justice?

G.H: Sajid Javid (Cabinet minister who is the first senior appointee of Muslim heritage) has brought up an argument for cannabis legalisation - why is it that white people can't do that? Why is it that we needed someone from a completely different class system and a different perspective, with some colour in his skin to say, look, it's not satisfactory - the policy on drugs in the UK doesn't suit patients, we need to issue some licenses. Over the last two months, there has been a new minister who has come along and started to change things for the better, fair play to him - we need more honest people like that who are not scared to tell the truth. He has the touch of being well connected to British people, he has his finger on the pulse of real life. I bet that he's not living in Chichester or whatever, he seems real. The white man is too scared to challenge the system, whereas the other fella said what was on his mind because he was lucky to have the job in the first place.
It makes my blood boil to think that these people are making decisions, The House of Commons doesn't have any common people in it!

Do you feel like being open with your kids is important? And what are the dangers of holding yourself back as a Man?

G.H: You won't be able to have a fulfilling life, unless you put yourself forward, you're not going to get anywhere are you?

Read more about Male Wellbeing:
http://www.hystericalfeminisms.com/voices1/2016/10/22/male-circumcision-is-a-feminist-issue-too
http://www.blackhealthinitiative.org/mens-health-and-wellbeing/
http://www.menshealthresourcecenter.com/mental-health-well-being/
https://thepsychologist.bps.org.uk/volume-28/february-2015/unheard-victims

'...challenging and raw, thank you for prompting me to do something this healing with my Dad.'

Gregory Hill photographed outside his old home in Norfolk (Hempnall), 2016

Words and Photography: Yasmine Akim

'*Mujer (WoMan)*', **FEMI OSHODI / MOONCHILE**

-

I learnt manlihood through my mother's pain
in my father's absence

see my hands are good at digging holes
but not so much at filling roles

what does it mean to be a son? a brother?
simply a being who cares for another

i learnt manlihood through a broken mirror
when you see half the picture
the rest is yours to paint

your own story
your own words
a true reflection
not society's curse;

the pressure to be, all that you are not
we too are half woman, have we forgot?

i learnt my masculinity is not defined by the width of my jeans, nor annulled
by the grace in my steps
the water in my bones

i'm learning to unlearn - to let go

i'm learning to speak soft, to speak true
and remember when you're taught not to be tender
paper beats rock every time.

'Since January 2014, my life has been upside down; Autism of my son, I had got used to it and helped my son since a young age to cope with this and he seemed to me more or less a Happy person until mental health struck. The ups and downs with Mental health of my son has changed our lives - not only his life but also all our families. Life is not anymore the same - uncertainties, anxieties, sadness, sleeplessness, not knowing what comes next - next month, next week, next day and even next hour - so unpredictable my son has become. I try to adjust constantly and keep my hope but it is tough! I feel at times drowned and wonder whether the psychiatric hospitals and drugs given to alleviate his mental health - anxieties and depression help him really? whether the solution is somewhere else? but where? how do we turn things back to where we were a few years ago?

But then sometimes my son gives me hope; he seems almost recovered and talks and jokes as before - this is when I say to myself, let me keep fighting; it is not all dark and he will come back and laugh - his weird and happy laugh which I miss! Yes it will - he will learn to manage it! My wish is to see him recover, and do things as before and laugh and quarrel with his twin sister and me seeing them from the corner of my sofa being happy both of them!!!! I want to see that before I depart from this World - so that I can rest!'

'Y's mum' , SHOA ASFAHA

'Untitled', CONNOR MCLEOD

-

A never knew ma Granda'
But he 'wis a grafter'
Fell fae a ladder
and died shortly after.

A barely know ma Faither,
But he 'wis a grafter'
Couldny stand ma Mother
so left shortly after.

A wis lucky a had ma Mother,
She made me a 'bit safter'
A platted ma sister's hair,
Played with My Little Pony
and bathed it.

-

The Descent of Man explores male gender stereotypes and what it means to be a 'man' today. Looking at masculinity and the perceptions and anxieties that come with it. It is a collection of works on working class masculinity. Reclaiming words that used to make me feel de-masculinised and putting them in the context of the ultra-hyper masculine world that I no longer inhabit.

'My furniture production job consists of a lot of strategic and practical thinking; this personal project gave me the freedom to design furniture with no boundaries. Giving myself opportunities to ignore reality gives me an escape from being pragmatic. Furniture plays a big part in everyone's day to day. Involving emotion just takes that to the next personal level.' ,
JOSHUA CHECKLEY

Pipe Mood Chair

Acrylic tubing filled with thermochromic ink that reacts to its environment and how you are feeling, :) or :(.

Defrost Affection Bench

Lonely times this winter can be cured! This acrylic and steel tube bench, customisable with heating element design of your favourite message from a loved one, provides a small amount of warmth and is just uncomfortable enough to remind you to appreciate human embrace.

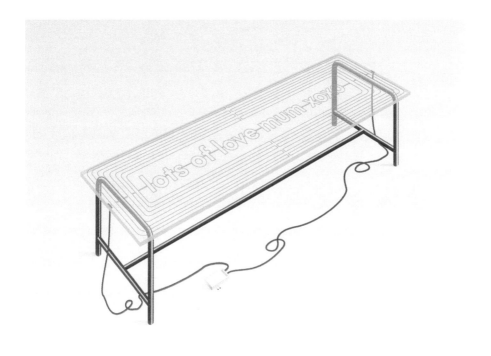

'Creativity for me is an authentic release or provocation of emotion. I had something to prove to them before, that I'm okay, and then they were both gone. I wrote the book before they were gone. The weight of what I've been through is incomprehensible to people, so the go to is going out. Creativity, I think it's just emotions, feelings, more than creativity. That's what we label it as today, as a society. I wasn't trying to create anything; it was mainly about release.' , **KHARIIS UBIARO**

-

The Noise in My Head

I just need to quiet the noise in my head
the noise that doesn't belong to a particular voice, the noise of insanity, I dread
I dread, I dread, I dread what's being said
influenced and infiltrated, engulfed and emancipated
the noise in my head has taken over
a cacophony of sounds, an anthem in the round, screams, sirens, pure vulgarity
        and violence, I can't deal
the noise in my head disabled my ability to feel
to feel and thrive but caused a lack of emotion
a crowd of consequences from noises within my head
this noise tells me that I'm better off dead better off sitting in a gutter, flickers
        and flutters
onomatopoeia I need it to stop
headed in and hearing from the wrong direction an ultimate inception
I just need to quiet the noise in my head

My Mind's Dark Party

there is beauty in death
changing states, passing though this life into the next
souls changing, passing through liberal matter

Imagination is an Eye

imagination is an eye within itself
positive thoughts and ideas sustain good mental health

realms that manifest pigments from extraterrestrial entities dissected fractions
and segments from another plane influencing the way we live,
a poisoned potential
– one that doubts surrealism
it is disbelief that creates a corrosive heart
imagine, imagining is the key to seeing externally what we as people
       internally desire
synergy between thoughts to summon our ambition
our hope
our freedom
freedom to dwell within another dimension
not to mention that we are products of our own making
induced with digested doctrines
yes
but we have a choice
a choice to listen to that subtle subconscious voice that speaks
speaks to no-one but ourselves
to create ideas that become viral and spread like disease, a rapid growth
       of franchise and branches, to create paper from trees
the origins of all came from one mind
to share thoughts and feelings and plans and meaning
from mind to mind
but I don't mind sounding peculiar and abnormal
realise and recognise that everything happens first inside
so know that thoughts create paths that steadily create literal roads
playing with paper planes in plain sight, a stimulus to build and unfold
the highest form of creativity through thought is imagination
imagine a nation of people that thought and fought for themselves,
emancipated from mental slavery
it is no-one but ourselves that can free our minds

cascading cans of cans and can'ts creep into calm minds
can'ts corrupt and cans congratulate
conflict is caused between the clauses
the collateral damage is us
convicted by crude conversations that congregate in our minds
so-called coincidental casualties conspired with our beings
castrating crystal clear thoughts
these are the thoughts of others that try to influence our own

imagination is an eye within itself
positive thoughts and ideas sustain good mental health

'The pilgrim & the vortex', 'Chamber of reflection',
'Golden Teacher IV', 'Lunar feelings for the new born',
'Transcending of Malcolm X', 'Untitled Series', 2015, 2016,2018,
CHRISTIAN QUINN NEWELL VIOTTO

-

Peace of mind is a stable foundation for starting any piece of work.

We all want to bring about something that can help us out.
Art is the science of transcendence, to go beyond and rise above, it works
on our mind, body & spirit.

We can bring about balance in our being if we are willing to
cultivate self-discipline towards following healthy practices.

I favour automatic drawings and collage making when planning to
create bigger paintings.
You're dealing with archetypes so you understand straight away what's
going on, it's not dogmatic, rather open to interpretation, like a Rorschach
test, you learn a lot about yourself whilst creating.

In that moment you share the power of God, not in amount but in kind, you
can decide how you want things to turn out. It's up to you how you want to
feel.

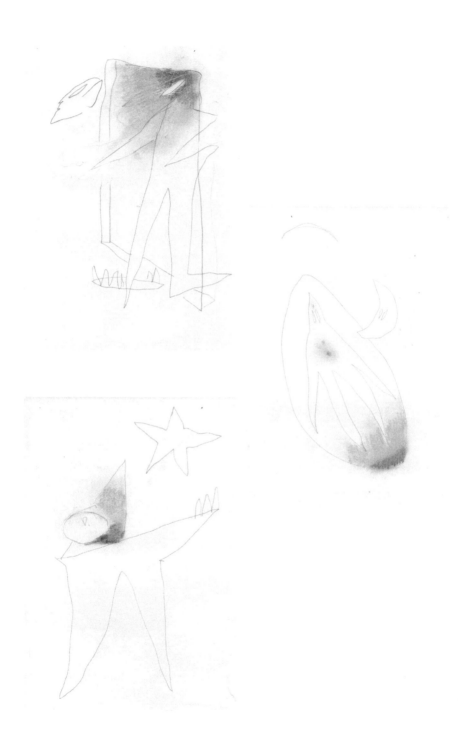

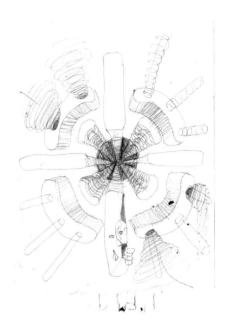

TRANSCENDING
OF MALCOLM X

M

We're constantly taught in our western society to seek manifestation, to bring about this and bring about that.

We like to play tricks on ourselves to help us forget that all objective things will eventually come to an end, if we cannot see the essence of a thing and only focus on its form, we will never find true, everlasting happiness or enjoyment in that thing or in anything.

But if we direct our attentions to seeking clarity in all things, in the present, through selflessness and meditation, this is the art of happiness.

'A call to love', 'Regressions of youth, the troublesome encounters through the walls of hell', 'To awaken from dream-like slumber',
'Untitled (notes) ', 'Untitled (subconcious)', 2015, 2018

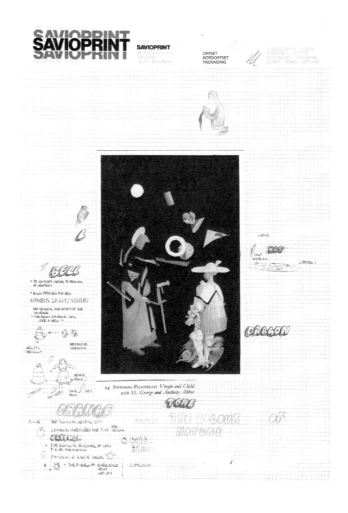

*"It's just the way I'm Feeling; Me, myself & I; Fragile;
Pull yourself together; Man Up; In Pieces; the state I'm in;
Putting on a Brave Face..."* , **MILO MAX**

-

It's hard to write a description, as I want the viewers to take away what they want for themselves. I was looking at multiple personality disorder and how we judge people on their exterior without really knowing what they are feeling or thinking inside. I love the use of colour and naivety when I'm painting and try to keep things as simple as possible. Bi polar Alone.

'Backstory' , **BADÉ FATONA**

-

Back story - Every story being told has one of its own to tell.
There is a background to every story that mightn't ever be told.
The rear is sometimes more telling than the front; more storied.
For it influences and drives the tales played out in the act of life.

These are the men of Backstory.

Paris, Tokyo,
2017, 2018

'Boy Brain', GAL AMIT

-

I didn't try to portray the male brain.
It's not flat like this. It's not multidimensional neither.
I've never seen one, really.

I asked him, what's in there? 3000 minutes later he came back with an answer.
Chains? "Yeah, chains. It's locked in."

Can it move? How do you navigate such a thing?

"I don't know. I don't have permission to explore that."

You need permission? I asked him.

"Yeah. It serves as a key."

'can I call you for a sec' , **ROXANNE FARAHMAND**

-

An exploration into human interaction, through the eyes of technology.
Are you ever really alone when everyone you know and care about is on your
screen? Are you comfy answering these questions? Why are you looking away
when you answer that? Have you done this before? Why is this the first time
you're doing this? What's wrong with you...

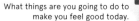

What things are you going to do to
make you feel good today.

Do you sleep well.

What was the first thing you think about
when you wake.

What's an important part of the day.

How often do you eat.

What's worrying you.

Are you worried now.

When was the last time you cried.

How has your day been.

How often do you think about your
mental health.

Do you do anything to help yourself.

Are you going to sleep well tonight.

What will you do to ensure that you do
sleep well.

If you was an animal, what would you
be.

-

In 2016 I started a postgraduate job interning for documentary distributor Journeyman Pictures. During my time there, I discovered a short doc in their archive titled 'Radio Colifata', which tracked the beginnings of the now famous institution in Buenos Aires, Argentina. The film follows 'Radio Colifata' founder Alfredo Olivera, as he recounts his journey to set up the first public radio station to broadcast from within a psychiatric hospital. His hope was that the patients of the hospital would find an outlet of expression through the project, and that its broadcast would help raise awareness and further conversations about mental health in Argentina.

I was struck by the film's portrayal of the necessity of the discussion in Argentina; the way the project had changed the patients' experiences in the hospitals, and the content of the radio programme itself, which included original songs, and music by the patients. Olivera was largely prompted by a desire to confront the stigma surrounding mental illness in Argentina, issues equally in need of discussion in the UK. I wanted to dramatise the story and pay tribute to the impetus of 'Radio Colifata' in some way, and so began work on a fictional piece following a parallel character's introduction of a similar project in Croydon, London. The play's linear narrative tracks their attempt to set up a station similar to 'Radio Colifata', looking closely at the obstacles they face and the concerns raised. This broad structure is then interspersed with excerpts from the show itself, i.e.: monologues and performances from patients. This submission for 'Him+His' is an early construction of that central character, as well as a monologue and scene detailing the initial inspiration for the project.

When I was approached to submit to 'Him + His', I was keen to present something from 'Voice Box'. The completed work will explore mental health issues from a variety of angles, but the core plot of this play focuses particularly on a man's experience of mental health. We see this in the challenges the central character encounters in discussing their own mental health, as well as the mental health of loved ones, and society as a whole. It is continually pressed into young boys and men via the demands of hyper-masculine stereotypes, that talking about your feelings or showing emotion is a sign of weakness. I hope this piece will rebuke that notion, and illustrate how expressing yourself, connecting with others, and asking for help, can so often be a positive step towards recovery for men, women and non-binary people alike. I hope the central character's voicing of his experiences of mental health, and his commitment to support, encourages and champions the voices of others, demonstrating a better alternative to silence, for all.

Protagonist 1

Jay is 35. After a brief stint as a music producer/MC in his late teens and early twenties, he married young to please his parents and made a living as an office temp, doing admin for various companies. His wife left him a few years before, after falling for a man who made it very clear he was in love with her. Jay never made it clear. When she left him, Jay felt lost and vulnerable, though he did not miss her, and the combination of these feelings made him doubt an essential goodness in himself he had always prized. As a child he was loud and extroverted, but sensitive and fundamentally kind, particularly to his school friends, who looked up to him. He is quieter now. He has spent the last few years itching to be more involved in volunteering in the local community, doing social work of some kind, but at present he has pretty abstract ideas of how to do so. His father died when he was thirty, and though he loves his mother, he is in limited contact with her, phone calls here and there. He has an older sister called Carolina (who he calls Cee, or occasionally CC), who emigrated to an unknown location in South America and is estranged from the family entirely. Carolina suffers from borderline personality disorder. Jay and she were very close as children. They shared bunkbeds. Jay is possessed by his work / aspirations and presently unbothered by his singleness, though we get the sense that he would like a child, someone to mentor, teach and care for, and that this would be his preferred way to express his feelings.

We meet Jay at the peak of an anxious and slightly manic period. He feels he is seeing more cases, and hearing more stories of friends and acquaintances' mental health deteriorating, of traumatic things happening which they do not recover from - maybe a specific example prompts him. He's also been becoming more interested in the work of his current company, and social work in general. They organise group therapy sessions for those suffering from mild to moderate mental health conditions. He knows he wants to help and get involved in the work that they do, and he spends a long time trying to work out exactly how to do so before inspiration strikes. He reads about 'Radio Colifata'. He decides he wants to try something similar in his local area in the UK (Croydon, South London), and begins working on a proposal.

Monologue 1

Jay: I got my first tape recorder when I was five. God I was so chuffed. It was a chunky plastic thing with gigantic yellow buttons on top, and it had a little microphone on it. You could speak into it and record yourself. Rewind, press play and just like that, the thing was speaking to you. The shock of hearing your own voice played back to you never gets old huh? Of course when I was five I would mostly repeat gibberish to myself, bleh bloo blah blah, nah na na naa naa, blow raspberries, make fart noises, you get the gist. Occasionally though, I'd speak into that mic like it was a portal into another world. Hello? Is there anybody out there? That little voice in my tape recorder was a friend to me. A hidden presence, there for sure. How are you today Mr Tape Recorder Man? (chuckles). I reckon it had all the answers. That was only the beginning for me and that little cassette player. Next big discovery was the voices inside that spoke all on their own. [The magic, sheer magic] of radio. Who were these people? Did they know that I was there too, laughing at their jokes? When I was sick in bed with tonsillitis, I would lie curled up around that thing, ear pressed to the speaker, listening to the breakfast shows [in total awe.] I swear they made me better all on their own. The voices, and the songs. I used to get so excited when I heard something new, or when I heard something I recognised. Would always try, and fail, to sing along. Never could hold a tune. Not like the singers, not like Cee. But I'd give it a good old go. Just to annoy her. I swear there was never a moment in my life I couldn't pair with a certain song. [Never a time I couldn't match with music.] And now it's like I hear those songs and those moments come alive in me. (pause). I think that maybe, you know you're in trouble when that trick stops working. When you hear a song and nothing happens. When you hear the voices and nothing happens. (pause) I know that's what it was like for Cee. She couldn't hear the music.

Scene 1

We are in a cluttered study. It is hot, Jay enters, turns on a fan, walks to the window and looks out with his back to the audience. Pause. He approaches a record player, previously invisible beneath a pile of papers. He shifts the papers and pulls a record from a blank sleeve, Street Fighting Man by The Rolling Stones. Pauses. Listens. Changes the record to something slower. Maybe Pieces of a Man by Gil Scott Heron. He goes to sit in his chair, at an angle away from the desk and window, looking out diagonally at the audience. He picks up a microphone and a tape recorder left in a pile by his chair, lifts the microphone to his lips and presses record.

JAY: Testing

(Pause)

JAY: Testing, testing, 1, 2, 3.

(Longer pause).

(Exaggerated impression)

JAY: Good Morning Croydon

(Laughs ironically, clears throat, turns to look at digital clock on the desk)

JAY: The time is 6.32, and uh, we're feeling good this morning.

(Pause)

JAY: Feeling positive.

(Pause)

(Exaggerated impression)

JAY: I know you think this is a bad idea Caroline, but we're doing it anyway. You're not always right.

(Pause)

Sometimes you're very wrong.

(Pauses and pushes his desk chair over to the window where he peeps through the blinds with two fingers, then returns to his previous position, holding the microphone to his mouth as he speaks)

JAY: My name is Jay Phoenix. I'll be your host today. I haven't done this kind of thing in a while so you'll have to bear with me. I used to be quite good at it. I think. My friends say I'm a little washed up at the moment. Maybe they're right. Despite what appearances might suggest, I actually feel better than I have in years. I feel like I might be able to do something, something good for some other people, for once. Maybe reach some people that need reaching. Speak to some people. My problem, the problem I guess I'm facing with this is, uh, I'm what some might call a man of few words. I've always found it easier to write things down, or to put my feelings into things which aren't words, I guess. But I am trying to be more open. This is me trying to be more open. We need to get better at talking about the things inside us I think. I'd like to give it a go anyway. Got to lead by example, haven't I? Which brings me to my theme:

(Pauses to remove a folded piece of paper from his pocket, clears his throat)

JAY: Songs to start the day right. I first heard this little number when I was seventeen. Tried and failed dismally to perform it myself. Never could get the hook right. Now I want you to enjoy this one folks and please do ring in with your own requests. We love hearing your thoughts here at uh (cough) this as-yet-unnamed station. Thank you for tuning in...good day and uh, take care.

(Small pause. Phone rings)

(Blackout)

'Dear Friend', SIENNA KING

-

Everyday I think of you,
I think of all the times we spent laughing, bussing the most jokes
Crying,
And arguing
Together. Man those arguments that left us in tears

You are strong, you are Loved for every bit of You, and what You bring to
this world
Never give up,
Your spirit keeps us alive!
You may not notice but your Future is Golden, matter of fact its Rhodium

My Friend
It's short and sweet b'cause I know I can go on at times
But
I Love you,
I Miss you,
I care so much about you
A never ending hug

With Love from Your Friend

-

'Untangled', **BENJAMIN TULLOCH**

-

This tight knot
That binds your thoughts
This tight knot
That bites your heart
Can be undone
Let your pain unspool from your mouth
All tangled and frustrated
So helping hands can unwind
And untie
Day by day
Those dark threads
It will be hard work
But in time
Thread by thread
Freedom

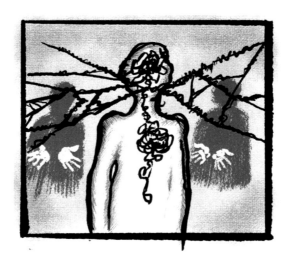

-

I wake up at 5AM with a feeling of great unease and insecurity. I turn on the lights and check my email, a reply from my therapist in London acknowledging my request to reschedule with a link saying: "You may find this helpful, it relates to what we talked about during your last session." I feel embarrassed and I light my candle and attempt to meditate to calm my nerves. I read my book that contains too much logic and not enough emotion, encouraging my inability to focus and my fear of the past. I get dressed as I receive a text from my mother: "I'm up - I can drive you up to Upaya if you want." I reply: "No I'm walking to photograph someone." I run out the door dismissing my mother's financial fears and her urge to control me by not letting me go on my own. It's cold, dark and I feel free. I feel the accumulation of power as I glide through the crisp air. I blast 'Hold on Tight' in my headphones as I fantasize about men I'm in love with and the type of life I want to have. I get extremely friendly "hellos!" from my neighbors walking their dogs as I jog downtown. The color of the sky gets lighter and I begin to move faster. I meet the seemingly care free opera singer at 7 AM on the mountain located by Santa Fe Spa. The sun rises while I sit on a curb and wait as he approaches. He greets me with elegance, he strutted himself with a graceful type of scary that made me want to be his friend. His self-assurance and accurate sense of speech screamed ACTOR. I asked: "What's your preference of genre when you act?" He said: "I like to play the psychos, that's why I love theatre it encourages the mentally unstable, the freaks." The notion of "freaks" made me feel at home. We walked to his car so he could light a cigarette. He talked about how smoking is sexy and underrated, I agreed on a superficial level with the knowledge that I only enjoy kissing a smoker when I'm not sober. I was reluctant to fully engage because of my fear. My fear didn't come from the fact that he had one arm or that this town tiptoed around him because of his past mental breakdown. No, my fear came from allowing myself to be attracted to a straight man. The fear of letting fantasy alter my reality and I lose focus. I told him about my exploration of fear through my recent film of me eating and shitting a scorpion, and how fear is self-caused and technically fiction. He said: "Sick!"

His enthusiasm struck my envy. Generally, I surrendered the power as he directed what type of headshots we wanted for his television auditions, as I wanted to be assertive when creating more drama. Like when I moved his cowboy boot for better composition and we said "woah woah!" I didn't know whether it was because I shouldn't have touched a valuable piece of footwear or because he thought I was hitting on him. Regardless, I became fearful. The conversation with the military offspring remained at a relatively shallow level until we began to dive into the subjects of addiction, vanity, judgement, and creativity. I told him I came back home to have a break from the partying and I needed to recharge in solitude, also known as emotionally burnt the fuck out. I thought about how much I'm suffering, suffering from nothing, the epitome of banality. I said I wake up every day with so much fear and angst. He said me too. He said: "One thing that I also wake up with is self-hatred." I said me too. He said: "Where do you think that comes from?" I said: "Well, for me it comes from my fear of judgement and my obsession with perfection." He said: "People are so fucking judgmental, I'm bipolar and I had a mental breakdown, and even though I've been fully dedicated to caring for myself (taking my meds) for the past four years without incident, hardly anyone in this town will get to know me. And as for perfection. That's bad. You have to let that go and realize we're all human." I nodded in silence but I knew how judgmental I could be, especially since I'm always judging myself. While, letting go of the idea of perfection could slow down my ambition. However, slowing down is something this generation needs to be slapped in the face with. He continued: "I was at dinner the other night and I saw a group of kids all sitting across from each other and all on their iPhones. Not talking at all! How fucking sad is that? Keep your friends close, keep your iPhones closer." I thought so sad and so me. He told me: "I think you're one of those people who needs extra one-on-one time with a human being." I said: "Yeah I do; I get so intense sometimes. And I feel so much more comfortable talking deep than making small talk, bullshit, conversation." He said: "I hate small talk, bullshit, conversation. And I like people who can think of something and have a rational point behind their thought." Our eye contact was strong. And in that brief moment I felt a connection. It was humane and it was raw. He showed me humility and kindness with no agenda. A rush of security filled my arms. Due to this connection I didn't feel the need to beat around the bush when I asked: "What happened to your arm?" He said: "I'll let you read my memoir. It's called Consumed." I said: "I will" with the utmost sincerity. He told me about his 80-pound weight loss and how he felt this year would be the breakthrough for his acting career. I told him: "It sounds corny but you have to believe in yourself, and the self-hatred sets you back." He said: "I know, I know..." Then let out a grumble of frustration. I related, knowing I would give the exact same response if someone said that to me, grumble included. He insisted on making sure I send him all the pictures I took of him, he felt the need to explain why or to justify an actor's love of self-image, when it was not necessary as I'm evidently aware that my own obsession with self-beauty can be crippling. Our last shots were the most dynamic and I felt the power return to me. My second film roll turned out to be less photos than expected and I turned off my camera with disappointment. He lightened the atmosphere stating: "We got some good shots!" I clung onto his positivity replying back: "Yeah we did!" We walked back to his car and made the small chat that always returns at the end of an encounter such as, "I'll let you know how long the photos will take" or "I'll send you the name of my book". He offered me a ride I told him I would walk. He said: "Are you sure?" I gave him a friendly smile and said: "Yes." I walked down the mountain feeling more grounded and aware. I sent him a text saying: "I forgot to say Thank you - too caught up in my own head." He replied... "My pleasure, Santiago. Thank you, as well. Simply send as many as you're able, per email. Be well, and I look forward to seeing your work from today. Enjoy family & friends. Todd."

'Âme Filtrée - "Talk to the hand" ' , **LINO MEOLI**

-

I'm fascinated by them
They're like angels to me
Watching over the streets

'David: Lucifer's flower' , HÉLÈNE SELAM KLEIH

-

Crisis

7 years --- Mental health issues, 7 years

23 years old - I couldn't see day - noise in my ear - it means nothing to me - I was normal -- my head was trying to tell the person that I wanted to throw myself off the bridge --- I was working back then as security at the foreign common wealth office

I was not supposed to have mental health problems - they knew I took the Medicine to put me,

The second you take it you fall asleep - you sleep in the wrong time / wrong place - on the street

Everything you do becomes awkward. You can't play football.

Olanzapine

Now he is not ill.
He is Grounded - Ecotherapy.

191 - 10th

You need to meditate your thoughts - open your ears

2nd Timothy chapter 2 verse 7

The dictionary talks about your birthday

23rd October - birthday

Lucifer's flower - red

77 - power

Often people are not wise enough to protect themselves
from mental health

We are all disturbed ---

What are you - I choose rose - rose will choose me

You look like an oak tree, but you chose palm tree

A pineapple, a mango, a cherry?

David is grounded.

Providence Row and *Grounded Ecotherapy* have maintained Queen Elizabeth Hall Roof Garden, London since 2011. It is looked after by volunteers who have previously experienced homelessness, addiction or mental health problems.

-

-- those people who have strong spiritual beliefs that they don't need a doctor or another person to tell them what they're like, define, diagnose them and prescribe treatment.

You need to teach yourself not be taught

I'm open to opinion, outlook, judgement on what it means to be healthy - spiritual, physical, Mental -- What is it about?

When does mental health start and finish?

By law a crime is committed by emotion - a feeling on an emotion level - that's what a crime is considered to be

Crime in general is defined by emotion

Emotion is Human being = to be, they are, she is, he is

-- Not human thinking -- but then how do your thoughts separate from feelings

I relate to Buddha's -- emotion is in the belly -- thought is in the brain

Spirituality is defined by having thoughts and feelings - and their intrinsic connections

e.g. Daytime = sun represents thoughts // man

Nighttime = moon represents feelings // woman

24 hours -- the whole day is a combination of the two

These are not facts or beliefs but impressions - make of it what you will

Trauma makes you stronger, wiser, and more aware of problems, attitudes

What pushed you to get help - almost desperation
I struggled - I didn't know what I wanted to do - it made me have no purpose

What if's

I tried - I extreme to the other - ignored, misunderstood

Controlled, told what to do, blamed

If there was a problem - it was my fault

Until I had a moment of realisation -

Ideal help would be - counselling, GP

1 session 1 hour a week - a weight had lifted - very rewarding

No stigma // regardless of things

I am a person; I am walking into an office - looking for support + help

I am not a diagnosis looking for a doctor or a prescription

Different strokes for different folks

There's no beginning // no end --

What shocked you?

How many people have mental health problems who are in the same boat, that... the suicide rate of men... either psychosis, psychotic disorders schizophrenia or bipolar... they have more risk of suicidal thoughts than a normal person would, which I can understand from my own experience. I was sleep walking at Vauxhall train station, where mum used to work at London Bridge... the incident that happened at Brixton train station... and twice what happened at Clapham North (yes I need to take my medication...) yes I suffered a lot. I was put in hospital for three weeks.

It was an experience for the whole family to endure and what I've realised is... mental health doesn't define who I am. It's just...It doesn't define who you are. It's just a state of mind where the person is confused on certain things, but they will recover by talking openly about it... or psychology sessions... or therapy or medication as well.

Do you think you've recovered?

A lot yes. Before I remember I was really restless, aggressive, agitated... the words I used to say used to hurt the family a lot.

Do you think you''ve completely recovered now?

So... I have recovered quite a lot 'cos I say to myself "75% I feel okay" it's just 25% that is a bit missing. I just need more psychology sessions to talk openly and to get advice from my psychologist as well. Otherwise I am just taking it day by day and thinking about the present as usual... being assertive...

You remembered the word.

People have told me to be more assertive but I am doing a lot these days... it's just thinking... just being selfish... not thinking too much about how the family are affected and just to recover at your own pace, in your own time. You can't rush these things so quickly. It takes a while to understand how to recover and then be fully confident to go back into the community... taking time... for example, even though they said before December I will be discharged but, I am saying to myself "No. It could happen but it depends on me." It could take until... to accept the pros and cons about it as well.

Do you think you will ever fully be recovered?

Maybe. I will see how it goes. Got to take it step by step. I feel optimistic I will feel fully recovered and back to my normal self, but it will just take time I think.

You're better than your normal self. What is your normal self? Your normal self, you were in and out of schools - reception, primary, secondary, sixth form, uni.

Hmm.

And you were stressed. You didn't have this understanding of yourself that you have now at this moment, that's... I'm saying you could change yeah but right at this moment, the way you talk about yourself... in my life... in our life, I've never heard you talk like that.

That's true. I don't even notice it myself because it's my own experience of mental health... sometimes even in my psychology sessions I don't realise that I am speaking a lot more openly

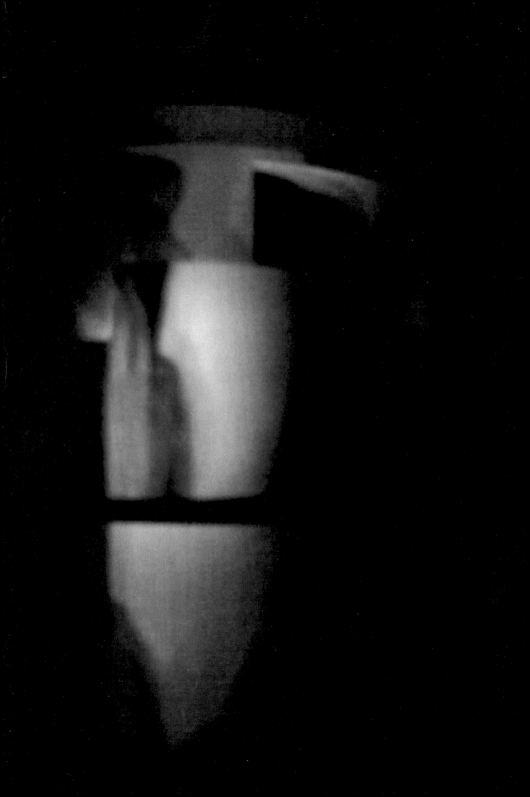

and seeking advice from psychologists and the consultants... like I have the ward round tomorrow morning... and I'm compliant with medication... but then, I ask myself "okay - there should be more talking therapies than taking medication" because, from my own understanding, me taking a lot of medication since five years ago up untill now - a lot of anti-depressants and anti-psychotics - some of them have helped me, some of them haven't, but then... one important thing is that the staff told me at the hospital is "If you stop taking the medication you would relapse" so... it's important to take the medication on time and ... that's one thing I find difficult because... the amount of medication I'm taking... it's too much. It gives mte a big headache. The night medication knocks me out and I fall into a very deep sleep and the next day I wake up at 12 noon... so basically it's a sleeping tablet that I take at night... that's one thing I hope at some point... after looking at these housing placements, when I go back, I just hope at some point I stop taking medication at all.

At the end of the day my body is affected physically...

It stops me from having hallucinations and delusions which is positive but the side effects are that I gain more weight and get a big appetite

Don't pretend like you don't already have a big appetite

I do have a big appetite but it's also...yeah that's true you're right. You're definitely right there. (laughter)

I think it's important that even if I recover fully from my mental health, I will still be taking medication because maybe I could have another relapse but you can't predict the future... you never know... expect the unexpected. It's from my own past experience that... especially last year it was very difficult for the family, I remember, I kept saying to mum and dad "oh, they're lying to you" this and that... but they took it literally... it's one of those things that I learnt my lesson from it. You've already seen from last year, I visited ten supported accommodations, neither of them worked... but this time if I move forward slowly...

What did mum always used to tell us?

Hakuna Matata.

Yeah. Hakuna Matata. Also, what else did she always say - the French word?

Merde. Quelle Merde.

It's true. "Don't give a shit!" Things will happen.

Exactly

Give this to dad.

You didn't even drink much of it, you just bought a whole one -

Okay I'll keep it then

Why do you wanna give it to dad, he'll just come back on Sunday with the same Tango

It's true (laughter) You are right Helene, I think I need to take my medication now. (laughter)

Gosh! Oh Gosh.

On previous page, still from 'Network', a video by Josiane MH Pozi and Hélène Selam Kleih

Index

Acknowledgements

In the process of making this book, I have had the support of more names than I can mention. Firstly, my endless love and thanks to every contributor who parted with their time, their energy and their privacy. It's exhausting as much as it is therapeutic to verbalise and physicalize feelings and experiences, especially when they are ones that have been suppressed for so long. Most of you started as strangers to me, but with your trust, have created a community. A thank you to every person who shared and donated to the crowd-funder, a thank you for the interest even in the early days , a thank you for the conversation : a thank you for faith in HIM + HIS. This book has been an all-consuming labour of love and a lifeline that I will always be grateful for.

Special thanks to:

AKINOLA DAVIES. ALEXA WRIGHT. ALEXANDRA BARKER. AMELIA ABRAHAM. BADÉ FATONA. CAITLIN LATIMER-JONES. DANIEL ASFAHA. DAVID IGHEN. DOUGLAS ALONGE. ELIZABETH MORROW. FELIX CHOONG. HUGO VOLRATH. IZZY CLIFFORD. JAMES MASSIAH. JOSIANE MH POZI. LAUREN DUFFUS. MAHNOOR HUSSAIN. MARK. MOWALOLA OGUNLESI. NINA CARTER. RIAZ PHILIPS. ROMANY-FRANCESCA MUKORO. SAGAL BULHAN. SALEM KHAZALI. SAMI ASFAHA. SARAH ASFAHA. SENAI ASFAHA. SONIA MENGHESTAB. SOPHIA COMPTON. SOPHIE DEACON. STEVEN SHAPIRO. STEVE SALTER. STEVEN HAYNES. TIFFANY R. CHAN. WILSON ORYEMA. YASSER ABUBEKER. ZEBIB ABRAHAM. KAMANI.

And of course, to my immediate family, Shoa Asfaha, Ulrich Kleih, Abrehet Asfaha, who have taught me that there is joy even in desperation, your laughter carries me always.

Yohannes Gabriel Kleih, my twin, my soul is yours, thank you for being my best friend, thank you for teaching me patience - TAKE IT EASY.

About the Writer

HÉLÈNE SELAM KLEIH is a writer, presenter and mental health advocate. Her works primarily explore the trauma of displacement and post-colonial language and art. She graduated from the University of Warwick in 2017, and founded Prosperitee Press in 2018. HIM + HIS is her first book. She lives in London and was born in 1995.

For resilience

Senai , and what is
+ Yohannes , and what will be